LASTING CITY

ALSO BY JAMES McCOURT

Now Voyagers: The Night Sea Journey

Queer Street: The Rise and Fall of an American Culture, 1947–1985

Wayfaring at Waverly in Silver Lake

Delancey's Way

Time Remaining

Kaye Wayfaring in "Avenged"

Mawrdew Czgowchwz

LASTING CITY

THE ANATOMY OF
NOSTALGIA

JAMES McCOURT

LIVERIGHT PUBLISHING CORPORATION

A Division of W. W. Norton & Company   New York · London

"Smoke Gets In Your Eyes," from *Roberta*. Words by Otto Harbach, music by Jerome Kern. Copyright © 1933 by Universal–Polygram International Publishing, Inc. Copyright renewed. All rights reserved. Used by permission. Reprinted by permission of Hal Leonard Corporation.

In one way or another everything represented in *Lasting City* happened. Certain names have been changed to protect the author from the innocent.

For information about permission to reproduce selections from this book, write to Permissions, Liveright Publishing Corporation, a divison of W. W. Norton & Company, Inc., 500 Fifth Avenue, New York, NY 10110

For information about special discounts for bulk purchases, please contact W. W. Norton Special Sales at specialsales@wwnorton.com or 800-233-4830

Manufacturing by RR Donnelley, Harrisonburg, VA
Book design by Dana Sloan
Production manager: Anna Oler

ISBN 978-0-87140-458-9 (hardcover)

Liveright Publishing Corporation
500 Fifth Avenue, New York, N.Y. 10110
wwnorton.com

W. W. Norton & Company Ltd.
Castle House, 75/76 Wells Street, London W1T 3QT

1 2 3 4 5 6 7 8 9 0

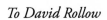

To David Rollow

CONTENTS

When we speak about the past we lie with every breath we take. Whoever turns biographer commits himself to lies, to concealment, to hypocrisy, to embellishments, and even to dissembling his own lack of understanding. Biographical truth is not to be had, and even if one had it one could not use it.

—SIGMUND FREUD

All one's inventions are true, you can be sure of that.

—GUSTAVE FLAUBERT

ONE

1

The world around him was like a silent noise.

In the Beginning was the Word, and the word was *Shazam*. (His first word—not "mama" or "papa," either, but, prompted by his older brother David, his lifelong hero, *Shazam*.)

New York, New York. New York as it is, in and of itself: the rumor. As over and against the New York he invented. Long division.

The rule is fast: life is short and art is long, but the transformation of a life into literature necessarily prolongs it.

". . . and this gives life to thee."

Corrigenda discouraged—no callers; rapt adherence to the family romance: the tendency to defensively glamorize one's family of origin in order to avoid hating them (thus incurring retribution).

A traitor to memory? Memory is treason itself. The facts of any past are moving targets.

The moral right of Author had been asserted.

(How clever. Pull the other one, darling, it's got bells on.)

2

*T*ell *everything.*

"Tell everything," his mother said only weeks before she took the final stroke in the room in the Kateri Residence, the room she'd occupied for the past eleven years.

"Everything?"

"Everything."

Everything—and why not? What did she have to lose? And anyway she'd be dead—and apparently, in the process no new terror added by the undertaking, which unquestionably smacked of publicity, something she felt had been unjustly denied her in the degree she'd deserved—by her father, who ended up living under the same roof with her all his life and who despised her relentlessly and without mitigation, the determining factor that made her a fighter.

He was the only one (the know-it-all) who knew it all, and she knew she was the last of them, had outlived all the others, friend and enemy alike.

"Well, in that case, we'd better put together the book of evidence." (They never did over the holidays and then the coma; it was too late.)

"It's no such thing," said Jack Burlison, his analyst. "Talk to her, in a dutiful manner, the way you talk to me as you lie there on that couch. She can hear you. The more you sit in silence the more the fear and anxiety for both of you. Recite as much of her story as your story permits, 'thinking out loud' as she used to do at home, and absent the obscenities—you can keep them in your head, at some peril, but try to."

And in his haste to make of her a vivid and memorable literary character—turning the tables on birth—he'd neglected to read the small print, added by the Introject. "Tell everything—to yourself, but if you *publish* a single word of any of it, I'll hound you down to your grave."

. . .

The four year old at the window in the front car of the El train, his head just above the metal panel, just able to see out of the bottom of the window, the city skyline looming up, coming closer station by station— closer . . . closer . . .

"Then this one day," "Then this one night:" the double helix of the tale.

They come by air, by bus, by train and driving themselves while driven.

Of all the Biblical cities, he chose Nineveh to enshrine the myth. Undoubtedly because of Jonah swallowed by the whale (what was the old fuck preaching against anyway—the usual he supposed).

Then when he looked at the "Manatus" map he saw a right whale— then Manhattan swallowed him up. He left Jackson Heights behind forever and by way of Brooklyn and the Bronx (doing nothing involving Staten Island but ride all night back and forth on the ferry—that once) and descended for the life they offered down into the innards of the right whale.

Daydreaming. The Goodyear blimp had been a familiar sight for years over the city. As he looks down from the gondola he sees small planes flying banners behind and others looping in the bright blue sky emitting skywriting messages in which nearly as soon as the last word was written, the first had dissolved. Life.

The first time his life dissolved, the terror was greater than anything ever after.

For a bright, clear Sunday morning in early August the humidity was strangely low. The mosquitos would not . . .

His father Big Jim's fortieth birthday, August 6, 1945. Big clam- bake on the narrow beach in the harbor in front of (Charlie and Flossie)

Moore's Hotel in Northport, Long Island. Half the village there for the event, people singing "This Was a Real Nice Clambake" from Rodgers and Hammerstein's *Carousel* ("The *vittels* we *et*?" What did *that* mean?) as the sun sets out over Eaton's Neck. The party is moving inside for continued festivities, singing, dancing, all centered around his mother Kitty's playing show tunes, old songs, and current pop numbers on the old barroom out-of-tune upright.

Hours earlier, early afternoon at nearby Crab Meadow beach, the boy had been sitting at the water's edge (Long Island Sound) building the Flatiron Building out of wet sand, just at the high tide line.

"What-cha building there, Jimmy, a pyramid?"

"The Flatiron Building—my grandfather built the real one, you know."

While on beach chairs arranged in a circle with a pitcher of sidecars and all four glasses nearby, the boy's mother and his Aunt (and godmother) Elizabeth, former classmates and sometime sparring partners at St. Lawrence Academy in Manhattan, his Aunt Florence and Dorothy O'Sullivan, resident of Northport.

("She came from money—old money, and was married already, but she walked out of that house across the sound, leaving her engagement and wedding rings in a little china dish in the master bedroom, wearing the clothes on her back, taking her cosmetics and nothing more, no alimony, not one thin dime, when she fell in love with him. Maybe you've heard 'He swept her off her feet' as an expression. Well, in this case it was an actual fact; stormed into that house, grabbed her up in his strong arms, and carried her out the door, down the marble stairs to the "suicide seat" of his truck, and he gunned the engine and thundered down the gravel driveway like it was something out of a '30s screwball comedy. Only he was no screwball, not then, not now, and she had a mind of her own—still does, in case you haven't noticed—and would rather have lived in a shanty by the freight tracks than be suffocated in her own room looking out over a spacious lawn, which she always kept locked."

"He has a son locked up in prison for murder out in Walla Walla, Washington."

"What a funny name for a place."

"Jimmy, you have just got to stop this listening at doorways."

"I don't listen at doorways. I lie awake at night while you all sit under my window burning those citro–citro–"

"Citronella candles?"

To fight off the mosquitos, while they drink their high-balls, and I listen to everything and pass it along to Andy (the stuffed-toy panda) the next day. Andy was a little hard of hearing and was always asleep next to him in the bed—but he wasn't, not ever, not until they've called it a night. When he heard his mother playing the piano nothing could ever be bad or go wrong.)

. . .

"Northport is so peaceful, Catherine," his Aunt Florence (Florrie) said, "so relaxing, don't you think so?"

"That it is, Florrie, that it is."

Banzai! Banzai! Banzai! Banzai!

The boys came from the east and south, like a surprise-attack platoon over the marram grass-covered dunes.

Banzai! Banzai! Banzai! Banzai!

And the marauders stomped his Flatiron Building flat.

"It had to be done, Catherine," said Dorothy O'Sullivan.

(Destroy his Flatiron Building—why was that?)

"Yes, I know—but a whole city, to disappear just like that one morning."

(A whole city—Who? Where? New York? Just like *that*?)

"They had it coming," his Aunt Betty declared with conviction.

"It's true, Catherine," said his Aunt Florrie, "they did."

The boy froze, then stood and staggered up the beach.

"What's the matter, Jimmy?" his mother asked.

"Didn't you see, Catherine?" his Aunt Betty said, "those boys destroyed his sand castle."

"It was the Flatiron Building," the boy said, still in shock.

"There's more to it than that," Dorothy O'Sullivan declared. "He heard us talking about Hiroshima. Jimmy, come here."

The boy walked over to Dorothy O'Sullivan, who felt his forehead.

"Catherine, the boy is burning up, and shivering all over at the same time. You'd better get him home and get Jacobi. It's a Sunday, but that won't matter to him, he'll come. I'll call ahead. The boy's had a pretty nasty shock."

. . .

After the war, when the Soviet scare was at its peak and the atomic bomb had been replaced by the hydrogen bomb, he would ride his Schwinn bicycle up to Northern Boulevard, to the top of the only hill in Jackson Heights and watch the New York skyline and all the buildings his grandfather had built be consumed by an immense fireball, then having blanked out he would race the Schwinn—and later the three-speed English racer—down the hill, through traffic (more than one witness attested the one time he swerved to avoid a car coming straight at him from the right on Thirty-Seventh Avenue. Had he jammed on the brake, he'd have been pitched head first over the handlebars and cracked his skull wide open. The incident had been reported to his parents, but he'd insisted he remembered nothing but standing at the top of the one hill in Jackson Heights and seeing the fireball explode over Manhattan).

"It would have been too bad," his older brother David said, "but on the other hand with his brains spilled out all over Polk Avenue, somebody might have gotten a clue as to what was *in* there—what made him tick."

. . .

The screen test in Astoria. Eleven years prior to "Tell everything," she'd entered the N.Y.U. Rehabilitation Center Medical Center on Second Avenue after she took the first stroke, and he'd introduced her to her doctor, "Mother, this is your new doctor—Dr. Handel."

"Halleluleah."

"She's quite a quick-witted woman, your mother."

"There was a legend in the Moore family that an ancestor—a boy called Toby sang the alto solo 'I Know that my Redeemer Liveth' in the premiere of the *Messiah* in Dublin in 1742. The Moores were ships' chandlers in Dublin, and a branch crossed the ocean to Philadelphia in 1763—result of the Treaty of Paris; they'd spied against the English in the Seven Years War—or the French and Indian War, as some prefer."

"Even in her condition she has the air of an actress—and something too of the command. Was she in show business?"

"In the theater of her mind, always—always the lead, and it must be said she was value for money."

"She's always been like that?" Dr. Handel asked.

"Always. They gave her the green light after a brief screen test up in Astoria when she was just a young girl. They were looking for a fresh new type after a terrible little monster called Mary Miles Minter gunned down her director "lover" William Desmond Taylor. They found what they wanted in Brooklyn's wonderful Clara Bow, who (with Valentino) became the biggest movie star in silents, the 'It' girl. Then talkies came in and that was that, a screeching halt for Clara Bow who went out with Twenties. But in the talkies Kitty Moore—that's the woman lying there, Catherine McCourt. She could have been Jean Arthur or Irene Dunne—she had the singing voice—although she herself always said she'd likely have ended up in the Joan Blondell category."

"Then her chances are excellent, she could live to be a hundred. Women like your mother who tend to dominate whatever group they find themselves in, however wary the group, unvaryingly thrive."

"Whenever we'd go someplace far away from the city, from the noise—the traffic, the horns, the 'Bungalow Bar' ice cream truck, the pushcart-vendors—"

"The rag sheenies."

"She called them that, yes."

"Sociology—the melting pot. Unique in the world—same as the rocks."

"You also a geologist, doc?"

"Rock climber."

"Funny—so was she—imagine. As kids they all came over from York-ville and climbed the rocks, especially the ones in the Ramble. Ironic that."

"I get the gist."

"And the schist, doctor."

Cura personalis. Nihil humani alienum pute. Sympathetic to every species of human being.

"Whenever she was in a peaceful place out of the city she'd say, 'Nice place to spend the last three days of your life.' So, no last three days for Catherine here, huh?"

"On the contrary. Stroke victims, especially women, and especially women as sharp as your mother, are capable of making remarkable recoveries. She will always be paralyzed on her right side, and always be to some degree aphasic—the residence you've found for her has a full rehab program, so I'd be hopeful."

"Only a Jewish doctor would say such a thing as that."

"Don't you want her to recover?"

"I'm of two minds."

. . .

There used to be, when the Second Avenue El they tore down in the '40s ran down to the "Jewish Rialto," theaters, restaurants, all of them thriving, which Catherine's father Dave Moore (1875–1958) had frequented in that period early in the century when Tony Pastor's music hall was doing a land-office business and the raffish Bowery had not descended into Flop House Central—a history all the more galling to contemplate in the mind of his only child, the vicious hypocrisy of his refusing to let her have a shot at a career in pictures, being selected as possible star mate-rial in the very same arena where Clara Bow had tested: Astoria—directly across the East River from the neighborhood around Gracie Mansion where Kitty had played as a child, sledding down the hill in winter with among others Bobby Wagner, who called her a dumb, cockeyed Swede when she ran into him with her sled and who decades later became Robert F. Wagner, Democratic Party factotum and mayor of the City of New York. ("That's how much *he* knew, even then.") In her mind there were things happening in Astoria, directly across the East River, so that the meaning of "so near yet so far" slapped the convent schoolgirl in the face. If only she'd grown up in the streets her father had come from (like his schoolmate Al Smith), and the heroine of Stephen Crane's *Maggie: a Girl of the Streets* ("I like your looks, Mag, they're outa sight"), chewed gum, smoked and spoken with the accent of Hell's Kitchen instead of sounding like some road company Katherine Cornell or a far less saccharine Helen Hayes, she'd have been famous—and happy—or at least had a shot at it. She hated her father, the man who had held her back.

. . .

In the ambulance with her after the first stroke. Paralyzed on one side, but still able to talk.

"You know, I never asked you, that test—was it before or after you and your mother sneaked you both off to see Jeanne Eagels onstage in *Rain?*"

"After."

"I figured—after I watched her in *The Letter*. It was Jeanne Eagels, not Davis or Stanwyck or God help us Joan Blondell who gave you the stigmata."

"Listen to the writer."

"Well, what do you think? She was forty when the doctor killed her with an overdose of heroin, and you were the age she'd been in *Rain*. She dropped dead right at the charlatan doctor's feet when he shot her up one time too many with heroin. What a cover-up *that* must have been, even for the Walker administration. Did you ever meet him—Walker?"

"She was tall—she was a tall woman. Eagels."

"Could you have matched her?"

"Nobody could match Eagels—nobody could hold a candle to her."

The ambulance had reached 40th Street. Looking out the window, she'd given the United Nations the fish eye, jerking her head in interrogative fashion. It was hard to make her out, he had to be patient, but he was fascinated at her willfulness.

"The United Nations. You took us on a tour of it once—Pop wouldn't go."

"Stubborn—right in many respects, though. Your brother David fought him tooth and nail."

"Your father—"

"Kept *stumm*. There he was living with us all those years and your father never addressed him as anything but 'Mr. Moore.'"

Then the ambulance, siren silent, and almost soundproof so that traffic passed by on either side in virtual silence, headed north up Second Avenue.

"Think they'll ever get the subway built? Take you for a ride on it if it is—of course there'll be no place on it you'll want to go—your old neighborhood has disappeared into the mists of history."

"Other places."

At 86th Street: Yorkville and beyond that the river and across the river Astoria. The ambulance turned left, headed for the West Side through Central Park. He watched her look out the rear window, her face calm, her blue eyes registering everything, as Yorkville and Astoria and all that had gone with them grew ever more distant, then disappeared. There were always memories.

Sunday, January 12, 2003, after the final stroke and coma.

"And the family—what—"

"You're on, doctor, I'm it."

"There are in your mother's case official difficulties."

"I'm aware of that, doctor, the DNR due to a mistake on the staff's part—stress of the holidays no doubt—has not been reaffirmed for 2003. I leave it to you, doctor, to make the correction."

She was in effect, as they used to say at Christmas, in deep and dreamless sleep, while above the silent world rolled by—so unlike the days of her prime, the days of all their primes, when they would have music wherever they went—music drifting out of open windows all over the city: popular standards, novelty numbers (like "Mairzy Doats"), advertising jingles, the big band sounds. The opera broadcast direct from the Metropolitan every Saturday afternoon, the New York Philharmonic symphony direct from Carnegie Hall.

They do say the hearing is the last to go—so maybe a little song, maybe "Smoke Gets in Your Eyes," or might that cross the threshold of memory to disturb her deep and dreamless sleep?

(Question: had anyone remembered to pray to St. Joseph, patron of a happy death?)

"She might last a week or she might go tonight."

"Let's split the difference and give her three days and nights. I think she's found a good enough place in which to spend the last three days of her life."

"This isn't quite a package deal."

"Funny thing, she was on one of those, on a Labor Day weekend in the Catskills, when she took the first stroke. Well, at least it wasn't Port Jervis."

(Port Jervis: the dark shadow, never to be forgotten.)

Passim.

. . .

In wieviel grauen Stunden, in how many gray hours: Thoughts like haunting melodies other than Schubert and "Smoke Gets in Your Eyes" (such as "Vilja" from *The Merry Widow* and "This Nearly Was Mine" from *South Pacific*, "Strange Music" from *The Song of Norway*, "I hear singing and there's no one there," from *Call Me Madam*).

"Put another nickel in, in the nickelodeon, all I want is loving you and music, music, music."

Her magical piano playing of the standards at parties . . .

Can there be a time line when Time drops its lines all the time?

Writing about them having been alive, about one's having been alive with them; death is catching: one is simply no longer alive.

. . .

Some time in the late afternoon—the pale sun setting in the southwest, over Staten Island, but he can't see it. It is the second day she has spent in a nice place to spend the last three days of her life—she must die tomorrow night at the latest, a consummation devoutly to be wished.

He dozed.

The skies over New Jersey have darkened, there's lightning in the sky. . . . He is with the man in the sky-blue suit and the scarlet cape and dark blue hair sailing above the city.

At any time the man wishes to, he can fly close to the speed of light in counter circles to the spin of the earth and thus move backwards in time to when he was the boy from Krypton under human guise, leading a double life.

Then the sleeper as a young boy is riding in the Batmobile, which, when its enormous batwings open, carries the passengers—that man in the bat costume, his "ward" Robin and himself across the Hudson River (the North River as it is known to those who work on the waterfront)— all the ships in below, the *Queen Mary*, the *Queen Elizabeth*, the *Aquitania*, the *Mauretania*, the *Île de France*, the *Flandre*, the *Leonardo da Vinci*, the ill-fated *Andrea Doria*, the *Raffaello*, the *Vulcania*, the *Stockholm*, the *Nieuw Amsterdam*, and in 1962, entering the harbor at last, under the Verrazano Bridge, in all her glory, the most fabulous of them all, the *France*, the great vindication of the sabotage of the *Normandie* two decades before—out through the four spacious skies, over Los Angeles, sailing out over the Pacific, out over Pearl Harbor and the Hawaiian islands, the volcano Mauna Loa, over the thousands of miles of deep blue water, then over Okinawa to the south end of the Japanese archipelago, to

Hiroshima. Over the city, the bomb hatch in the floor of the Batmobile opens, Little Boy is dropped, exploding 1968 feet above the unsuspecting city and the mushroom cloud rises. The man in the bat costume is joined by the man in the sky blue suit and scarlet cape, who takes the wheel, switches gears and as the Batmobile assumes the velocity near the speed of light, flying in circles west to east around the planet, reaches New York on the evening of January 13, 2003. With the precision of a stealth bomb, the Batmobile flies down to the hospital on the Upper West Side, close by St. John's, the unfinished Episcopal cathedral, and Columbia University, passing through its walls as theologians said the infant Christ passed out of his mother's womb like light through a glass, leaving her *virgo intacta*, to the small white room where the woman lay dying.

Whatever the truth value of the Freudian dictum, the surest way to see it in motion is to begin at the beginning—as if there really were a Big Bang to life (*Shazam*) from which all does follow as the night the day (and seems absolutely incandescent in the middle of the night, least illuminating in the hour after waking—"Oh, I don't dream—or if I do I never remember them").

Records, endless varieties of.

Lacrimae rerum—auribus
lacrime meam. Exaudi
orationem meam
Domine et deprecationem meam.
The tears of things—accept my prayer,
Oh Lord, and my supplication:
Give hearing to my tears.
(Conflating Virgil and Psalm 29.)

Catherine's haunting unavailing guilt over Port Jervis and its sad and terrible aftermath.

"Whatever moves or toils or grieves hath its appointed sleep." (Shelley, "Remorse.")

As she lay dying, he thought of her, the expression she'd always used when she was late, which was often: "The time got away from me."

The time had begun to race ahead of him in 1945 out at Moore's Hotel in Northport, and all the lovely voices of a summer night drifting up from the garden and through the bedroom window, which he imagined with delight being allowed to go down to join.

He might stay up so long as he behaved himself like both a clever boy and also a polite one. For instance, "Don't go chasing fireflies to put them in a jelly jar—it may be fun for you, but you're preventing them from making whoopee, and if they can't make whoopee they die."

Fireflies? Lightning bugs for as long as he could stay in charge of his expressions and words for things (like as not secretly). And the time raced on like Nashua the racehorse with nobody in any brightly colored satin get-up in any saddle on his back.

All the voices from the front porch, drifting around to the back of the house where the child is in the victory garden—whatever hushed conversation or talk of silent words not uttered in the moment in the rose garden (and Maud never did come down—or did she?) And the black-bat night flights flew on in V for victory formation. ("We won the war!")

The excursion on the New York Central to the New York Botanical Garden in the Bronx: all the voices in all the other gardens and rooms, in outer halls and secluded rendezvous over cocktails for two, become again one voice giving one stern and implacable command—"*Get out.*" (Adults only.)

The past is another country where they do indeed do things differently, and chief of all the differences is to give no thought whatever to the future.

(His father, called Big Jim except by his sisters, was in general a taciturn man, a graduate of the Jesuit Regis, the finest Catholic secondary school in the country, well spoken and extremely well thought of, which embarrassed the child. Every once in a while Big Jim would stand to attention and recite:

Tell me not in mournful numbers
Life is but an empty dream . . . etc.)

Too young for World War One and too old for World War Two, Big Jim's theater of war was his life, his battleground his bewildered sense of what it was all about besides weary toil, three-week summer vacations, pinochle and unruly children.

Big Jim at seventy to his second son and namesake (dead drunk) ". . . hopeless, pointless and ridiculous," reducing the sodden sod to wailing tears and maudlin avowals ("I love you and you reject me").

Eleven years earlier in a desperate ploy to elicit sympathy (song from Jerome Kern's *The Firefly.* Catherine: Sympathy? It's in the dictionary after "simp") his loud and drunken and Dexamyl-driven confession of impotence (absolutely untrue as a result of the Dexamyl).

The facts are these.

The evening of each of the three days spent at her deathbed, and when not, walking all over New York thinking about walking all over New York thinking about walking all over New York . . . by then the personal self has disintegrated—losing any interest he might once have had in the winged mysteries of divinity—and the self that matters becomes the page (and, yes, the sidewalk) written on—in silence.

The Residence private room, that *locus solus*, or lonely place, for the next eleven years.

"Nice place to spend the last three days of your life."

Had they "slipped up" at the Residence on the flu meds, offed her, either because she'd become just too much of a pain in the ass, or just because they needed the room?

No chance accusation, much less proof, only the urban lore that insisted such things happened every day—culling the hopelessly afflicted—as did the surcharged morphine drip.

They should've given her a fighting chance to reach a hundred and one.

Author's stream of consciousness—and speaking of which the matinee performance at the Winter Garden of *Ulysses in Nighttown*, a play made from Joyce's novel, with Zero Mostel and Fionnula Flanagan, is the juxtaposition of the sexual reminiscences and dreams of woman, reminiscences centered on the Rock of Gibraltar (*vide passim*), which rock, part of the plot, will be coming soon to a page near you if it's plot the reader's after. *Plot* how are ye. The *temerity*.

He'd been reading to Catherine about the geological history of New York and its peculiar schist—after all the McCourts had quarried it in the nineteenth century, supplied the architects with finely cut sections of it—perhaps for instance Stanford White for the original Madison Square Garden and many stately mansions—carved it for St. Patrick's Cathedral (the neo-Gothic fretwork over the west door), in case she gave a fat rat's ass, which he doubted. Rock was rock and she'd climbed enough of them in Central Park.

The story of the Moores was far the more interesting picture in the family double feature (free dishes Tuesday nights). Starting with the dying woman's own. The screen test in Astoria, the affair with—

How could it even have been told or spoken of, that frantic, compulsive and in its own way nearly comatose whoopee and shenanigans, yet fatal (to the stability of young married life), that act of adultery in a commercial travelers' hotel in the tri-state border town Port Jervis on the banks of the Neversink. The unthinkable, an affair—an affair with a Jewish man, her traveling salesman partner at L. B. Furriers.

He sat there recalling the pitch of his vileness in the waking nightmare (later inextricably woven into the nightmare of the frightening darkened room of they two having at one another in the Pinewood, his college bar up in the Bronx, he in an alcoholic blackout and consequently absolutely unaware until informed next day by shocked classmates and Paddy the bartender himself who had never in his life seen such an attack by a son on his mother and was thinking seriously of banning the miscreant from the place altogether), raving, shouting at the top of his histrionic lungs, shouting something like "Mother my ass—some run-of-the-mill castrating Irish Catholic bitch with her legs wrapped around the neck of some short, dark and smoldering Jew boy Lothario with wavy hair, no doubt of the Ramon Navarro type, in a sleazy hotel room in fucking Port Jervis—what a dump—where three states come together, two words, comprising the fevered dream of delirious *ménage à trois* lovers—you, the yid and Christ himself, body and blood."

(For what did anyone think the Eucharist was really about in a hysterical, now menopausal woman's life? Check with Teresa of Ávila, or go to Rome and take a long and reverent look at Bernini's treatment of the only woman Doctor of the Church, rendered by his genius in polished marble in the church of Santa Maria de la Vittoria.

Besotted she'd been, trapped in an orgasmic ecstasy (and she no doctor of the church, merely a communicant, later to climb step by step to dizzy heights, become at different times former president of Blessed Sacrament, Jackson Heights Parish's Rosary Society, its Mothers Club, a Third Order Franciscan and the highest rung of all, a pinnacle in fact, the producer-director of the all-woman Blessed Sacrament parish dramatic society, the Genesians), an orgasmic ecstasy never served in bed either on her honeymoon or in that first apartment on Mosholu Parkway in the Bronx.

(*Tell everything.*)

The wise fool hath said in his heart, there is no God, no justice, and above all no eternity—only now and now and again.

They got one thing right though, we have here, even built on monumental schist, no lasting fucking city, or to be more accurate, the city has no rock-like lasting us.

Time goes, you say? Ah no!
Alas, Time stays, we go . . .
　　　　—Ernest Dowson

In any case no weight of expectation: a sure thing: a line finally drawn under things.

As has been remarked, since the dreamer was at the time of the scandalous fight—nobody had ever heard a son say such things to his mother—in a total alcoholic blackout, one of his first, the contents of the dream dreamed not only the gist of what he had screamed while so out of control, but also the amplifications that the bottomless well of the unconscious and its contents spews up in any nightmare had by a violent nature—and his was manifestly that—the amplification of the contents of the dreamer's reconstruction—asleep and awake we lie with every breath we take—due to the alcoholic blackout, adumbrating the events on the banks of the Neversink whatever they might have been, piling Pelion on Ossa like a terrible child in a towering matricidal rage, piling up wooden blocks that spell out obscene words.

Now far removed in time and mileage from the voices coming up from the front porch of Moore's Hotel in Northport. What he did and does remember shouting was "You know it's really a pity I despise you, when we have things in common—you're a whore and I'm a flaming faggot—and really we should meet on a regular basis in some rat hole like this and get shitfaced drunk as quickly as possible—and all you have to do, mother dear, is sniff the cork—and work on hammering out the basis of our relationship." (If this wasn't a homosexual's re-creation of the closing line of the first act with which Jeanne Eagels brought the house down at Maxine Elliot's Theater on West Thirty-Ninth Street, 1922, "I have the right to stand here and say to you 'to *hell* with you' and be damned," it was nothing.) Also the explication of the living text of a life that has been far from an open book: Author's uncanny attraction to Eugene O'Neill's play *Mourning Becomes Electra*, the Orestes myth and his "take" on it leading eventually and in the light of the contemporaneous thesis of David Isay on the etiology of male homosexuality to Author's invention in fiction of the "Orestes complex."

. . .

"So are we talking? Here we are at your deathbed, as if by prearrangement, as if to have dinner and take in a show.

"I just remembered the old joke you liked about meeting at the corner of such and such a street and avenue. 'If you get there first make a mark on the sidewalk, if I get there first I'll rub it out."

And of another deathbed—his paternal grandmother's, at home on 1912 Loring Place off Burnside Avenue in the Bronx, two blocks south of New York University's Hall of Fame. His godmother, Aunt Betty (his Aunt May kept on saying, "Elizabeth is a sister of charity"). The old woman had kept not one but two daughters home with her, forcing them to give up their lives "to look after mama."

It was a crowded death watch (give the people what they want) in contrast to this one, but then again, he remembers, there's nobody else left.

Catherine always thought the McCourts were cracked, and after her husband's breakdown early in the Depression, barely four years after their wedding, on November 18, 1929, at the Church of Our Lady of Good Counsel in Yorkville, and two years after the birth of their first child, a boy, David, when the bank in which he was expected to make his career went bust.

The woman lying in front of him having an interior monologue—who knew?—or maybe singing "The Moon and I" from Gilbert and Sullivan's *The Mikado*.

For many years every performance of *The Mikado* he went to would irresistably bring to mind a high-school girl singing "The Moon and I"—a pretty and highly intelligent girl who should have gone on to be something other than his father's wife. (And remembering that as a child, in view of the canon of permissible and impermissible words, being both troubled and bewildered by the lyrics to "Tit Willow." Why was the bird called Tom Tit? And what about his big brother David's expression "useless as tits on a bull?")

. . .

When one is lying in the final coma, life does not flash before one's eyes, one flashes before its eyes . . . and then one's place knows one no more, full stop. What anyway was Orestes doing here at Clytemnestra's peaceful deathbed when for uncountable years in dreams (after falling in love with *Mourning Becomes Electra)* he had beaten bloody, slashed to ribbons, stomped on the face and hacked to bits the very she-devil introject who bore the dreaded name *mother.* Because otherwise it just wouldn't have been *fair,* her dying there among kindly but impatient professionals. Surely Clytemnestra can never have been called Kitty. Or Clitty. Speaking to the woman in the coma as per directions given by his analyst Jack Burlison. "Massage the back of the neck, etc.," while Author's own interior monologue in the manner of O'Neill's *Strange Interlude* (another favorite) runs on. In three nights he could have recited the synoptic versions of both her life and his, but forbore for fear of creating the unnecessary and unwanted excitation of countless lives swimming before countless victims of drowning—for he himself was just keeping his head above water, treading until the moment of rescue, the woman's death.

"My she looks lovely," one of the nurses said. "How old did you say she was?"

"Ninety-five, and she still is—they say every minute counts. Yes, ninety-five last November 13th—a real Scorpio and no mistake." (With her head wrapped in a blue-bordered towel, which when he'd finished carefully arranging startled him: it made her look like a follower of Mother Teresa, of whom he had once said, "If the perfection of the soul is achieved by suffering, and especially in the Hindu caste system, sacred to the primary and very ancient religion of the subcontinent and adamantly concerned with reincarnation, who is she—who is anybody, really—to impede that progress?")

"She must have been a nice lady for you to—"

One among many such misconceptions of the nature of the deceased.

"She was not a nice lady—nice ladies finish last, same as nice guys—which is to say they die first." (The last shall be first, Christ said—a statement born out by the consideration of contemplating any stacked grave in Calvary cemetery, where she'd be heading.)

The nurses by then had gotten used to him—his humor melancholic as it happened, but very well concealed over the years. Nobody in their collective memory had ever spent three days and nights (give or take, time out for dashes home for naps) at a mother's deathbed. He told them it was an old Irish custom and that if somebody connected didn't do it, it was a slap in the face, and if you ever dared slap your mother in the face, that hand would stick up out of your grave until she came and beat it down with a stick. A couple of the nurses were Filipino and that frightened them.

The Mexican Dominican priest called in for the last rites. "Oh. Isn't she beautiful!" Then the Cheyne-Stokes breathing.

"Come on now Kitty Moore, they're waiting for you at the party."

"Roll over, Catherine, you're snoring."

And so she did, and so she died, at long last (although it would have been a kick, that hundred and first birthday party).

. . .

The night world as it presents itself as he walks out of the hospital. Looming shadows *Casa Italiana* and the dormitories of Columbia, St. John the Divine (unfinished still), whereas his great-great-grandfather George Moore had carved the fretwork over the west door of St. Patrick's cathedral down on 50th and Fifth a hundred and fifty some odd years previously, Morningside Heights overlooking Harlem (where his maternal grandfather, Dave Moore, had lived as a child with his older sister Katie Duffy, her husband and their son, his cousin Charlie Duffy).

(Should there be a time line when Time drops its lines all the time?)

Walking through the theater district—out of the doors just shutting down, the voices of past performance—Ezio Pinza, Mary Martin, Ethel Merman, Gertrude Lawrence (at the St. James) "Whenever I feel afraid . . ."

Wandering the streets of New York—the Grid (murder investigation), the Incident Room, etc. Hushed were the streets of many-peopled Thebes, but never those of Gotham.

Walking the Grid. If the streets of New York all put together comprise an area six times the size of Central Park, then Central Park is one-seventh of the city and seven is a lucky number second only to eleven.

Central Park where the grid gives over to the Civil War between the East Side and the West Side.

"In the Lasting City nothing except the city lasts."

Not going to any fucking wake to see her stuffed in a box with ALLOW CONTENTS TO SETTLE stenciled on the side.

. . .

Crossing Amsterdam Avenue, he hailed a yellow cab headed downtown out of the realm of darkness, into the realm of light.

"Broadway and 44th, Johnny, if you please."

"My name is not Johnny, sir, it is Pramit—Pramit Banarjee. There it is, with my identification photograph—not very flattering, my wife declares, but you know women, sir."

"I'm sorry about the name, Pramit, but you see, when I was a child, returning with my parents to our home in Jackson Heights, my father, having hailed a taxi, would say to the driver, 'Take the bridge, Johnny, and out Skillman Avenue to Northern Boulevard. . . .' This was such a regular occurrence that I concluded my father knew every taxicab driver in Manhattan and that they were all called Johnny. Tonight for some reason I've just spoken in his voice."

"It is a very moving story, sir. That was a wicked bump you took on your head, sir, getting into the cab. Are you sure you're all right? Should I not perhaps take you to the hospital?"

"I've just come from there—my mother's deathbed. I'm not going back tonight."

And something wicked this way—Moriarty, Author's archenemy: that cocky grin in the rear-view mirror.

"Fed up with the light ones, famished for dark ones: that old black magic rising in the loins. Ah, the tortuous caves in the Central Park of a faggot psyche."

"Of which you do not have one, you're merely an incubus."

"Oooh, *burn*."

"Sorry."

"Skip it. Go on, disbosom yourself to the kindly gentleman: he will not be eating pieces of you and in all likelihood you'll not see hide nor hair of him again in this life you so little prize."

"Balls!"

" 'Balls,' said the Queen. 'If I had 'em, I'd be king.' 'Shit,' said the Jack. 'I got 'em and I ain't king.' Ah, such fond memories of Jackson Heights gutter talk."

"You're a sick fuck."

"You could be in better fettle yourself, dear."

"Get off my back."

"I'll wager I'm the only man you've ever said that to, and I'm not even factual."

. . .

Across the road, invisible beyond the wall in the white headlights of the traffic moving north, lay the dark expanse of Central Park: scene of the crime (as once was said of far off Eden). Impossible to walk the grid—only to be led down (and up) the garden path and to sit on a rock like the topless gossamer fly-winged White Rock girl, and watch for slimy things to crawl out from under it and a thousand others—now in his nostalgia, out of the little car in the Ringling Brothers, Barnum and Bailey Circus in Madison Square Garden which they always got into free of charge and had the best ringside seats—but he was in the taxicab, driven by Pramit Banarjee, late of New Delhi.

The Maine Monument in Columbus Circle (seemingly led on by

the beautifully carved boy at the prow) was the southwest entrance, and the southeast just across from the statue of General Sherman, mounted on horseback and led by Victory. (Katherine Anne Porter, the once-famous Texas-born writer, upon seeing the monument in Grand Army Plaza for the first time declared, "In't that just like a Yankee, lettin' a lady walk!")

North to the Ramble, by day a favorite children's play area, although somewhat treacherous, and by night the haunt of the sexually intrepid male homosexual horndog on the scent—various scents: Man Alive, *Calêche, L'equipage,* Chanel *Homme, L'eau sauvage, Poison de Dior,* Bill Blass, English Leather, Givenchy, *Gio,* Versace, Amyl Nitrate . . .

And the Old Spice bosuns, those Neanderthal knuckle busting gladiator numbers: "Got a match?" whispers Mam-zell *L'eau sauvage,* convinced she'll score.

"Yeah, your face and my ass."

"What's your line—do you deal in services?"

Musing on the stories heard on the opera line of songwriter Cole Porter and his pal Monty Woolley cruising the park in hansoms for hustlers who would suddenly appear from behind the trees as the cab approached. The hansom cab boarded at the southeast portal, directly across from the Plaza hotel (which his grandfather had built in 1910), carrying Monty Woolley and Cole Porter, tongues pendant, pulls up next to the college sweethearts. Monty to Cole: "When will she get his message?"

The '50s crackdown on homosexual desire.

. . .

Orestes complex. The fascination with murdered, mutilated women. Then there were the forty-one whacks Lizzie Borden gave her mother, and later still at the opera the scene offstage where Orestes hacks Clytemnestra to pieces, and the thrilling and sexually charged finale of *Dialogues of the Carmelites.*

"Blessed St. Margaret Clitheroe pressed to death, oozing charm from every pore—and more. Santa Lucia with her eyes on a plate—is that detail in the song? We don't think so. Santa Barbara, breasts on a plate. If they only knew out there. The terror of mastectomy.

"Mary Surratt, hung out with the laundry, her eyes plucked out by ravens.

"Ruth Snyder, Ethel Rosenberg—got the hot seat.

"Bonnie Parker riddled with bullets, squirming in the hail-of-bullets in the sitting-up dance of death in the front seat of that old jalopy.

"And our all-time favorite, from the childhood realm of comic books—in this case the EC horror comics of the early '50s, finally banned by some authority. Right thing to do for a change. Child molestation, no question, in which the vast majority take place among relatives in the home—in what the Roman Catholic novelist François Mauriac has called 'the serpent's nest of blood ties.'"

"There were a lot of fat ladies around then, especially in the opera," Moriarty said. "'It's not over 'til the fat lady sings.' Your mother's dearest friend was a fat lady who conformed to popular type. Wonderfully kind, always laughing. Alma was her name, Alma meaning soul."

"To the traumatizing story in the EC horror comic. Man married to fat woman forever eating Whitman's Sampler chocolates, and nagging, nagging. Finally husband has enough. Chops her into pieces and arranges the body parts in a handcrafted Whitman's Sampler box."

"You have always been fascinated by the mutilation and murder of girls and women," Moriarty observed. "It started with your grandfather's story of the maniac who bashed in a prepubescent girl's head with her own skate. And then there was the one that took place in the polar bear den . . .

"You haven't yet gotten over the Black Dahlia and probably never will, although strangely enough you took no interest in the Sharon Tate murder by the Charles Manson gang. Years later, sitting in the backroom of Max's Kansas City under Dan Flavin's neon orange triangle illuminating the notorious Round Table you said (illustrating your Donald Lyons know-it-all quick-study cadet status) that the Tate murder wasn't glamorous enough to qualify, as was the failed actress Peg Entwhistle's fabulous nocturnal swan dive off the H of the giant HOLLYWOOD-LAND sign, but merely sloppy and sordid like so much coming out of Hollywood at the time. You were of course shitfaced, but managed still to make the better part of your audience find you truly sick, perhaps dangerous.

"Then Sid Vicious killed his girlfriend Nancy in the Hotel Chelsea, and you said the location itself made it immortal—they should put up a plaque outside, next to the one commemorating Dylan Thomas's death."

So Dave Moore and little Davey were sitting in the kitchen having lunch, when the woman's body flew past the window, headed in the wrong direction for blue skies. Dave Moore prevented Davey from looking out the window, while screams erupted from housewives at their kitchen windows all over the building. The story circulated like measles all over the parish, and for years was periodic table talk on 95th Street.

And when his mother would say of an acquaintance in hospital 'for a rest' (alcoholic detox), 'It all got to be too much for her, she went to pieces, everything seemed, well, of a piece, but as fragile as a piece of peanut brittle. And that is all that will be said on the subject."

Send in the clowns.

. . .

("Marie Sherman made me up as a clown for Pop's party."

"She was trying to cheer you up after the Hiroshima business."

He remembered most the red hair and the rouge circles—and Marie Sherman had brought along from L.A. a red wig from a costume shop.

"I suppose that gave you the idea for the red hair," David said.

"Gorgeous, isn't it? I inherited this auburn hair from our Grandmother Moore."

"At the age of forty?"

"Late development.")

. . .

Moriarty said, "I'm perfect for the ringmaster role—they can't put me in hell."

"You're mad—you seriously think I believe all that hell shit?"

"You can take the boy out of the Church, but you can't necessarily— tell the world you didn't consider making a clean breast of it all with that Mexican Dominican priest who came to send Kitty Moore off to seventh heaven."

"Get out of my sight, ringmaster."

"But not out of your hearing—and hearing is the last to go, remember?"

Moriarty assumed the position: no megaphone.

"Not that it matters lost in the mists of time, but can you remember was it here in the legendary Ramble or down at the Everard Baths that you first learned the meaning of the word 'palpate' and gloried both in the word and in your expertise at it?"

"I really can't remember."

"Test your memory, my dearie, do you remember the mad queen down on Bank Street ('"Penny Candy" was written for me, you know') and the bunch of violets he always wore in his open neck lavender shirts, and his great claim to fame? That elaborately constructed game 'Central Park.' Properties: Seal Pen, Big Cat House, Simian Sanctuary. Hippopotamus, Rhinoceros and Crocodile House. The Polar Bear Cave. The Boat Lake, the Pond, the Bird Sanctuary, the Reservoir, the Boat Pavilion, the children's model boat pond, the Alice in Wonderland memorial, the Angel of the Waters, the horse trail, Cleopatra's Needle, the Ramble . . ."

. . .

His mother said the Ramble was the Yorkville kids' favorite spot. Had he ever once of an afternoon (to go in at night was to court disaster) gone into the Yorkville children's favorite spot without recalling what she'd said and thinking of children? Is the charge true—are all homosexuals potential child molesters? ("Woe unto they who scandalize my little ones, for it would be better for them that a millstone be tied around their necks and that they be drowned in the depths of the sea!")

(Oddity: the name of the most notorious gay bar on Long Island's South Fork: The Millstone.)

One card in the mad queen on the Bank Street's game of Central Park read, "Child molestation by distant time and close proximity, even as imagined: Go to Jail for Life, then to Hell for all Eternity."

One needn't be stroke ridden to deliberately or otherwise conflate time, place and incident.

Nightmare scenario based on a vivid occurrence. One afternoon Author is cruising the Ramble when he comes upon a group of boys with their short pants down around their ankles, engaged in the kind of sex play that was common in his youth in Jackson Heights—the circle jerk—the ritual rite of passion from sporadic thought to aching obsession vigorously as each built as quickly as he might to his climax, groaning, as potent jolts of sensation throbbed deeply through their engorged helmets.

So far so true, actual and satisfactual but in the dream . . .

From his point of vantage on the high rock he can see them but unless they look up they can't see him. He is riveted and sits down on a rock to watch. He compulsively drops his pants and is about to start masturbating, intending to shoot his load down on one of their heads, when an undercover vice cop pulls him up, cuffs him and drags him to an unmarked squad car parked on the curb in front of the Metropolitan Museum of Art. Back in the Ramble, the boys pull up their pants, put on their St. Ignatius Loyola uniform jackets, collect ten bucks apiece from a second plainclothes cop, and walk away laughing.

The little shits, decoys. Will they testify against him for the prosecution, bearing false witness? How false? Well, he never saw any of them look up, so how could they have seen him. But what did that matter to Lillian Law?

At the very least, each post-meridian entry into the Ramble occasioned feelings of extreme unease.

"Child molesters often murder their prey, usually by strangulation."

How often had he wanted to strangle his mother. All homosexual men unconsciously or consciously want to murder their mothers, who are inevitably the rivals for the sexual union they seek from their fathers. The fabled overprotective mother of the sissy boy is trying to protect herself; the father in question most often flees in terror.

"You stayed with your mother for three nights, throwing her sins in her blank face until finally you told her to die, and she promptly did so."

"You're trying to make me kill myself, but I refuse to."

"Behold the wilting lily—listen, St. Teresa heard a lot worse from *her* devils."

"And as usual you're full of shit—men who wear Givenchy, *L'eau sauvage*, Yardley and Bill Blass do not molest little girls."

"So the dragnet is out for the Old Spice crowd?"

"Evaporate yourself, conversation truncated, we are no longer on speaking terms."

"You have never understood. I come when called for and don't depart on demand."

"Alas."

. . .

She'd said as children they went to Central Park all the time after they outgrew Carl Schurz Park. They went ice skating on the Pond, looking up at the Plaza and afterward drifting through the Egyptian room at the Metropolitan Museum. Later she remembered the society bandleader Eddie Duchin's grand Central Park Casino at 72nd Street, the big lake where rented gondolas drifted lazily about, within shouting distance of the magnificent Dakota Apartments, prowling through the Ramble searching out secret places and sitting on the rim of the little lake where boys sailed their model boats, the rich kids' store-bought miniature yachts coursing over the same bounding main as the other kids' often homemade skiffs and sailboats— one of the few places in the city where the classes mingled freely, the rich kids always accompanied by their nannies, who kept a protective eye on their charges lest they mingle too freely with the lower orders, coming home with their mouths full of dirty words and their little heads swarming with head lice.

From the southeast entrance across from Grand Army Plaza, his grandfather walked with him down to the Pond where the bird sanctuary you could never go into was, and showed him the bust of the Irish Romantic poet Thomas Moore, songster and friend of Byron ("Tommy loved a lord"), a kind of ancestor, and told him how a forward-looking party of Moores had come to Philadelphia from Dublin in the year 1763, well before the War of Independence and a century before he, Dave Moore, was born down on Grand Street. (In later years in St. Stephen's Green, a tame but pretty park on Dublin's South Side, he decided he'd much rather have been related to another Irish Romantic poet of the nineteenth century, the amazingly beautiful James Clarence Mangan, author of "My Dark Rosaline," whose bust—open neck shirted, brass hair flying in the wind—sat majestic on its plinth of Wicklow stone.)

And as for George Gordon, Lord Byron, who boasted of owning the biggest cock in England; it was said that when some sacrilegious party exhumed his body they cut the whopper off: it's supposedly somewhere in a jar, suspended in formaldehyde.

. . .

The rocks—schist: Manhattan, Washington Heights, the Bronx—a couple of them outcropping on the East Side in the back yards of townhouses. Also said to be connected to Gibraltar.

Molly Bloom's soliloquy and "Aw, rocks, tell us in plain words: metempsychosis, psychosis . . ." The Prudential insurance man coming to the house: company logo, big rock ("Own a piece of"). Death and fear and desire for inheritance all mingled together. *Double Indemnity*— the young boy's fascination with film noir. Picture based on the Ruth Snyder case in New York, the classic case, they called it in the apartment on 95th Street. She got the chair (the picture on the front page of the *Daily News* of her strapped in, smoke rising from her leather helmeted head—everybody going to work: headline *DEAD*).

Women fainting and men throwing up their breakfasts.

Brünnhilde's rock: rock, matches, paper? The White Rock girl. Club soda. Scotch and soda, "mud in your eye." Why? Rock 'n' rye, the Big Rock Candy Mountain. Rock Hudson and the rumors—legs wrapped around the necks of hustlers . . . forbidden sex, Author as top and then bottom, the remorse over battling the lethal maternal introject using his mother's real life story: *how to bear it?* How could such a thing be beneficial as Jack Burlison insisted it was?

Rock/Cock. "Cock of Ages, cleft for me, let me hide myself in thee."

Upright Protestants with all the fucking money (Mrs. Gotrocks). Rockabye baby . . . the cradle will rock, the cradle will fall. Rockaway . . . under the boardwalk. Rock 'n' roll. Rocking the boat being a queer. The linguistic ridiculousness of the pun in "Thou art Peter and upon this rock I will build my church" (what Galilean fisherman spoke Latin. What Jewish rabbi for that matter).

His Central Park stories in the college literary magazine; his ideas of sophistication: hansom cab rides after the senior prom, giving his date and nominal girlfriend Claire his class ring.

The wild and subjugating sound of the park's chief emblem, the carousel. Steam calliope music at night? Impossible, like hearing the songs of the fairies—"The Good People," "The Other Crowd"—while out walking on a summer's night in Mayo. And yet he heard: hypomixilydian mode as far as he could make out. Something deeply queer about the steam calliope; what? Every ghost of every past—the lasting place.

In other words his whole life represented. Central Park an essential *topos* in our text, a trope.

Topos: literary critical term, from the Greek, meaning place; plural, *topoi.*

The essential allure of Central Park: a lifelong vision of the green world (in which all the predators but men and snakes have been put in guarded caves and cages) enclosed in oblong garden walls. "Beside the garden wall . . ." ("Stardust," Hoagy Carmichael)

Come into the garden, Maud,
For the black bat, night, has flown . . .
   (Tennyson—"Anyone for?")

The precinct of the unruly, of the rambling jaywalkers, they whom the grid has driven mad.

Every statue originally bronzed and gleaming like pure gold the morning sun, long since weathered, creating a patina of verdigris—save that of General Sherman led by Victory, rebronzed and covered with some newly invented protective coating that would keep it gleaming for as long as the city lasted (or was made to disappear in seconds in a ball of fire a thousand times more devastating than that which leveled Hiroshima), so unlike the statuary in the Metropolitan Museum of Art—white as white, the bleached bones of antiquity, misrepresented in that antedating their rediscovery they'd all been rendered vividly in every color (Athena for example, with bright blue eyeballs) of the painter's palette applied to the white marble, making the Sacred Way on the Acropolis, leading up to the Parthenon, a riot of color as erotic as the world of the Hindu pantheon dancing over Pramit Banarjee's yellow cab dashboard, in which the shapes of the deities are more imaginative and evocative than those of any other religion currently working the planet (and their numbers seemingly as great as the population of the Indian subcontinent itself).

All reminiscent of the exotic Technicolor of his youth—although the fantastic color *Cobra Woman* (Maria Montez) and the Ali Baba pictures were not Hindu—but he had seen Bollywood pictures and television documentaries of the floating gardens of the Punjab and of the blazing funeral pyres of Benares, reminiscent of those January bonfires of the dead Christmas trees up in the overgrown lot on Polk Avenue, on which no house had ever been built. (And as they stood around them Johnny Zillich—called by his brother David "Johnny Zilch"—would talk of the sacred duty of the *Aghori*, eating remains on the Ganges, eating the bits of unburned flesh off the charred bones of the incinerated.)

And finally, instead of a revolting Catholic wake out in Jackson Heights, a vision of pall bearers laying his mother's body, garbed in Franciscan robes, on top of a pyre of Christmas trees in that vacant lot across from the Polk theater, where he'd first seen Technicolor on the screen.

. . .

His grandfather once showed him the site of Hooverville (and each Thanksgiving Day, before the afternoon meal, Author and all the children of the neighborhood dressed up as bums and went around the neighborhood singing

Thanksgiving's coming, the turkey's gettin' hot,
Please put a nickel in the old man's pot,
If you haven't got a nickle, a penny will do,
If you haven't got a penny, then God bless you.)

The boy became so fascinated by bums and his grandfather's stories of the Depression and the Hooverville shanties, he asked for a model Hooverville.

"They don't make model Hoovervilles," his mother said, "and anyway there are things best left forgotten."

"By some people maybe."

He remembers her looking at him then with something like fright in her eyes.

He tried to build a Hooverville in the vacant lot where they burned Christmas trees—he used cardboard boxes, but unpopulated it looked like nothing, and his brother refused to lend him his old soldiers to make up a National Guard, so he and his friends burned it down as Hitler's bunker (a game that continued for some years after the war's end).

. . .

The taxi goes around Columbus Circle, left on 57th to Seventh Avenue, right on Seventh Avenue, Carnegie Hall dark and empty.

"You see that building, Pramit? Carnegie Hall; my grandfather built it."

"That is most impressive, sir, most impressive."

"I was impressed, Pramit—I was then only four years old. 'I built Car-*nay*-gie Hall,' he said, 'and went back to listen to the music— Tchaikovsky, don't-cha-know. In person—the reporters called him Pete. No trouble with the Russians in those days—no trouble like pesky Uncle Joe—and of course I had help.'"

. . .

From Carnegie Hall to Howard Johnson's.

"If you will forgive me sir, you seem a trifle upset."

"No trifle I'm afraid, Pramit. Survivor elation—brings on frightful anxiety. And as I think we have become friends——since, I think, we negotiated Columbus Circle—you must call me James."

"I will so, Sir James, from this moment on."

You and me, babe. The echoes are everywhere.

"But as we are friends, Sir James, may one enquire into the nature of this survival anxiety, which in Hindu culture does not exist, for we accept the fact that there is none—survival, Sir James."

"Nobody gets out of life alive—but where's the harm says you, when if you have been a good person you will surely come back in a higher estate."

"You know the Hindu religion, Sir James? Few do."

"I can't help looking at the pantheon on your dashboard and pinned above it. Pramit, I have just survived my mother—no easy thing either. I closed her eyes for the last time less than half an hour ago—and please don't tell me she is going to come back improved. I want her stuck away safely someplace in heaven. There is no more purgatory."

("Didn't you tell me that when you stopped them taking the Lord's name in vain down at L.B. Furriers they started calling you Mary Magdalene? Well, good old Mary Magdalene was the first to see the risen Christ on Easter morning. 'Don't touch me,' he said, 'I've been through hell.'") Missing places: the Taft or any other name did not have Vincent Lopez and its renowned dance floor, and Birdland, the jazz mecca, was no more. What about the I. Miller shoe company building, east of Seventh with its frieze of Mary Pickford, Rosa Ponselle . . . etc. . . . actors, singers . . . who else was there, wearing I. Miller costume footwear—somebody who played Peter Pan . . . Maude Adams, yes, Maude Adams. . . . "Come into the garden, Maud."

Was even the I. Miller building still there? Was Luigino's pizzeria, frequented for decades by operaphiles after the curtain had come down at the Met, with its photographic diptych of Licia Albanese as Butterfly and an ape in identical poses reaching out to each other—and how long was that diva going to live? Was the plaque noting Eugene O'Neill's birthday still on the wall of the building that had once been the hotel in which the birth took place? (EON on his deathbed: "Born in a hotel room—and God damn it—died in a hotel room!")

3

The dream of the culinary service provider. Over on Broadway the Paramount, the Astor (and the Astor Bar) were gone, but there was the Howard Johnson's where after a show they might go for fried clams and ice cream.

"More coffee, hon?"

"Yes, please, that would be nice."

"Always a sad time of the night when the theaters are all emptied out and the traffic jams in the streets have broken up."

"It didn't used to be when after the show you were headed out to late supper and the night clubs—that's when the New York night went on till dawn."

"Yeah, and the Broadway baby got to sleep early in the morning. I remember it well. Where are the shows of yesteryear."

"I'll drink to that if only with black coffee."

"I don't know why, but I get the feeling you've got a long night ahead of you—working the night shift so to speak—I don't mean being a bad boy, because baby, it's cold out there. Of course there's probably no business either, what with the Internet and everything gotten so sophisticated. *We* were sophisticated."

"Throwaway swank."

"That was the stuff."

"You're still sophisticated—a sophisticated lady."

"You remember the day—anyway, not only can you find out everything on the Internet, so you don't have to know anything anymore—frees you up to lose your mind—but you can get anything you need too; you can get a hot pastrami sandwich online, delivered in ten minutes. Plus all that other stuff—which is no longer remotely sophisticated."

"I figured you hadn't made me for a market researcher from out of town who'd come for the boys upstairs at the Gaiety, only to find the doors bolted and the joint gone out of business."

"Oh, honey, you've got dyed-in-the-wool New Yorker written all over you—you could sew on a label. Your first time at the rodeo was a long time ago."

"When it gets dull I sit down with my coffee and polish up my French verbs—time was French was the second language around here."

"I remember—'Fractured French' cocktail napkins 'Carte Blanche,' 'Pied à terre . . .'"

"Everybody said 'Pardon my French.' after using a profane expression, like 'tight as a crab's ass.'"

"You weren't born yesterday."

"I was born five months before Pearl Harbor."

"You never!"

"Sometimes I feel that way, but City Hall doesn't lie."

"You kiddin'? It lives by lies. So, there's a portrait hanging in the attic?"

"My mother never looked her age—She died about half an hour ago up at St. Luke's and I had the odd feeling she was headed right down here to the bright lights before the theaters went dark. She always said she'd have more energy when she was dead three days than we had at any time."

"Oh. Gosh, hon, I'm sorry—how old a woman was she, if I may ask."

"Ninety five."

"God bless her—she must have led some kind of life. Boy, are they in for a shock at the wake."

"She buried them all—all the McCourts."

"She must have been kind of lonely all the same, but aren't we all, one way or another? I miss the girls at the Latin Quarter and the Copa— we were some bunch—and a lot of the ponies I danced with. Guess that's why I took another job on Broadway—probably would have tried the dime-a-dance joints if they'd still been around. This may look like waitressing, it's really performance art. People from all over the country take my picture—I'm a Broadway *attraction*."

"Bet you don't go home to an empty room."

"Alone, yes, hall room no, I've got a nice one bedroom over on Tenth Ave. These days they call the neighborhood Clinton—no more Hell's Kitchen. I'm sentimental, and I once did 'Slaughter on Tenth Avenue' in the *On Your Toes* national tour—so you could say I was a Balanchine dancer first and foremost.

"I did Graham, ended up a Fosse dancer—made my last stand, so to speak in the all-Fosse show."

"Marge and Gower Champion."

"Aces—tops."

"Bambi Lynn and Rod Alexander."

"Phooey—zero. It is sad though—the Gaiety Male Burlesk certainly did not go out of business for want of steady customers."

"Giuliani."

"Who else? Hypocritical sonofabitch."

"I went to high school with him in Brooklyn. We were both in the opera club until I found out he was a dumb-ass wop Tebaldi fan, pardon my French. He would have excuse the expression knelt down and eaten her out while she was singing '*Vissi d'arte*,' I lived for art."

"'Spine tingling adoration,' huh. I remember her, she had a big gorgeous voice, half the time she sang flat as a Child's pancake.

"I don't think it was ever sinewy spine tingling love for those wandering boys up there on the runway—plenty of flippant ass, God I loved them when they'd come in after the last show—the ones who hadn't scored—but, no bells ringing."

"Now, that was a show—and Judy Holliday. The original live wire."

"The only repose in this town is for the souls of the faithful departed."

"Faithful—faithful to what?"

"Good question—you'd have to wonder, wouldn't you. I suppose what it comes down to is the repose of the souls of the good eggs, know what I mean?"

"Yes, I guess so."

"Of course you do. Your mother, for instance, was a good egg, I can tell—what else would make you sit at her deathbed—you're no sap."

"It just didn't seem fair, that's all, leaving her to die alone up there with nobody talking to her, urging her on."

"There had to be a lot more to it than that. I'd have talked to her— you know talk is supposed to be the waitress's stock in trade, the real talk of the town. And I was never that breathtaken by the thought of limitless possibilities that it snatched the voice right out of my throat. The only thing that ever did that was laryngitis from strain on the vocal chords, like a opera singer. I was seldom indisposed."

"Well, here are a couple of strange stories about my mother you can tell: The room at the Residence was not one with a view—I used to tease her 'What on the Upper West Side would a Yorkville girl be interested in looking at anyway, Grant's Tomb? New Jersey?'—so everything from the outside came from the television screen. In one case, six months before she died, we had been watching Peter Jennings covering the attacks on the World Trade Center.

"'Hispanics?' she had asked. Word had already reached her of the death of her granddaughter's fiancé. And she was hurt and bewildered. 'Hispanics?' she asked, looking intently at the replay footage (terrified of the answer, she having given so much of her life as a primary-school teacher and an active parishioner talking down with righteous ire all the old Irish biddies in the parish back in Jackson when they objected to the two-language Mass schedule and bemoaning the influx of Colombians and the diocesan decision to institute a Sunday Mass in Spanish in every parish with a significant Hispanic population).

"'No, Arabs.'

"'The bastards—who's *that* guy?'

"'That is nobody less than my former classmate at both Loughlin and Manhattan, His Honor the Mayor of the City of New York.'

"'Italian.'

"'Yes.'

"'Republican.'

"'Yes.'

"'Sneaky.'

"'Very.'

"'Honest, though.'

"'More or less—no Fiorello, however.'

"'Good show *Fiorello.* Tebaldi fan.'

"'You remember.'

"'Of course I remember—I've got a few marbles left as yet, you know. What's he doing, campaigning for election?'

"'He's making his presence felt.'

"'They all do that—goddam nuisances; let the police and fireman do their jobs.'

"'And go home to Gracie Mansion, put his feet up, and watch it all from there?'

"'Exactly.'

"There is of course a back story to all this," he added, by way of explanation to the waitress.

"Any time you want to tell it—I was always a great 'This is where I came in' girl—got to prefer watching the pictures that way. Even if I came in on the second feature and it was lousy I wouldn't leave after the main attraction, but always sat there until the 'This is where I came in' moment. Funny the things you do."

"And the things you say. Whenever they'd be sitting around telling family stories and got past the Depression to the war, I'd say, 'That was where I came in,' and my brother David would say, 'loud and clear.'"

"The Moores lived in a railroad flat on East 88th Street, near East End Avenue and Carl Schurz Park. There was a hill in the part on top of which sat Gracie Mansion, deserted in those years, later as we know turned into the mayor's official residence."

"For La Guardia, I remember."

"Odd thing, my grandfather always called him 'La Gardia.'"

"Good thing they waited for him—if they'd given it to Jimmy Walker it would have been the biggest, bawdiest speakeasy in town. But back to your mother."

"Yes, she was a highly intelligent, flashingly temperamental narcissist, who could also, and often enough did, turn on a dime into one hell of a good sport."

"I've got news for you, hon—*don't touch that dial*—you loved Kitty Moore. What about the gay thing?"

"We now say queer."

"We now say culinary service provider—a riot, all of it."

"Interesting . . . ending with the Gay Pride March on the TV last year."

She inclines her head.

"No," he told her, "I went once or twice early on, but I can't do crowds anymore—in fact I can't even do parties or dinners of more than eight. The only time I can be with a room full of people; I know what I'm there for then. I can play the author on stage, but offstage no. People ask sneaky questions. But if I'd known you were interested, I'd have gotten an afternoon pass and taken you down there, pushed the chair up the Avenue and you could have gestured to one side and then the other like the Queen Mother."

"Bit of irony there, hon."

"She didn't pick up on it—kept looking at the parade as if she'd missed a great opportunity. 'You remember I told you about my Uncle Jimmy O'Keefe. Sweetest man in the world . . . had the Irish falling sickness, good man's failing.'

" 'Died of it?'

" 'No, he got off it and joined A.A.'

" 'Well, Jimmy had an A.A. friend who used to visit once in a while; later Jimmy died. Came out to Northport, and up to Windham too. Maybe you remember him, Eddie Midwinter. Had been an actor. Always made your father nervous, although he never let on.'"

"It's the strangest thing, hon. You had the strangest look in your eye—as if you were talking in a blackout, but I can tell you don't drink—

or else you'd be down at Dave's or one of the other newshounds' establishments. You really don't remember what you've been saying since the part about the gay—queer parade."

"Something about the family histories—I guess I've told them so often I'm practicing forgetting them forever and have gotten to a certain stage."

"There's something more to it than that. You go on automatic pilot. Your whole life has been one of sprints and intervals, right? Do you know what an absence seizure is? My brother had them—more and more as he got older. They never bothered him at all—in fact he would become more and more light hearted. Saw no reason to see a doctor, he never fell down. Then one day he was walking through Schubert Alley to pick up tickets to a show he was taking me to for my birthday—Judy Holliday in *Bells Are Ringing*—and he fell down dead on the pavement. Not a mark on him anywhere except for the bruise on the side of his nose.

"Everybody said it was an amazingly lucky death—I didn't take it quite that way. I did go to the show, though, and didn't sell the other ticket."

"Now which story do you find more interesting?"

"You can't make a decision along those lines. Left to itself your story and theirs could be shot in black and white and Warner's realism, but the dramatic rise of the city, building by building, is definitely B-picture material in relation to your family, the Moore story—which is strictly Metro, in Technicolor, with historic costumes, transatlantic ships, the American Revolution, and original score with takeoffs on Irish melodies—Academy Award material."

"I've often thought it was like those old movies."

"You should definitely write it up—you'd look swell accepting the Oscar, that old New York accent might remind people that not everybody in New York sounds like Scorsese and Bobby De Niro, eating Chinese food and sending out for pizza."

"At Yale they said I sounded like Helen Hayes."

"Ridiculous. If you sound like anybody it's Alfred Lunt mixed with

Elliott Nugent—classic stage actor and tough guy at the same time—now go figure how old I am."

"I'm vague on time, on eras, but it brings a new terror to death to imagine oneself captured on television for all time standing on the same platform with Meryl Streep, each of us handling identical gold plated statuettes—of a eunuch yet."

"I know what you mean. The days are gone when you could find actresses who called themselves that—actresses—who could play Kitty Moore."

"That's why Bette Davis was asking so much about her. I interviewed her for *Film Comment* when she turned seventy. My mother always said Davis was class."

"She saw a great part from the past she'd never play. Your mother was right, Davis was always class, and so was Kitty Moore."

"Einstein says time bends."

"It certainly bends you over, I can tell you that much—and your father."

"Another story."

. . .

"You had your eyes closed the last few minutes."

"Oh, sorry, hon, I often do that, rest the eyes while letting a story wash over me. You must have thought you were back with your mother, going on and hoping you weren't talking to the wall. Anyway it's no bedtime story you've got to tell.

"Y'know I have the strangest feeling we've met before—and not in here; probably just a common New Yorker feeling."

"Did you ever work at the Burger Ranch on 40th and Seventh?"

"No, but I used to go in here with the girls—I was dancing in *Aida* and *La Traviata* at the time. God, how long ago was that? I wasn't steady, only 'between Broadway engagements.' I was a showgirl most of the time. You went there a lot, didn't you, from the old Met. I thought I remembered you when you walked in. But I said to myself from the look of him he can't be old enough to have been part of that crowd—gosh, honey, you sure are well preserved."

"And you don't look nearly old enough to have been a Latin Quarter girl sitting up there hanging from the ceiling in a birdcage—"

"With peacock feathers sticking out of my ass, warming up the audience for Kathryn Grayson. Good thing too, since even in this humble profession when you turn sixty-five, it's the heave-ho."

"Do you remember Rhoe?"

"Rhoe? Who does not remember Rhoe? Not remembering Rhoe is like not remembering Lucille Ball. A legend in the profession. I remember you saying something funny about her, but I don't remember what."

"I said she was probably a waitress at the Last Supper, which I got from my mother, who used to say it about old nuns that seemed to have been around forever."

"I remember you clearly now, the kid in the dark blue cape coat— you told me your big brother used to date Latin Quarter girls. You used to sing arias."

"Mainly mezzo soprano ones—like '*Mon coeur s'ouvre à ta voix*,' my heart opens at the sound of your voice, '*Printemps qui commence*,' the beginning of spring, and the whole of the Judgment Scene, Ortrud's curse and the '*Che farò*,' what shall I do without Eurydice?"

"I remember—you weren't bad at all—a little screechy, but you had some pipes on you, a top that could peel the paint of the walls, a wobble you could walk through and a chest voice like a transmission turning over on a cold day—and you certainly did throw yourself into it."

"My voice was my weapon of choice."

"And you were scrappy too. Everybody else in that crowd was gaga for Callas, but you were in love with Victoria de los Angeles. I remember you got me to go to *Madama Butterfly*—it was the most gorgeous thing I'd ever heard in my life."

"Tuesday, November 4, 1958."

"And then the next day there was this crazy old guy—"

"Sachs—we called him Doctor Sax after the character in Kerouac."

"He had this insane idea for the second act, when Butterfly is singing the big aria—"

"'*Un bel di*,' one fine day."

"Yes—Kathryn Grayson sang it at the Latin Quarter, in a shimmering white dress that must have cost a thousand dollars—big money in those days—saying her costumes had been lost in transit. She sang with a microphone—sweet little voice, but Victoria de los Angeles was better—she delivered the goods, all right, you got the message."

"That's just the word."

"And she sings how they'll see a puff of smoke—"

"From the ship coming into the harbor—"

"Yeah, he said they should flash the mushroom cloud over Nagasaki on a scrim upstage. And you started shaking like you'd had a bad shock—you were a shaky kid anyway. And I asked you what was the matter and you said you'd been—"

"Traumatized—yes."

"By the first atom bomb they dropped on Hiroshima—and the crazy old guy said, 'But darling, I'm talking about the *second* one—on *Nagasaki. Madame Buttercup* takes place there.'

"You asked me did I ever work at the Burger Ranch. I'm surprised you didn't ask me had I ever worked in the Coliseum. Years later I used to see you in there drinking with your father. You used to get pretty emotional—you weren't the cocky little number you'd been in the old days. Your father was a handsome guy, a real Mister Pants, the whole works.

"Then one night I saw you come in with both your parents—in fact I was working your table. I remember you didn't drink and the three of you all laughed a lot. That's the last I ever saw of your father or yourself until tonight."

"That night you're talking about—my father dropped dead in the bathroom after they got home. I got the call at about four in the morning, 'Your father's gone, dear.' I guess I was surprised at how much it tore me up. It was the only time I ever picked out a casket for anybody—I went expensive."

"He was an expensive-looking guy, your dad."

"I figured you only die once, so go the whole hog. Do you remember the other woman—what type of woman was she?"

"Oh, so you cottoned on to that, huh."

"They had these friends, the Nallys, Kate and Charlie. Kate had a laugh like a longshoreman. My mother used to say. 'Kate Nally is the salt of the earth—a little Tenth Avenue, but what does that matter?' I always imagined the Other Woman was like Kate Nally—Tenth Avenue is convenient to the piers."

"No, as a matter of fact she was a real lady—quiet and demure."

. . .

Match the inhabitants in Column A with the quest items in Column B.

Column A
    Father
    Mother
    #1 Son
    #2 "
    #3 "
    Grandfather
    Gorgeous delinquent cousin.

Column B
    The Lost Chord
    The Holy Grail
    The original Shaggy Dog story
    The point of it
    The 7 last words
    The perfect batting average (1000)
    The Day of Judgment

4

The original old fuck on the park bench. As the pale gray light of a January dawn came up in Madison Square, he spoke without turning his head to the old man sharing the bench facing south-southwest.

"My grandfather built the Flatiron Building—and the original Madison Square Garden over there."

"That wasn't the original he worked on, not the original Madison Square Garden. It would have been the second, the skyscraper one with the statue by Saint-Gaudens of the goddess Diana perched on the top. Designed by Stanford White, the society architect who kept an apartment there for purposes other than domestic—as did David Belasco in his theater uptown—for which White was shot dead by the mad Harry K. Thaw, while having dinner in the rooftop restaurant—but you knew that. He probably worked—your grandfather—on the third one too, when they moved it up to 50th and Eighth, rendering the name ridiculous in a particularly New York way. And now they've got a fourth rising tall and hideously ugly over the second Pennsylvania Station, pardon-me-boy, a profanation. It's number three that you'd remember as the scene of many exciting experiences—the circus, the rodeo, hockey games, and track meets. Boxing matches you would not have attended, although your father and your older brother undoubtedly did."

"I come from people over there on Gramercy Park. They tried to keep me confined behind bars at Payne Whitney, but the doctors said I'd be safer here from the voices."

"You're talking here to the original old fuck on the park bench, whose distinction and allure has always been associated with shabby appearance, not to mention paranoid schizophrenia, which is no more thanks be to God, Stelazine, Thorazine and Zyprexa. One finds a bench the most logical place to catalogue benchmarks."

"I don't suppose your name is Moriarty."

"No—you know if you turn your head my way I'll still be here. Now and then I'm taken for a stiff sitting up, but that's not so. The brain whispers 'Your vitals are registering.'"

"*Did* you like it so much better when everybody was alive?"

"It had its points."

"So then you did."

"Seems one must have. Let me tell you something about the story you're now telling."

"It's my story and I'm stuck with it?"

"That's neither news nor the point. The point is your contribution to the history of what might have happened, or did, or didn't but always will have, is like your grandfather building the Flatiron Building. There are many contributors, but in the race against time you have the inside track, and history is written by the winners."

"I'm not much of a winner—except for the door prize."

"You know it was a great mistake taking down the Second Avenue El—and never mind the steel was sold to the Japs who gave it all back to the vendor at Pearl Harbor, it was the tearing off of the roof the thing made, leaving the Avenue exposed to the flat glaring light."

"Glory be to God for dappled light, and that bright light drove Second Avenue mad."

"Ever been to Tangier?"

"No—I don't go in for teenage Arab boys or opiated hashish, and Paul Bowles is wildly overrated, as William Burroughs knew—as both a writer and a composer—although Jane isn't, even if she was batshit."

"Ever watch science programs?"

"I used to drink and watch them—would wake up to something about black holes."

"Want to hear a long story about New York?"

"Actually I was hoping to write one."

"And why not; be our guest, but know this one thing: you can neither dictate nor control the rollout on your own. Restless laws and fast control each small portion of the whole. When you come to think of it, that was then and so is this.

"The planet Earth is a woman—a woman who has never made up her mind exactly what she wants to look like . . ."

"We come to a crux, New York's newly discovered foundation myth: at the geographical center of the last great supercontinent on earth, the land mass emerging from the womb of Pangaea, as far inland from Panthalassa as could be—and following the great tectonic split that cleaved Pangaea in two, New York's other half geographically speaking is presently located at the northwest tip of Africa, in Morocco, and across the Straits of Gibraltar, just within the Pillars of Hercules, the Rock of Gibraltar itself. New York now lying directly across the Atlantic that eons ago poured into the cleavage of Pangaea over millions of years until . . .

"Thus New York's destiny all the while lying in becoming its exact opposite, the greatest of all world coastal cities, its destiny as maritime as Venice.

"If the polar ice cap melts later in this century and the tides (ruled by the moon) rise to engulf both Venice and New York, what lives will swim before their eyes. . . . Geology: Deep beneath the buildings, the city streets, beneath the subway tunnels and stations, lies the geological foundation that makes New York City unique in the world. Consequently, there can be no doubt whatever that the notorious New York native personality is more than a metaphor, it is an emblem and essential reflection of the geological evidence: native New Yorkers are unique in the world."

"I was telling the Hindu cabbie earlier that although we have no Big Ben, we do have here and there ringing bells—such as those up there on the Prudential Life Building (the Rock of Gibraltar)."

"For whom the bell tolls?"

"The worst of Hemingway's many bad books—'*I obscenity myself in the milk of your mother.*' And the earth moved, for fuck's sake. Who ever felt the earth move?"

"I couldn't agree more—and at least you know when the earth moves under this little garden of earthly delights it's the Lexington Avenue Express and the BMT up to Carnegie Hall. Remember when that and a nickel would get you on the subway."

"We jumped the turnstiles."

"Ever listen to those shows on the radio: The Shadow knew. Lamont Cranston, voiced by Orson Welles; and so did innumerable other detectives and private eyes. The only significant swerve in this activity was in the greatest classical film of the era, Orson Welles's *Citizen Kane*, in which Chicago is justly represented as the most distinctly American city—even though in the history on which it is based, William Randolph Hearst was a New York yellow journalism mogul and Marion Davies a fetching Ziegfeld chorine. But nobody would have bought the idea of a tycoon building an opera house for a single singer, which is exactly what did happen in Chicago, where Samuel McCormack, the urban streetcar czar, built the Chicago Opera House for the Polish Soprano Ganna Walska. The very preposterous 'frontier' quality of the gesture appropriated by Welles, but actually having no bearing whatever on his Hearst-Marion Davies story line.

"Just as Hollywood became necessary to New York as given over to an industry of mirroring in every metropolis *the* Metropolis, so in radio, the fantasies emanating from New York studios 'peopled' the alternate New York with fabulous fauna—not only a man from the planet Krypton ('Secret World') but the vampire turned benevolent Batman with his captive adolescent, the exact parallel of the enslaved acolyte vampire. Only rather than Dick Grayson's neck revealing the puncture wounds from fangs, it was a rosary of rosebud welts, called 'hickies' by the vulgar—for Bruce Wayne, although a respected socialite, was obviously a slave to love and everybody seems to have known that Robin was a three-ring circus in bed."

Archaeology with teaspoons. (Eliot: "I have measured out my life with coffee spoons.")

Spoons: soup, serving, tea, coffee
Forks: meat, dinner, cake, ice cream (old-fashioned and
    southern)
Knives: carving, steak, fish, bread and butter.

Considering his ability in later life to "looking back" create anachronisms at will, imagine the boy of eleven looking up at the ceiling in the Hayden Planetarium and seeing New York shining like a blue sapphire at the center of Pangaea, and imagining how far it would be and how long it would take to spend a vacation at the beach on Panthalassa. Whatever may be cast concerning the births, lives and deaths of himself and of the others, they all live and breathe entirely between hard covers and anybody who wants to know more or otherwise is going to have to find out for himself (the women may rely on intuition).

Once one has reached a certain age, if instead of seeking out his own couch for an evening spent reading *Moby-Dick,* or taking in the latest Joe Gage porn-video extravaganza—should one find it necessary to go out after dark, especially on the West Side below 14th Street, he should never do so, mark you, except in the company of a familiar of Moriarty's distinction and allure.

The moon in its flight—ghostly galleon behind a veil of cloud thin as a wisp, with all the others gone aboard, whosoever they may be or might have been shining down on the metropolis. Not since Nineveh, on the banks of the Euphrates, had such splendor shone.

That morning he had drawn the Tarot King of Pentacles—so his power that livelong day lay in responsibility. He could surround himself with the conditions he wished to create—*what?*—all depends on so much else—and therefore had everything he needed to be successful and independent according to his values and purposes.

What a shell game.

He who would consider the welfare of others is a master of production. He would be empowered by it and it would be his honor—

Or . . . question . . . nobler . . . mind of man . . .—generous in offering or reproducing security, stability and protection by his virile—

Hah!

—and reliable example. Hidden assets were perennial trust, respect and validation that were well deserved—

Hah!

And his own mother had—a particular way of compromising the universal myth of descent from a high place, for when in the *Mikado* Yum-Yum sings "I mean to rule the earth, and he the sky," she is singing in the persona of Kaguya, the original and originating moon goddess of Japan.

Memories are made of such things, but never the things themselves— he has never once talked of seeing Margo Channing in *Remembrance* at the Schubert Theater in San Francisco. Mooning over countless men. *Qot homines tot sententiae.* So many men, so many opinions. Moreover, the records, tapes and discs he owns bring reminiscences too difficult to bear. Nostalgia is dreadful, its victims enslaved by it in its baleful presence and their dread obligation to it.

And they are fleet of foot, swift as the gazelle: futile the attempt to head them off at the And-It-Came-To-Pass. Let's get this thing started.

(Give him a minute to polish his plectrum and we're off.)

He was going to go out and grab happiness, or as much as anybody had to spare anyway, Now he no longer follows people anywhere, so for now where they used to lead him is irrelevant: he is alive. He neither bugged nor tapped nor sought to catch big-bang events in clamped ellipses, bent on deceiving most of the people all of the time.

Assess load, do not bend, assume Fifth Position, breathe from diaphragm.

Half squat to lift, *demi-plié*, pull out load, and carry away.

Free association: employment of no longer restricted to analysands on analysts' couches, has become a godsend to memoirists with uncertain but compelling goals. The Age of Chaos (which thoughtfully provides at its inception its own theory). All chaotic familiarity is familiar in the same way. When everybody's someone then no one is anybody—but that's the whole point.

Studies have shown everything, and it's all true, natch, but irrespective and regardless of the fact—that (the case found true) and a nickel will get you on—still holds.

The world is everything that is the case, according to Wittgenstein; the will of God is what happens. Rumors keep circulating and that's all one can say about that. *Und Morgen wird die Sonne wieder scheinen*, and the sun will rise again tomorrow, God willin' and the crick don't rise— not your stuff exactly, is it my love.

You got that right, dear, one's never even read *Huckleberry Finn*.

. . .

Roses are red and violets are blue, and how can that be the case when on the spectrum of colors found in the rainbow, blue is one color and violet another, with indigo, which is a mood, between them, but if violets *were* blue, and you mixed their pigment with the red of red roses, you would get the color purple, the color of loosestrife and of heather on the hill. This was an example of metaphysics, a game for rainy days.

However, such questions are epidemic, and he's not been in an epidemic for decades now. And never forget the best boy electric, the rigging key grip or the unit publicist either—"You think they're doing this for their health? They are not, have been taken on, put on the payroll to protect and assist the workings of the stable sites of contestation."

"Watch out—you are leaving your performance in the dress rehearsal," the wise old fuck said.

"We did it once."

"I take it you mean by that once upon a time rather than one time only."

"Well . . ."

"Tell the world you're not a sucker for a pair of pouty pink lips."

Used to be was—he wore lipstick, not kiss-proof.

"Heaven on earth with the angel of one's choice."

"Angels fall, if not to hell, by the wayside. It's tragic."

"'*Rough winds do shake the darling buds of May, / And summer's lease hath all too short a state.*' That's Shakespeare."

"Nice—I couldn't have said it better myself."

"'*Les sauvages dansent sans cesse la fête de la nuit.*' The natives dance their all-night festival without stopping."

"Affrighting the wildlife—squirrels."

"Beasts. *Bêtise.*"

"Quiz question. Rimbaud, Jean Arthur Nicolas, a dirty foul-mouthed little savage at loose in a civilized city—ever see them together? as the snappy saying went in those madly sophisticated days in the twilight of everything.

"'He is identical twins in one body' is what people said of you. 'He is looking for a man who will love him for himself as he is, not what he thinks he ought to be—especially if what they think he ought to be is snuffed.'

"'He wishes the unseen parts of his slender body to be handled, with care—This Side Up.'

"'Say hello, you never know,' is his mantra—especially when he got a full snoot in him. To say he'll cross the wide avenue to prove his point is insufficient; he'll walk out into the middle of traffic if the prospect is walking briskly up the other side."

"And then there are gifts."

"*Petits cadeaux.* Little nothings.

"'*Je vous en prie, prenez cette bourse qui me gêne.*' I beg you, kindly take my wallet, which only weighs me down.

"Of course there were no barons, no earls, no diamonds, no pearls, no ermine and—no trip to Harlem (unless you count the Mt. Morris Baths) until taken there under protective custody of one's beautiful black college roommate—straight but hip, and he looked like a male Lena Horne."

"Bet that French ventriloquist taught you a lot, didn't he."

"It was reciprocal, a two-way street; I taught him how to make lasagna."

"And then there were all the suits and overcoats and camel skin shoes and watches showered on you by your father. 'Mahdeah,' they said to you, 'with a father like that you do not need a john.'"

"I needed a john a lot in those days—the bitter fruits of sin."

"Shall we compare thee to a summer's day burned scarlet in the sun, as you had been as an infant when your Aunt Elizabeth, your godmother, fell asleep in the sun while holding you in her lap and turned you both into boiled lobster."

"I told that story."

"It was your explanation for always sitting under the beach umbrella."

"The sonnets don't tell the half of it, do they—what happens."

"One often wondered how many of you boys carried those cards in your wallet in case of a lethal assault I AM A CATHOLIC. PLEASE CALL A PRIEST, and if the uniformed branch was able to rouse one at the local rectory, working the death-at-the-hour-of-the-wolf shift, would he be one who'd sucked your cock at the Everard Baths. You used to say you'd like to be a fly on the wall when Tim Tyler fucked Chuck White, but you were no fly, baby, you were the fucking *wall*."

"No. I was no fly—never really, not when I remembered the rhyme they'd taught me in Northport."

"The rhyme—another sonnet?"

"No, more an elegy."

Little fly upon the wall,
Ain't ya got no home at all?
Ain't ya got no suit that fits?

Don't ya get no Christmas gifts?
Ain't ya got no friends t'play with?
Ain't ya got no folks t'stay with?
Awww—*wanna see God?*

"*Splat.*"

"Now Nineveh was a wicked city and Jonah preached against it and he was swallowed by the whale—although since Nineveh is hundreds of miles inland, whence came the whale, in the cloud that Hamlet taunts Polonius with? In any event the whale threw Jonah up back on shore. History does not record how Jonah lit a fire in the whale's belly—but Pinocchio did in Mostro's, and *Pinocchio* was your favorite child's story. After all, you doubted your carnality and perhaps as a consequence became what your friends called an invertebrate liar, but you got the message about the nose in record time, long before you read Freud—in German, you insisted—and went into analysis. Do I give a fair illustration of how your mind ceaselessly works—and fuck 'em all if it disconcerts them, they could eat shit and die?"

"I believe a copyeditor, or a fact checker at *The New Yorker*—they are such dears—would find a few errors in the publication of your illustration, but there you have it, don't you—I mean to say, this is it.

"Whereas others, many, declared '*Mirabile dictu,*' strange and wonderful to say.

"And I 'Thank you.' You know Zinka Milanov said it all. 'Look, I tell you, I luff my public and my public luffs me—we understand each other very well.'"

"You luffed them, and in a manner of speaking, fluffed them. You were out to grab as much love as anybody could spare. And you always were without question always a hard worker in your chosen field of endeavor.

"And of course it's true, we do all end up in the garbage pail—which is why it is so important to find the most accommodating garbage pail one possibly can—down by the trucks parked overnight on the waterfront. All through the night men came by to haunt the place, known back in the day as 'the filling station,' New York's most famous outdoor summer night homosex arena from midnight to dawn's early light."

LOADING ZONE.
NO OVERNIGHT PARKING.
LAW STRICTLY ENFORCED.

"Scruffy."

"And as for this fair chunk of Eden, operating the same hours it must have been the statue by Saint-Gaudens of old Admiral Farragut over there—Saint-Gaudens got a lot of work in those days—"

"Damn the torpedoes, full speed ahead!"

"It was then as now the middle of winter—although as sometimes happens warm for the season—the January thaw, not quite midwinter spring. Do not you chide—Friday's Child, loving and giving. 'Love is not love that does not show itself'—and sitting on a park bench forty years ago with a stiff dick sticking out of your chinos certainly qualifies you for service to your countrymen. I take it you have not come here as before, waiting to meet some interesting people—make new friends and have more good times. Well, not anymore—gone are the days when they came in their hapless and unheeding droves, damned the torpedoes, barreled full speed ahead: the lavender flotilla.

"And in the end you made an impact or you didn't—simple as that.

"*Neurotic Counterfeit Sex* was the title of the book, a polemic. *One* was the magazine of the Mattachine defense. 'We find the term "straight" demeaning. There are no straights, all men are bent, being either of the heterosexual bent or the homosexual one.'

"You've seen me here before—is that what you're implying?"

"Your inference is correct—there are no clean getaways—but not in a very long time, not since you used to stalk terrified tourists on hot summer nights up and down Greenwich Avenue, shout solidarity avowals up at the whores hanging out the windows of the Women's House of Detention, which you called Tehachapi, and calling every third manifestation of the burgeoning queer culture *chronic*. And what was that little saying you scribbled on a stall in the can at the Cherry Lane?"

"I forget."

"Really? And you renowned for your memory."

"It may come back to me—lately I'm preparing to telescope things that happened between Pearl Harbor and V-J Day, with some postwar spillover—not much."

"Well, before you shut out the rest of your life, I remember what you wrote. '*They also serve who merely lick it off the floors.*' Even though you were generally thought of as a labeled loser. You had your ways, you were not lackadaisical—in fact you were quite famous for your unshakable, remorseless patience."

("Jimmy," Donald Lyons, who really knew it all, had said, "you have the patience of Job—and the temperament of Medea.")

"Still recognizable to those with a memory in that you still sit looking down and to the left, indicating the determined recollection of past events. At such times you would read quiet, soft spoken and confident, and not the tremulous neurotic wreck you actually were.

"You were interesting to listen to, but you put a great strain on people, even on seasoned big city folk who were witness to your antics."

"There's now't so queer."

"You had a certain reputation, game but not entirely real—like the taste of take-out coffee mixed with the taste of the paper cup it came in. Also apparently too young to know fear, but we know all about that, those of us born too old to know anything else except how to mask it, lest the rank odor of flop sweat close our show before it makes it to Broadway.

"Sex on a pogo stick, they said—sucks a mean cock, swallows copious amounts of spunk, takes it up the wazoo like a trooper, and falls hopelessly in love accepting dates to meet at the Plaza fountain, ones he knows in his hollow heart are bound to be no-shows."

"Unrequited love's a bore."

"Like Chet Baker—in 'I Fall in Love too Easily.' In life you fell in love too easily with love—'blah-blah-blah-blah-blah-blah-blah-blah-love.' In your attempt to make a splash socially, you cannonballed into the pool like a naughty child and got everybody poolside wet. You did everything in those days to attract attention but yodel—maybe you should've taken lessons. You really did get to be like gum on people's shoes."

"You're awfully judgmental, you know that?—I haven't met such a judgmental old fuck since the night I sidled up to John Carradine at the bar in Pete's Tavern down on Irving Place where Washington Irving lived and wrote—and who gave a fat rat's ass about that?—and started chatting him up—he really was a great actor and had worked with Douglas Sirk—starred in the movie *Hitler's Madman*. 'I perceive, sir,' he said in that famously deep, resonant voice, 'that you are homo-*sexual*.' I asked him did that matter, and he said something like, not if I behaved myself—governed myself accordingly is what he said—and showed good manners. I asked him would that be good homosex-ual manners or good manners as construed by famous old actors when approached by their admirers, 'You can't think I'm trying to put the make on you—you're a grand old man.' He laughed out loud—I think if I hadn't stuck the 'grand' in he'd have told me to fuck off and get lost. We were rough and ready guys—"

"Yes, on the corner of the square—Sheridan Square."

"—but oh how we could harmonize. '*Libiamo*,' 'Drink, Drink, Drink' from *The Student Prince* and '*Giovinezza, giovinezza, primavera di bellezza*,' youth, oh youth, springtime of beauty, the Italian Fascist drink-ing song."

"A bold move with Carradine—you knew he'd already clocked you?"

"Definitely. What I did not say was the only grand old man I'd try to put the make on was Alfred Lunt."

"You'd have had to get past her."

"I had a plan for Miss Fontanne: they said she took a nap every afternoon, after she'd hung her head backwards off the side of the bed for twenty minutes to fend off gravity, and he went for a walk. I figured I'd shanghai him on his walk, butter him up in all sincerity on his truly great performance in Dürrenmatt's *The Visit*, and take him down to the Everard, which I'd heard he frequented on nonmatinee afternoons."

"Ah, the Everard Baths—your home away from home and dormitory in those far-off happy days, you enjoying the company of mature men in various aspects, night after night, and sometimes taking in a matinee on a rainy afternoon, favoring always gentlemen of the ebony persuasion."

"True enough—except I don't think they had been persuaded black; but *Happy Days* is a play by Samuel Beckett. And when I got him there— Alfred Lunt—I'd fuck his lights out and then lay him out to whale shit for letting that second rate English comedienne prevent him from playing great roles and sticking him in piece after piece of Mandarin philistine theater shit until—actually she was pretty good in *The Visit* too."

"You never saw them in *Idiots' Delight*."

"And you did, right?"

"I did. And they were both wonderful—I'm very old, dear."

"The world is waiting?"

"The world waits for nothing, my dear—neither does its mother. Not since you quit graduate school and had a nervous breakdown, spending every afternoon back home in Jackson Heights watching soap operas— *The Secret Storm* and *One Life to Live* were favorites—getting tanked and going to the real opera or the ballet every night."

"Ergo zero. Would you say not since the last time you saw me here?"

"Rolling around in the predawn light on a cardboard carpet with a bizarre assortment of similarly driven inverts of all ages—*quelle galère*, what a pain. Like piles of second cuttings ready to be bailed and ready to be wrapped tight—a new experience for them all. As often as not involved in fantasies involving great quantities of Spanish moss dripping off tall thin live oak after you'd all lost *Belle Rive*. You said you were going to be a writer and I predicted a brilliant career in custom content magazines."

"Then how would you know—?"

"That your life had taken one dog-leg turn, then another, charting a 180-degree reverse course move just in time before your fragile bark collided with the rocks? Word got around that you'd beaten the odds—people were amazed, actually—New York is a famously acoustic town or was before the diabolic coming of the Internet."

"*Gracias por pararte a mirar mi perfil,* thanks for showing me my profile."

"You haven't got much use for the Internet. You know, when the telephone was invented, approximately a century before the Internet, people commenced to think they actually had something to say. Look what end *that*'s brought us to.

"You know they say you read the book you're in at your own risk of being infuriated—but I'm delighted—to be uncovered for instance as your Doctor Sax: so much more interesting as you declared, than Kerouac's. And who could fail to recognize the revelation of your first clear memory of sheer terror."

"Hiroshima."

"You talked about it all the time. I must say though that under the rubric 'Coming soon to a page near you,' you've flashed rather a lot of coming attractions—more than you get at the pictures these days—not that I ever go, but my informants do—and that's saying a lot. Perhaps you ought to run the reel backwards at rewind speed to that very day, the Sunday we dropped the bomb on Hiroshima. And you brought in Nagasaki, which nobody ever talks about. Nagasaki is definitely B-list."

"I don't do rollbacks at rewind speed, thank you very much. We'll get there in due time—perhaps after I've visited the site and made my amends, perhaps sooner. Yes, mine—it's as if I was there. It was my father's fortieth birthday."

"Adumbration—memories, dreams, reflections as C. G. Jung put it—and sixty years of Karaoke sex in Tokyo: we taught them more than baseball and automobile manufacture."

"*Je n'ar jamais vu Hiroshima.* I've never seen Hiroshima. Or Nagasaki either."

. . .

Pink cotton candy at the circus and the carnival made him nuts the first time he saw it, ate it—we had a carnival that came to the neighborhood once a year. Under the trucks . . . another story—

His eyes focused inward, intent upon a different time and—what have we here? A boy of eleven, fresh from his first nervous breakdown—see we're already losing the run of ourselves, shooting out of sequence, returning to the past at every opportunity as if that would fend off the consequences of—

Tell everything.

"Terrifying visions and hysterical polio symptoms—so we have him under the trucks, under the boardwalk, up the roof, down the cellar—and years later other fucks in other trucks, only not under them, inside them, like merchandise crated up and stowed away for someplace out there under beautiful and spacious skies above the fruited plain

"—but after a while I got used to it and all it did was make me sick to my stomach."

"Did you frequent the trucks on West Street?"

"Which of us in his day has not covered the waterfront?"

"Did you even like it—sex with older men in the most dismal, dangerous and demeaning situations?"

"*Nostalgie de la boue?* Longing for the gutter. Not always—sometimes I made it back to their apartments, remembering always an older and more genteel time when one would look at the books on their shelves and at their record collections and ask pertinent questions about Melville and Maggie Teyte, the English opera singer—the kiss of death, unless one was especially invited to Sunday pink tea matinees.

"As to liking it, all in all I preferred *Don Giovanni* and Balanchine ballets to entertaining fantasies of sex with Sergei Sarota and later Joey Marciano, and both the Buell Twins, one of whom killed himself—was it Joseph? One is suddenly *bloqué*, blank. And so far as the waterfront went, you might say somewhat ironically that I started there early too; my father was a suit on the waterfront, both on the North River and the East."

"A timekeeper."

"Yes, that's right—how did you know that?"

"The Shadow knows—did, still does."

"Knows that the timekeepers were the only suits on the waterfront."

"That and much else—"

"I wore a suit—blue and white seersucker—working for my father's company, John W. McGrath, Stevedoring Contractors, 39 Broadway. In the summers I worked as an office boy: 'You do nice work,' was the insistent jibe at the office—prime example of the subtle wit of the '50s."

There was something about the men's room on that floor, speaking of being clocked—urinal surveillance from the stalls.

One gave up that dangerous surveillance—whispers had started at the water cooler, although nobody nailed the kid in the seersucker suit. "Seersucker doesn't make a cock sucker" was the word. "Anyway the kid still goes to communion; he told me so."

He started walking the streets on his lunch hour. One day, looking up at the naked god recumbent in marble on the frieze of the Stock Exchange, he developed a fetish for him. He later told this to a priest—in the Everard Baths. "You are clearly attracted to men of stone—perhaps you ought to consider a career in Wall Street; it's inhabited exclusively by such creatures of a distracted God. If you can't get blood out of a stone, neither can you give one a transfusion—thus cold, hard, bloodless specimens."

And later, no longer the clean-cut office boy in the crew-cut and white bucks, but a still-young slut taken to prowling the streets all night—as he'd just been doing again—for old times' sake?—gathering up the remnants of lives torn to tatters and stained with sour secretions of mind and soul, like some queer sexrag sheenie?

"I remember you sitting on this very bench with your pants and underpants down around your ankles looking over at the action under the giant sycamore and edging for hours. That thing between your legs—

nothing to write home about it in itself—was so hard a cat couldn't scratch it."

"You thought I was just a pretentious hypocrite playing red-nose reindeer games with fools."

"Not a hypocrite, no, merely a somewhat sententious alcoholic guttersnipe with crooked eyes."

"Immaculate degeneration—I got it from my mother."

"And whatever you said, there always seemed to be a *theme* to it."

"Would you like to hear a funny story about an old woman's scrambled brains?"

"Comes to us all, if death doesn't come first."

"The Shadow knows everything."

"So does the Web. Photographs, reviews, interviews, author of. . . . The Internet has done away completely with the absurd device of the single narrator, bane of all telling, and with it the bollocks about beginning at the beginning—author born on the Fourth of July, 1941, a rainy Friday, in Flushing Hospital—well within the city limits—under the sign of Cancer, Leo rising, moon in Scorpio. 7/4/41: numerologically significant in world history, culture and myth—On the 7th Day He took His repose, the 7 nations of Canaan, the 7 wonders of the Ancient World, the 7 Against Thebes, the 7 Deadly Sins, the 7 Gifts of the Holy Ghost, the 7 Keys to Baldpate, The Secret 7, the 7 Hills of Rome.

"The Capitoline, the Palatine, the Esquinal, the Quirinal, the Viminal, the Caelian and . . . I forget. Does the Shadow know I've just come—Well, it's been a matter of hours by now—from my mother's deathbed, fulfilling a long-held ambition, long a restless and forbidden dream?"

"Of course he knows."

"Just slipped his mind."

"Speaking of dead, I was dead wrong to say begin at the beginning— 'In my end is my beginning' and vice versa makes for a short, breezy book, hardly value for money—when all you need do is begin and let the beginning of telling be itself, as the story of the poem is the poem—

'let be be beginning of seem' as Stevens put in in 'The Emperor of Ice Cream'—start *in medias res*: anywhere. Prick up your ears."

"The most beautiful of them all, the Aventine—there, I haven't lost that marble anyway, speaking of marble."

"I particularly remember the Scorpio rising part. When you were very young—a sophomore in high school, I believe, the night of the Callas debut in 1956, you were doing some kind of imitation of T. C. Jones in Mask and Gown imitating your favorite film stars Bette Davis and Talullah Bankhead, gassing to the whole crowd that you didn't go out for varsity swimming because they caught you smoking and heard the word that you were drinking as well and doing Bette and Talullah imitations in the lunchroom. Joe Hollywood was there and said 'What a camp, an aquatic scorpion,' in that way of his that could make the Lord's Prayer sound suggestive, and I told your fortune, advising you to avoid entrapping sentimental frogs."

"And I thought you meant Frenchmen who got drunk on Pernod, searched out old French movies, played Piaf records incessantly and bawled their asses off—hilarious. You should have said toads."

"And that you had no need of help crossing the stream. Your kiss would be the kiss of death for them and none of them would turn into princes, but only go under, and it could be on your conscience—if one could be located."

"I remember. I remember what else you said. 'Remember these are the early days of love's madness. So take them to heart and give yourself a little smooch—no harm in it; the glass may be cool to the lips, but you want to let yourself know what's up—hah, hah—and will soon need seeing to. Clear focus on what's what; you don't want spoiled for choice.'"

"Keep this in mind and hold to it; in spite of everyone's misreading of Schopenhauer: life is *not* an idea of life."

. . .

Pathetic subterfuge to begin a life at the beginning of a life, what with what's known, has been known since the beginning: that there is no beginning, that the measuring of time from the six days of creation on is only still what it ever was, a placebo, a palliative fiction—a dose of addictive snake oil exuded by the snake in the grass in the perfect lost-forever garden.

Because he told lies, because his thinking was not linear, nor lateral, nor circular, but corkscrew spiral, they told him to cool his heels and go stand in the corner in the round house; he went mad—there are some shames that must never be revealed on any account, even to those who would pay cash money for the details.

What the reader is faced with instead happened all right, to people, to persons of long remembered quality and estate, as well as to others less fortunate—and if "Ouch" is a one-word sentence, "Fuck" is a one-word paragraph. The upshot: quiz question in two parts (short essay, no multiple-choice distractions, there is a bell, it will ring, however avoid unwarranted stress): What the book starts out in the beginning to be about and what it turns out to be about in the end. Concentrate.

"Schubert, as you know, wrote the *Wanderer Fantasy*, but couldn't play it—there's some striking analogy in that pertinent to your case."

Life's a business that doesn't cover the costs.

Before he left home and went to Ireland his father let him know there had been a poet in the family, a blind poet called Seamus Dal—Seamus the Blind—who wrote bardic verse according to the old rules, in Irish, in County Armagh. (The McCourts have always had eye trouble, invariably ending in glaucoma and total blindness; he himself was born with monocular dyplopia—and sees double in each eye. When he tried to play baseball and they put him out in right field, the rare line drive that came his way, as the ball descended would turn into not two but four balls, a completely hopeless situation.)

"See you again sometime on the road to happy destiny."

"Read gender narcissistic alliances to fend off libidinal demands; 'if they get burned I'm not the one to blame, kiss me you brute.'"

"I doubt you'll be coming back this way again."

"Likely not—at least not from the same point of origin."

"The point of origin—"

"For the life to come."

"Would that be the mother's deathbed?"

"It would, or would that it were. It remains to be seen if it actually was. By the way who exactly is the world's mother?"

"Being no longer the great goddess or the Mother of God, she cannot be known, only inferred by the ubiquitous presence of motherfuckers in the world."

"I think you really are the Wise Old Man at that."

"Yes—Well, the eleventh prime is 29—keep such things close to your heart, and always remember, we know what we know strictly on loan."

5

He awoke with an excruciating headache; strangely, it was still dark outside the bedroom window.

They used to say I was dropped on my head when I was born. Doorbell. *Doorbell?* Downstairs doorbell. Who the hell is passing out menus in the middle of the night?

Must answer, possibly be another emergency. . . . Mr. Faria next door in the middle of the night that Christmas Eve.

"Yes?"

"James McCourt?"

"So they tell me, but I don't believe we've been introduced."

"This is the police, Mr. McCourt, please allow us prompt entry."

"Oh—yes, all right."

Nobody running up the stairs, the elevator humming, some reassurance surely.

Scant minutes later the apartment buzzer; he opened the door to admit two young policemen standing on either side of Pramit Banarjee.

"Hello, Pramit. No trouble, I hope. I myself have the headache from nether hell."

"You banged your head badly Sir James getting into the taxicab. I wanted to take you to the emergency room, but you said you could not possibly go back into the hospital that still housed your mother's corpse."

"Yes, sir, we're very sorry for your trouble."

"Thank you officer, that's very kind of you."

"You asked me Sir James, did I work at the Burger Ranch, and I said no I did not, but when I first came here from India, I did some rather menial tasks at the Taj Mahal in New Jersey."

(Trouble? Nothing was ever less trouble—for the moment anyway—in one's entire life.)

"You said if you were going to die you'd prefer to do so in your own bed. I am extremely gratified to see that such has not been the outcome. It has been necessary to call the police for you to open the door so that I may return to you your wallet, which was found by the workers cleaning out my cab, fallen under the driver's seat. You were very groggy and very kindly allowed me to enter with you and come into your apartment and see you settled comfortably in your bed.

"You kept talking to someone who wasn't there which I admit was a bit worrying."

"Moriarty."

"Moriarty? Who might that be sir?" asked one of the young cops.

"He's the bad guy in Sherlock Holmes, the *antagonist*, you know?" the other cop said. "Didn't you ever read Sherlock Holmes?"

"Moriarty? Moriarty could be anybody officer, but in this case he's an old enemy who won't give up tracking me. Thus conscience, thus coward, thus banging one's own head."

"Would you care to register a complaint, sir?"

"I would, officer, but I'm afraid it would do no good—I made Moriarty up, at my older brother's behest. Like the Creator himself or his older brother the author of *Genesis*, who must suffer like constraints, I can't unmake him. . . . I'm starting to remember. You, Pramit, asked if you could help me into my pajamas. I said I didn't wear any, and you turned your back while I undressed and slipped under the sheets. So I never got out of the taxi until we reached the front door?"

"No, sir, I would not allow you to—you will forgive I hope my effrontery, but I could not possibly allow it after such a bang on the head that you had to walk unaided in those empty streets, so we drove through them."

(One is supposed to walk the grid, not cruise it.)

"Up Eighth Avenue and down Broadway, in and out of all the theater streets, you asked to stop several times, and each time sang a song—or a part of a song. You have a very pleasant voice."

"Past its prime, I'm afraid. You don't mean to tell me we neglected the Belasco?"

"No sir we drove over to Sixth Avenue on 44th Street, then back across 44th Street, then up past a place you said used to be called the Latin Quarter, then around the corner again to Sixth Avenue, and again across to a Howard Johnson's, which was just closing."

"Do you suppose I was having strange visions?"

"It would be strange indeed Sir James if you did not have visions in—"

"In the wake of—of the wake I won't be going to."

"Yes, it would be strange indeed for a person of your—"

"Bent."

"Well, sir, if everything's all right here, we'd better get back on the job."

"Thank you officers, I think everything's copacetic."

" 'Copacetic.' Now there's a word you don't hear much any more. My father would always say things were copacetic—if they were."

"It's rarely comes up, officer, because, as words go describing things as they are today; to use my father's old expression, there's not the call for it there was.

"And Pramit, I want you to have this—it's St. Christopher, the patron saint of travelers, especially travelers in distress. I think he would be made at home in your pantheon."

"Oh, Sir James, I couldn't accept such a gift."

"You must—you see, you've been my Saint Christopher tonight, bringing the traveler home to safe haven."

"I see then that I must, and I thank you profusely. I am sure he will be fine company for all the others."

The younger officer brightened. "We've got a St. Christopher medal in the squad car."

"Be sure to keep him there, officer, he won't let you down."

. . .

"Well, that was entertaining," Moriarty said. "One supposes after such a virtuoso performance you're ready to return for a peaceful interval to a less eventful dreamland, courtesy of how many Ibuprofen, eight?"

"Four."

"Lovely number. Give me four and I can make the world. Sleep tight then."

"Thank you, and thank you for the courtesy of allowing me to sleep alone."

"No problem. Copacetic. In the first place I sleep in pajamas and in the second, more important place, you're not my type."

. . .

Followed by migraine. Three days in a darkened room—plenty of coffee, Ibuprofen, nothing else. Lovely fasting in a dark room riding the swoon of. Perhaps not the last three days of his life, but silent as the tomb. Wonder what's going on at the wake? All in the mind, but Moriarty will report back with all the phantom details.

And when intermittently he'd come round, he didn't know who he was—had never even heard of himself.

6

*T*he wake according to Moriarty.

"It all came out at the wake, and you missed it."

"I know—I should have had you wear a wire."

"You can't wire a metaphysical construct, even one that meanders, but having heard for the last three nights the dead going at it great guns—and they had much to relate indeed—I come to bring you both back to Jackson Heights and up to speed—to as they now say index you—so fasten your seat belt for the *Long Night's Journey into Mourning* in which a good deal of weather is expected.

Vision of the wake: The spinet piano from Jackson Heights where the coffin ought to be, surrounded by revelers as Catherine, back to the camera, tickles the ivories. Funeral flowers, all from little brother Brendan's school colleagues. Kitty Moore singing "The Moon and I" and "Smoke Gets in Your Eyes" and duetting with big brother David in "The Hostess With the Mostess on the Ball."

After the wind off the river and what was written on that wind (a faithless lover's kiss, a night of stolen bliss, an entire city obliterated in one atomic whirlwind) has died down. The North River, not the Hudson—not until the intersection of it and the Harlem River did it become the Hudson. He'd covered the waterfront and met face to face its gaunt shadows.

By the light of the silvery moon. And there he was, the man in the moon. But the man in the moon is a lady.

I mean to rule the earth as he the sky
We really know our worth, the sun and I.

For whatever reason, whenever his mother sat down at the piano to play and sing "The Moon and I" he was gripped with an inconsolable nostalgia coupled with a fierce tenacity and the overwhelming desire to perform something from Gilbert and Sullivan (Koko for instance, although clownish, he had from the very beginning found inexplicably mortifying).

If indeed there does exist any such thing as the Object, in the male homosexual infant that Object must of necessity be masculine. Can one speak of a tough, wary innocence?

Sitting in the dark/sitting in the light (but never in the sun except under an umbrella). Far more present in the dark, assisting at performances others had begun. In the classroom, passive, going into defensive trances, as if careful not to be detected, but all unconscious, as the only way to be the agent in the process not so much of learning as of plowing through the exercise like the little engine that not only could, in a walk, but did with a vengeance, at the end of which he had memorized everything but understood nothing—only to be told that this was a commendable state, that Socrates on television in *You Are There* with Walter Cronkite, a whole crowd watching him drink hemlock and say deep things just before checking out, had been prone to similar transports. (In later years Author, a tearaway born with a perforated margin, would glory in crowds at the Cherry Lane watching him get more and more shitfaced on stingers, spouting brilliant, hilarious thing after brilliant hilarious thing prior to passing out on the floor, dead to the world. People spoke of slow suicide, but he figured the longer he could draw it out the better—his suicide might run as long as *The Fantasticks*.)

And for what—why had he blabbed? A read? Remaindered as soon as published—you can hear them at it, the wicked. Man dear, who cares about you, specifically in the light of monumental things—about your feelings on the subject: depression (in which the shadow of the Object falls athwart the ego like the shadow of the cross formed by the post and lintel of the stable door in the moonlight athwart the manger and its occupant), or of the more eloquent, elevated condition that is mourning—blessed are they who go in for it, for they shall surely be comforted, whereas the depressives, balls withering in terror, will merely be stupefied on the flight deck for the length of Holy Week, then returned to the world. And if you hear me or anyone else declare I-feel-your-pain, you'll know it's because we want your drugs; nobody gives a fat rat's ass about you or your feelings surrounding such a monumental event. Mock, scourge and spit upon the Crucifixion? The devils in hell perhaps—*Gefallenen Engeln*, fallen angels—knowing that all the while not a blind bit of notice is being paid, nor none ever will—unless one among their number is selected as a candidate for that role of roles in infernal life, the entering into and possessing of a human soul, and then will the voice of the demon be heard in the land—capable of anything, capable of entering into the newborn child, so that howling obscenities aimed at blaspheming the Crucifixion may be heard from dozens of them in unison in the holding pens in maternity wards in which they are kept, as if they, the demon neonates, were suddenly grown into schoolyard tormentors of frail or "sensitive" boys—and girls too take part in these evil things. All of it you understand as a preparation for life—life itself and not an imitation of life—for that you skip to Easter Sunday, don your Easter bonnet and walk down the Avenue—Fifth Avenue. Photographers will snap you and you'll find that you're in the rotogravure.

(And also that God has somehow always had mercy on your soul and always will—but don't go telling people so.)

The story settles on the surface of forgotten dreams that rise in haste to meet it, like lake trout to the mayfly—or else they don't, and one's futile efforts are like those of the patrol boats during the Second World War, in the earliest years of life, the years of German submarines reported off Block Island, their searchlights sweeping back and forth across the black mirror surface of the waters of Long Island Sound. But if they are found to rise to the occasion, if they are successfully lured to the surface and captured, the work thereof is surely aided and abetted by the up-to-the-moment phenomenon of Netflix delivered in the mail—and that's another thing, the postman has stopped ringing twice, preferring to await with the faith of the medieval Christian the coming again of the iceman.

. . .

Moriarty returns to the darkened room, not unwelcomed.

"So?"

"I shall write an ode to Conway's Funeral Home on Northern Boulevard, and to the pertinence of two pieces of New York historical cultural information. Conway's is nearly diagonal from the Boulevard Theater where Bette Davis played in the Blanche Yurka Company in Ibsen's *The Wild Duck*, playing Hedwig. And Northern Boulevard itself—Route 25A—was the long, desolate road past the oculist Doctor Eccles's grotesque sign of two disembodied eyes on the way to the Eggs, West and East, in F. Scott Fitzgerald's *The Great Gatsby* (the book whose hero hid behind the "Jay" his real name, James)."

"You certainly did get in there with all the ghosts of those dead women hovering over the open coffin."

"It was a tricky job, but somebody had to do it. Got a lot out of them too, you might have noticed—after all, the show must go on."

"Why? Why must the show go on?"

"Because you would die if it didn't, that's why."

"It's what Bette said about, 'the ones who *beef* about the *necessity* of all the publicity—usually they're the ones who would *die* without it.'" I said perhaps it was that they never learned how to handle it. "It isn't *even* that—they would *die* without it."

"You often said your mother was like Bette—you even told Bette she was."

"I think I was probably the only one who ever went to interview her and was asked to '*tell* me about your mother.'"

And did he—everything? Alluded to. After all Kitty Moore often said that *mutatis mutandis* her life and the lives of all those women were very Warner Brothers—very Davis, Joan Blondell, Ann Dvorak, early Barbara Stanwyck. And then there was that marathon weekend-long cocaine-driven discussion with Miz Lansky at Punch and Judy Dilllard's place in Brooklyn, devoted in its entirety to an examination of the reasons Catherine was a Bette woman and Mrs. Lansky a Joan woman.

"Don't make fun of Joan, baby, Joan was deep."

(Essay project: "Deep Joan.")

Tell everything.

Not quite everything—after all that would have been a little too close to the bone for both of them, for both were driven women still very much alive. When he got back to New York he called her and told her Bette had said, "Say hello to your mother for me, and tell her I like her son very much," and Catherine's answer was, "Yes, Well, Davis was always class."

7

From commonwealths and cities I will descend to families,
which have as many corsives and molestations, as frequent
discontents as the rest.

—Robert Burton, *Anatomy of Melancholy*

It is rashly said that dead men tell no tales, or if they don't then ghostly women, if no longer wailing like the banshee, do indeed talk blue streaks. The narrative drive of dead women is implacable. The three fates do not keep silent as they work; there is nothing almost being said.

There is a tourist attraction in Palermo, an extreme example of that mission of enticement the Roman Catholic Church espouses alongside the recitation of the Holy Rosary, the ceremonies of Holy Week (although the office of *Tenebrae* is no more), the novenas to the Immaculate Conception and the Sacred Heart, and Bingo, the three-night open-casket wake. The sight of *I Catecumi* (the converts) horrifies the general run of visitor, but for a certain tourist clientele it represents the biggest Camp in Western European Roman Catholicism. In the Capuchin monastery in that city of extremes and *omerta* there opens a narrow door. An aged monk appears, to lead the pilgrim down a short flight of stone steps indented by the footfalls of hundreds on thousands of *pellegrini* into the catacombs themselves, where along the white stone walls row upon row the mummified bodies of thousands of the dead, dead of all ages decked out in the clothing in which they preferred to be displayed in anticipation of the resurrection of the dead and the General Judgment, are stuck up on plain sticks. In this ghastly literal *carnevale* each face is set in a grinning rictus that clearly whispers, "*Benvenuti, signori e signore . . . I santi morti!*" Ladies and gentlemen, the holy dead!

It is easy, in fact automatic, to imagine these fashionably dead Trinacrians, men, women and children alike, when left to themselves in the dead of night erupting in cackles and crooning, retelling time out of mind the same joys, sorrows, resentments and most terrible vendettas of the past yet present in them. ("Shoveling shit against the tide," Moriarty says.) An underworld from which the egress is only marginally more difficult than the ingress, with nondebilitating effect, unless one considers setting the clock for a psychic time bomb and being indelibly marked for life by debilitating effects. And Charon runs the Staten Island ferry.

8

The holy dead among the mourners.

"I suppose Kitty was always going to outlive us all."

"What do you mean—every time?"

"Don't blaspheme, Elizabeth—that's blasphemy."

"Elizabeth was always precise."

"That she was, Florrie, that she was," Big Jim said. "As to Catherine, she was never going to take an early call."

"Yes, Jimmy. Well, you know best."

"Elizabeth was a Sister of Charity—a Sister of Charity in everything but profession."

"She was, May, she was. By the way, is Tom here?"

"He is, he is certainly, somewhere. He's become a bit timid, don't-cha-know. And when all is said and done, you're with your own."

"Well, he was always fond of Kitty—and she of him. It was he that would have married her had he not been so arrogant and full of himself."

"I believe there are two schools of thought on that, Elizabeth."

"Well, yes Jimmy, there would be, wouldn't there. Elizabeth?"

"You were the matriarch, May, so yes, I guess there were, only—"

"Tom could never have stayed married to a woman who stood up to him. Ethelyn didn't really stand up to him. Not until she stood up and walked out on him—by that time he couldn't stand up unless propped up by a lamppost or a wall."

"Who just said that?"

"If I didn't know better—and I don't; nobody in this room does—I'd swear it was Kitty's voice. You heard it, didn't you Jimmy—wasn't that Kitty's voice?"

"Well, Catherine's voice always did carry, Florrie."

"Her voice carried, yes—and she carried it everywhere she went—but it didn't always carry the motion. That story of the screen test in Astoria never rang true to me—it's hard to believe she'd have wanted to be in silent pictures."

"You're terribly sharp today, Elizabeth."

"Don't forget, May, Elizabeth *was* Kitty's classmate at St. Lawrence Academy."

"So she was, Florrie—two little maids from school were they, who one day in 1926 played hooky to go off and see Mae West in the movie *Diamond Lil* at a matinee."

"Yes, May, poor Tom, face down in the gutter beaten to death is no way to go. Why they had to put that terrible red toupee on him to lay him out, I'll never know, except I suppose they had to cover the top of his head all bashed in like that. And let's not forget it was Tom Kitty was interested in to that night he stood her up and Jimmy happened to be sitting at the dining room table doing his homework."

"There sits our sister Marcy—what a fool she was to marry that Tom Newman, who was a bum."

"Elizabeth!"

"The Sisters of Charity were no patsies, Florrie, you know that, and it was Elizabeth who kept Tom's picture in the bottom drawer of her dresser until young James went rummaging and found it. "

"You'd have had a conniption fit, Elizabeth, so it was lucky Florrie found him doing it, and even though you were his godmother, she very wisely stepped into your shoes—you were so careless about buying shoes, Elizabeth—you'd buy them, wear them for a day, decide they didn't fit after all and give them to Kitty. And then that one time out in Jackson Heights, in the first apartment on 95th Street you got into some kind of hijinks doing the can-can, and off flew the right shoe—they weren't too tight that time—and hit the ceiling—why the mark was still up there when they moved to 94th Street."

When at the grandmother's last summons, the boy, rummaging by instinct in his Aunt Florrie's bureau, uncovered in the bottom drawer an 8 × 10 sepia photograph of a very beautiful man, Florrie, discovering him, didn't berate him, but sat him down on the bed and started to tell all she thought an eleven-year-old boy should know. "Oh, I know all that Aunt Florrie. I heard the phone ring in the middle of the night and Pop's short replies and him saying to Mother, 'It's about the other one, the one who stood you up. The Rochester police said they found him, as they put it, "layin' in the gutter next to his brains."' Somebody had caved his head in with a crowbar outside a gin mill.

"They had a couple of drinks (Scotch and sodas) and sat up in the kitchen until we got up for school. It was the first time I ever saw any-body drinking highballs at breakfast time." His father didn't seem either sad or happy, only relieved. He knew all the arrangements with the police and the coroner and the undertaker and the cemetery would be taken over by Loring Place.

"'Betty and Florrie at Loring Place will see to it.'

"'And if they need money?'

"'If they need the money, they'll get the money.'"

He wanted to go to the wake because of all the times when Pop wasn't around and mother would tell him, "You're just like your Uncle Tom—willful, arrogant, cruel, caring for nobody but yourself." He'd also known Grandma sat next to the casket the whole time saying over and over, "That's not my Tom."

He wasn't allowed to go and he didn't suppose they'd make a copy of the picture face down in Aunt Florrie's drawer, but at least he knew at last what he looked like. He was hands down the most handsome—beautiful of them all—and maybe even queer: that would be too fabu-lous: dead of a gay knock.

He also knew that were he still alive he would run away with him far beyond Port Jervis—all the way to California: he was beautiful enough for California—and get into bed with him at night and do anything he wanted. *Too* fabulous.

"I remember Kitty saying one time on Loring Place that she'd go into the convent when Jimmy died—it was after Aunt Lizzie's funeral, or mamma's, one or the other—and there was Jimmy sitting right there across the room. Was it the Charities she was going to go into, Betty?"

"No, Florrie, it was the Grey Nuns."

"Well, you sure put up a stink over that one, I remember."

"If you mean, was I offended, Florrie, yes, I was. Catherine could be infuriating."

"Well, anyway, she didn't. Nuns had gone out of the picture, as Kitty herself would say. I guess they were all dead by then, or walking around without their habits on—wearing those terrible clothes they wear now and trying to look like everybody else."

"You were always the best-dressed woman of the family, Florrie."

"Oh, May, I think we all tried our best to look smart, don't you?"

"Well, Marcie always said you were the clothes horse."

"Florrie looked smart. She always believed in keeping up appearances."

"Indeed."

"Now, Elizabeth."

"Not always such a Sister of Charity, after all, am I May. We learned more than charity from them. Kitty for instance always said that Marcy died in self-defense."

"Well, I certainly think Kitty looks lovely in the casket."

"I never cared for the open casket—not that it mattered a damn to whoever was in it."

"You make it sound like it was always the one casket."

"Well, wasn't it in a way, when you come to think of it?"

"I must say I never came to think of it."

Then there was the Fatima story. They were sitting on the lawn out in Northport having breakfast on Author's fourth birthday, Betty, Florrie, Father O'Pray, and Jimmy and Elizabeth. Miriam and Marcella had taken Author to the Park to look at the bandstand before the parade down Main Street started. It was Elizabeth who said she'd always wanted to go to Lourdes and Fatima, Kitty said Lourdes yes, Fatima no. "But why not, Catherine," Elizabeth asked with that look in her eye they knew so well.

"Because, Elizabeth, I don't accept Fatima."

Elizabeth was scandalized.

"Well, you *were*! Elizabeth, I was there."

"May was always there," said Florrie.

"You don't have to get up on your high horse, Catherine."

"Well, it's not *ex cathedra.*"

"Apparently not *ex-Catherine* either," Big Jim said.

"Am I right, Father?"

"Yes you are, Catherine, as with all apparitions accepted by the Church, she recommends belief but does not insist on it. There are so many claims put forth you see that Monsignor Finucane, an Irishman and one of the investigators at the Holy Office, says it's vergin' on the ridiculous."

"But, Catherine, *why* don't you?"

"Accept Fatima? That the Mother of God would show children the pains of hell—*that* I can never accept. I'm afraid I see the whole Fatima three-ring-circus rigamarole as just that, without foundation."

"So no tent pole for Fatima, eh, Catherine?"

"Speaking of things Irish, I'd like to tell Monsignor Finucane I find Knock more than a little fishy too."

"She would have said that even as a child, Kitty knew her own mind—and that was long before I.Q. tests."

"Actually, Catherine, you are partly right about Knock. The Church recommends belief in the vision, but does not list it as a Marian apparition as such."

"Some children *are* the pains of hell—and you call that a message from a Marian apparition—"

"*Marian McSherry!*"

"That is if the Marian in question had been sent to appear which she has not—only sent to sit here in the present company banked by a cascade of lilies that would suffocate anybody alive, to listen to the living as they traipse around poor Kitty's corpse."

Calling the Roster of the Also Present (Also Dead)
    Alma Buerro Monaco

Kitty Simmons Sullivan
Helen Fisher Duffy
Florence Mulligan Ten Eyck
Flo Carmody
Mary Daly

"You probably all know the story of Kitty and the Pleasure Car Service? She told it on herself any number of times."

"That was the trouble, Kitty just couldn't keep her trap shut."

"Marian—really!"

"Oh, I don't mean the Pleasure Car Service story, that was a funny one. I mean the rest. As she got older, put a couple of drinks in her—"

"That, if you will forgive my saying so, Marian, is the pot calling the kettle black."

"Marian was the first she told—and Marian never told anyone."

"You bet I didn't—never did about anybody including myself. That's how I was able to have a beautiful, gorgeous affair for twenty-five years and nobody ever knew a thing about it. The living think they owe the dead what they call truth; I insist that what the dead owe the other dead is party loyalty."

Marian held these things in her heart. She had been there at the kitchen table in Sunnyside when it all started, with the two of them poring over the want-ads. There it was: "Wanted, personable traveling saleslady, good wages plus commission. Apply L.B. Furriers," and the address in the fur district. Once hired and installed, whenever the Jews would come out with "Jesus Christ!" Kitty would upbraid them, and this happened so often L.B. started calling her Mary Magdalene.

From this day forward, forsaking all others . . .

"The one important thing missing in that casket is a telephone with her one hand holding the receiver to her ear while the other is wrapped around the rosary beads."

"They're her beads—Kitty was a Rosarian."

"She surely did go in for gathering information."

"To a very great extent Kitty lived our lives along with us—to a much greater extent than we lived ours along with her. That club woman instinct, I suppose."

"Those harpies—look at them over in that corner as far away from the casket as they can get. Do I note a hint of grim satisfaction—still probably not to do with Kitty in particular, just that every time one of them goes it's one less candidate for high office."

"But Kitty was ninety-five, Marian."

"You wouldn't know that—from that distance it could be Eleanor Roosevelt in that casket."

"Kitty tried serious politics when she ran for president of the Grandmothers Clubs of America, and lost badly, 'Vera Maguire warned me that if I ran I'd be crucified—what she neglected to add, however, was that she'd be holding the nails.'"

(Alma) "Although I remember when Vera died, Kitty was very generous, 'She left behind a legacy, with something in it for each of us.' Jim said, 'I hope she didn't leave you her mouth.'"

"And there were eyebrows raised over Kitty's flirtatious attitude with that bum you married, Marge."

"Not a bum, Marian, only ambitious."

"And remember, Marian, Marge was Kitty's maid of honor."

"And there are things you just don't do? A saying honored more in the breach than in the observation."

"I'll never forget Frank sitting alone at Big Jim's wake, looking as if he'd lost his best friend in the world."

"Remorse?"

"Oh, I very much doubt that. I think it was just that Kitty liked to drink a bit more than Marge."

"Things got bad after the forced retirement."

"Which got her landed in Amityville Hospital, for as we used to say, a little rest."

. . .

Forsaking all others? No, but then people change their minds, especially women on the road to Port Jervis, on the banks of the Neversink
(famous last words). Erie Hotel, 9 Jersey Avenue. Nice place to spend the
first three days of your forked life as a mother/wife and scarlet woman.

Hard to imagine what they talked about, the lovers on the road.

The Jewish lover on the road was true; was the abortion? Or did she
throw herself down a flight of stairs to induce a miscarriage, like Gene
Tierney in the movie *Leave Her To Heaven*?

Anyway the Pleasure Car Service story.

It's a pretty funny one, and characteristic of her famous moxie.

So?

"It was a while after Kitty had given up driving. They were going in
to the opera on a cold winter's night—"

"With snow so deep."

"Kitty, Helen Duffy and I forget who else, all dressed to the nines
of course, and they'd decided to use a car service called Pleasure, which
drove them in right up to the plaza, and would meet them after the
show across Columbus Avenue in front of the Empire Hotel. The opera I
think was *The Tales of Hoffman*, a long one with three intermissions, and
their seats were in the Grand Tier, the level with the big bar, and by the
end of the evening Kitty and Helen were looped, much like the hero on
stage, although not quite flopped over a tavern table.

"In any case a brisk trot in freezing weather, heedless of the ice—God
protects drunks and fools, especially when they're a gaggle of old bags
dressed to the nines—across the plaza to the hotel had sobered them up
in two shakes of a lamb's tail, and they were standing there in the freezing cold waiting for the car, which by then was ten minutes late. A car
finally pulled up, but Helen was sure it was not the same one. Kitty said
she supposed they used any car that was available at the appointed hour,
but that another driver might not recognize them, so she stepped off the
curb carefully through a path cut between the snow banks, still a little

wobbly, up to the car, and when the driver rolled down the window with a quizzical look on his face, she smiled that rather coy smile they knew of old and asked pleasantly, with a good deal of Scotch floating on her breath, 'Pleasure?'

"Needless to say, it was not the car service's car, and the poor driver hastily rolled the window up, gunning the engine, and sped off around the block, just as the Pleasure car pulled up behind. On the way home, Kitty said, 'I hope whoever it was that man was meeting finally caught up with him. You know, I don't think I looked that bad, do you?'"

And thanks for the use of the hall.

TWO

1

"Take the 59th Street Bridge, will you, driver, the upper ramp, and out Northern Boulevard to 93rd Street, then right to 35th Avenue—and be careful when you come down off the upper ramp to take the fork to the left or we'll end up on Queens Boulevard."

"The Midtown Tunnel is faster—the bridge isn't worth it just to avoid the toll."

"That's not the point, I like the view from the bridge—and let's have no arguments, please, I'm going to my mother's funeral."

His affection for the bridge his grandfather had built in 1909. His determination had been to go and live on the Manhattan side of the bridge—flash forward to the park at the floor of 57th Street: *Bells Are Ringing* and the "lost" boy at dawn in 1963, and a few months later his being the "lost" boy picked up in that same park on the night of the Kennedy assassination and taken home by a drunk and distracted gentleman over thirty . . . but he'd been that route before.

He'd chosen the bridge rather than the Queens Midtown Tunnel in order to avoid that morning the flyover of the LIE past Big Jim's grave right underneath, and where Kitty Moore would be interred that morning—they were probably digging the grave just then, or if they'd done it already, he'd no wish to ride over an open one already containing his father, Grandfather Moore and the Grandmother Moore he never knew. (Mae had made the remark at Big Jim's wake that it was strange that their Jimmy was being put in the grave with the Moores when all the McCourts—"his own"—were up in St. Raymond's in the Bronx. Jimmy had always been the thoughtful one. There was ever-so-slight a hint of henpecking to the remark, but you could never have called Big

Jim henpecked, in fact had Kitty ever seriously attempted it, you'd have soon seen a hen running around without a head.)

Then on the bridge, looking back out the cab's rear window with the view of the skyline in the winter morning sunlight with the sun traversing the blue sky far south of the Narrows and Staten Island, the story of his grandmother and his mother taking the Third Avenue El down to 59th Street, then changing to the newly extended Flushing line, over the bridge on which his grandfather had worked, over Welfare Island where his mother's cousin Charlie Duffy would end up a lifelong resident recovering from a life shattered by cocaine use, to Queensboro Plaza, there changing to the BMT to Steinway Street in Astoria where his mother would be tested in the studios there and found suitable.

Interrupted by his memory of the four a.m. ride across town in 1982 after the call, "Your father's gone, dear." The toe tag, selecting the casket for his father's wake—Author viewed by family members and friends as sober, which "would have pleased Jimmy."

Then to Jack Burlison. Father/Son—where is the Holy Spirit? Theology says he is an emanation of the love of the father for the son.

All the insipid fathers on television, and finally in 1956 Frederic March in a great portrayal of James Tyrone in the Broadway premiere of The Great American Play, Eugene O'Neill's *Long Day's Journey into Night*. And in this one every bit as important the older brother hero the sickly Edmund loves so. Author, the undiagnosed epileptic, was never very sickly in appearance, but always confused as to what was going on in his brain. His older brother David, who seemed to intuitively understand this, and especially after coming back from Korea to find an adolescent perpetually on the edge of a manic-depressive bout, protected him as best he could, which simply saved Author's life.

So many books and plays, paintings and musical compositions in that postwar era—William Styron in his first two books, the titles of which form a potent sentence, "*Lie Down in Darkness* and *Set this House on Fire*" (after which he summarily disappears into flatulence, simpering self-regard and irrelevance)—Jackson Pollock, Morton Feldman and

Elliott Carter, Eugene O'Neill, the stolid Arthur Miller and the inter-mittently resonant Tennessee Williams and William Inge, all went after the big questions, the shattering experiences of demolition and survival. No such concentration of existential broadcasting has ever in like degree troubled a New York audience since.

Then, after the session with Jack Burlison, stopping by at the apart-ment on 72nd Street around the corner from Harry Blair's old place—220 East 73rd.

Years earlier he had been talking to Harry Blair about his mother's adultery.

"Anyway I think Port Jervis has something to do with it, because when we were in the car with Marge Mooney coming back from Niag-ara Falls, we'd stopped at some dumbass place upstate that was supposed to be a refuge for Marie Antoinette but they didn't succeed in getting her out of France and she went to the guillotine. 'Let 'em eat cake!'" Marge Mooney said, and my mother said it was all just as well, what would Norma Shearer have done for a good part.' 'What they all do,' I chimed in from the rear—having heard they all do, the latest being Mar-ilyn Monroe, who grabbed me by the balls the first time I saw her, down in Vision Beach in *Don't Bother to Knock* which somebody down there said should be called *Don't Bother to Knock Her Up* because she was crazy.

"So anyway I was bored stiff and I'd seen the Norma Shearer Marie Antoinette movie and it stank. I remember coming home and saying, 'And they call *me* cockeyed,' which got a lot of laughs because everybody knew Norma Shearer got parts only because she was married to Irving Thalberg, Louis B. Mayer's nephew and a big-shot producer at MGM—so that proved that getting married was at least one way to avoid putting out to gorillas and still get star parts.

"So I'm looking at the road map and I see a place I've heard of in geography in school—Port Jervis, where New York, New Jersey and Pennsylvania come together. I like places like that, like Harpers' Ferry, where West Virginia, Virginia and Maryland come together, or that place out in the middle of the desert I haven't been to yet where you can be in four states at once if you bend over, Four Corners. One foot and one hand in each state—New Mexico, Colorado, Utah and Arizona. Come together—just like the guys down the cellar who won't let you in because they think you can't jerk off. You wouldn't give them the satisfaction, you said, which is pretty funny since you've been in love for years with Tommy Mendick ever since he dropped his pants standing in the stall with you standing by the sink washing your hands which weren't dirty, and showed you his cock and balls *and* ass."

"'So could we please drive through Port Jervis?' Right away I see this look pass from Marge Mooney to my mother and her look back and I figure there is something going on here, remembering my mother often said *deadlier than the male.*

"Well, anyway, we did—drove through Port Jervis without stopping, almost ran a red light. She looked like some dame on the lam—even Marge noticed. And I think I knew always their song had been "Smoke Gets in Your Eyes." I once asked her why she almost cries every time I play it and she said she can still see Tamara Geva in *Roberta* on the stage singing it— and later Irene Dunne in the picture, who was completely miscast—the character is supposed to be a Russian princess in exile in Paris, but after she had that big success on the national tour and then onscreen in *Show Boat,* she could call the shots and get whatever she wanted.

"Anyway, she loves Jerome Kern—my mother—she says there was a show right after *Show Boat* called *Sweet Adeline* that took place in a beer garden in Jersey—not as romantic as a show boat on the Mississippi— starring Helen Morgan. She says there never was and there never will be another Helen Morgan, certainly not Polly Bergen."

. . .

Big Jim's Death. You hear people say after a spouse's death that half their life is gone, that half of them is torn away, *et cetera.* And they must reconstruct it—there are even workshops on it now I hear and you can go on Oprah Winfrey. Not Kitty—all she had to do was *regroup* and *resume.*

"Resume being plastered at the wheel—frightened the bejeesus out of me more than once I can tell you."

"Which is why they finally took her license away from her—the boys, not the law, thank heavens—and she started taking the car service to the opera."

"The sorrows of theretofore."

"Such wonderful parties, though."

Catherine leaving for Conway's, the funeral parlor, tripping on the front steps of the house. "Let's not make this a doubleheader."

. . .

"Mother, there's someone on the phone in the office who'd like to speak to you—Girlie Doran."

"Girlie Doran, O my God,"

. . . .

"Hello, Girlie, how are you? Oh, I'm all right Girlie . . . yes, thank you, Girlie, that was very thoughtful of you . . . Yes, dear, very sudden . . . yes, a mercy. Well, thank-you, Girlie, it was very good of you . . . yes, bye now, Girlie."

. . . .

"Girlie Doran."

"From Yorkville—we were in the same class at Our Lady of Good Counsel. Very nice girl—she went to Cathedral, I think, so I didn't see very much of her afterwards, just around the neighborhood from time to time. She came to your grandmother's wake to pay her respects, and I remember just before your father and I were married, she called to congratulate us—said she heard your father was a fine man and she hoped we'd be very happy. As I say, a nice girl, Girlie."

"Have you seen her since?"

"No, I don't think I have."

. . . .

Then there was Frank Hennessy, sitting alone and forlorn. He'd made all the money in advertising and moved to Darien and at Author's college graduation offered him a job interview at Kenyon and Eckhart, only to be told rather airily that he, Author, after his upcoming European trip, was going into summer stock at the Surf Lite Theater in Beach Haven, New Jersey, playing Prince Dauntless in *Once Upon a Mattress*, and then returning to Riverdale to take up the position of editor of the college alumni magazine.

Just before they closed the casket, Author asked the undertaker (they'd jokingly dubbed him Digger O'Dell from the old Fred Allen radio program) "Would you take that ring off his finger, please, I don't approve of burying jewelry." Then when Digger, in his most solemn voice, said, "The family may step up to the casket now, to say their last goodbyes," Author called from the back of the room, "We can do that very well from back here, thank you."

"Well done, James," his mother said as they drove away for the funeral Mass.

No appearance by Big Jim's Other Woman (a stocky, full-breasted woman, he imagined, who could and did drink any man under the table at Toots Shor's). Would she swoop, or stalk or swan in in stone martens, or meekly creep into the back at the very last, wearing black with a big black-veiled hat. Would she once have been betrayed by a friend (perhaps herself in love with Big Jim) who'd called Catherine and said "Oh, my name wouldn't mean anything to you, but I believe it would be in your interest to meet and speak with me—I think considering the nature of what I have to tell you, cocktails would be preferable to lunch—shall we say tomorrow at four at Schrafft's on Madison Avenue? You can take the bus in from Jackson Heights."

It is a matter of lively controversy among experts which is more wearing, living two separate lives or agreeing to live just the one.

Was she a big, blowsy Kate Nally–Tenth Avenue kind of woman, Big Jim's Babe Shor, given to racy expressions of the soil? Who'd come right up to Catherine and embrace her, take a quick look, say a prayer, turn and walk out never to be seen or heard of again? Or possibly one of the—but that was not possible. Whereas Catherine could well have brought off an affair with, say, the aforementioned Frank Hennessy, Jim would not have been interested in any of Catherine's crowd, apart from Marian, who'd been anyway having her beautiful, gorgeous affair. (When Marian finally revealed it, after her lover Barney was dead, Catherine said: "All very well, if you want to put up with the *Back Street* performance.") Author, who loved Marian the best among the crowd, turned in a fury and said—"First of all Irene Dunne was great in the role and Marian would have been just as good, and being a back-street mistress beats visiting a back-street abortionist every time." (His many cruelties came as much out of the histrionics of the writer pose without which he could not seem to do until his late forties—forty-seven to be exact, in 1988—as out of his so-called nature, could the two ever be separated in what his German teacher Edmund Tolk had called a born writer? Most probably they couldn't.)

Big Jim surely couldn't have been having it off all those years with Girlie Doran.

Why Babe Shor? Big Jim was the kind of elegantly sartorial guy to be found in a John David suit at ringside and on the waterfront. The guy who'd heard with grave misgivings the krauts ranting at the Bund rallies of the '30s at the Garden. He'd had a great pal in Al and Katy Muller, the Bavarians who ran the restaurant right across 51st Street. But these were real Krauts imported to rev up the native fifth columnists (confusion: newspapermen and traitors). Finally, was the *Hindenburg* sabotaged by Zionist agents? But as a Catholic, equally troubled by the atheistic communism of Russia, by Stalin's show trials, etc. Anyway because of his position as head of the ticket takers union at the Garden and all the ball parks, and liking the ring, which Kitty Moore, convent-school-bred, would never go near, Author early learned about John L. Sullivan and Gentleman Jim Corbett, Joe Louis, Max Schmeling, the Rockys Marciano and Graziano, and later Ingemar Johannson (whom he would meet rather surprisingly in opera singer Victoria de los Angeles's dressing room at the Metropolitan after a performance of Massenet's *Manon*, accompanied by his countryman and then close friend the tenor Nicolai Gedda).

("Nicolai and Piaf, darling. Let's hope this hunk has better luck than Marcel Cerdan," Piaf's lover, the French boxer Marcel Cerdan, killed in a plane crash on his way home to her from the U.S.)

Author quickly learned the terms: right uppercut, left hook, glass jaw, sucker punch, punch drunk and reveled in a whole collection of fight pictures from *Golden Boy* and *Body and Soul*, on to *The Harder They Fall* and *The Champion*—all emblematic of his New York, hard, tough, fast and gentlemanly. He was always a welcome guest at Toots and Babe's place, a boxing club at 51 West 51st Street, and Author's greatest ambition was to come of age and go around the corner to 52nd Street, where love was rumored to beckon, to hear Mabel Mercer (the Povla Frisch, or perhaps the Maggie Teyte, of saloon singers and Empress of Gotham homosexual above-ground night life) sit in a straight high-backed chair singing Alec Wilder songs such as "While We're Young" in languid fashion while idly threading the trademark patterned silk kerchief through her svelte brown fingers, giving it the merest odd flick to indicate the whisper of an emphasis.

(Or as Victoria de los Angeles, as Massenet's Manon—several blocks south on Broadway, put it,

"*Obeissons quand leur voix appelle . . .*
Nous n'aurons pas toujours vingt ans!"
Heed their call when it comes,
we won't be twenty forever!)

The Kitty Moore "Mabel Mercer" song was "Smilin' Through" from the 1920 musical of the same name starring Jane Cowl, then the darling of Broadway. Then she picked up his sheet music of "Lazy Afternoon: and learned it—she sight read everything like a speedreader—and he *skeeved* on it every time she sang it, convinced she was trying to tell him something ("Silly boy, are you trying to keep things from me who knows you better than anybody?"), bringing on the *skeeve of all skeeves.*

Kitty Moore's different song repertory, Rodgers and Hammerstein (just let anyone dare ask old Mabel to sing "If I Loved You." The heave-ho) and Jerome Kern in a voice more like Irene Dunne's, and "Smoke Gets in Your Eyes," jocularly referred to as Joan of Arc's theme song, or torch song and none other than "their song," those fated lovers of Port Jervis.

They asked me how I knew
My true love was true.
I of course replied
Something deep inside
Cannot be denied.

They said someday you'll find
All who love are blind.
When your heart's on fire
You must realize
Smoke gets in your eyes.

(And all he could think after that for weeks, in the first of so many confusions between the sacred and the profane, was Ingrid Bergman as Joan of Arc, burning at the stake in Technicolor, and calling out "*Jesus!*" as her heart went on fire along with the rest of her and smoke got in her eyes. Had she been blind? Had she gone overboard with the armor and the horses and the chain mail and the spears and all that Hollywood demanded in a saint? Might she not have stayed still and seraphic, as in *The Bells of St. Mary's*, batting the ball around with little angel-faced hooligans instead of being sent to the stake by the terrible Francis X. Bushman, a bad priest? He had never seen a bad priest, never even heard of one, except maybe that Father Coughlin on the radio before he was born—his grandfather had called him a bad priest, or crazy Father Feeney up in Boston with his Slaves of the Immaculate Heart of Mary—the Pope had excommunicated the pack of them for maintaining that outside the Catholic Church there was no salvation. And in point of fact the name of the parish, St. Mary's, was a Hollywood solecism. The Episcopalians had parishes called that, but Catholics never referred to the Mother of God, considered as a result of the Assumption to reign over all the saints in heaven. There were parishes such as Mary, Star of the Sea and parishes named for her attributes, such as Queen of Heaven, Queen of All Saints, Our Lady Queen of Martyrs, Our Lady of Good Counsel, Our Lady of Sorrows, and Our Lady of the Angels. And there were St. Mary Magdalene and St. Margaret Mary—although one's never come across a St. Mary of Egypt, the subject of Respighi's lyric masterpiece *Maria Egeziaca*.)

But the smoke in this singer's voice was something else, something that bore no connection for instance to the smoke from the frankincense that rose from the thurible or censer at High Mass and got in young Author's eyes, tearing them up and strangely enhancing his ardor.

Joan of Arc died all right, but not her love for her Jesus or her saints—and Ingrid Bergman lived on, for a time in disgrace as an adulteress (in classier climes to be sure than Port Jervis), till she too was redeemed by the Oscar. (And Kitty Moore hated her father for Astoria.)

And this Mabel Mercer kind of postwar throwaway swank (greatly enhanced by the still-obscure guerilla tactics of homosexual outlaws and the burgeoning cult of passionate irony undetectable to the postwar wised-up and increasingly cynical and well-informed beneficiaries of the G.I. Bill, known for at least four generations as Camp) reconfigured above all other sophisticated pretensions and ambitions of social climbers in the New York Rialto, where for the first time in urban history, the lower and upper classes really did rub elbows and really did bump nasties and more or less right out in the open, and made Author think his father really was the stuff. As soon as Big Jim hit his middle fifties, he started spending all that time in the Barcalounger in front of the television watching the Giants . . . it never occurring to Author that the poor guy "working two jobs and putting in a lot of overtime" might have been just plain exhausted and in need of recharging before heading back to his own Babe. This must have also been the beginning of Author's getting along with blowsy women and by the age of sixteen, at the Floradora down under the El near the 74th Street station when every morning he changed from the IRT Flushing Line to the Independent Subway, the IND, to get to high school in downtown Brooklyn (and some nights on the way back home after being a schoolboy, he'd drop into the joint where he always felt protected by the butch dykes, who'd taken a shine to him because they thought it was a riot that here was a flaming teenage faggot with no other message to be given), who had two years earlier out in Northport let an older teenage girl sit on his cock and get him off and see stars—something he never forgot and never repeated.

. . .

Somehow, perhaps purposely, the cabdriver had taken him onto Queens Boulevard after all—there was the Elk's Club. Down to the right was Maspeth, terminus of the journey he and his grandfather had taken sixty years ago on the old trolley line that had started at La Guardia airport and run down Junction Boulevard to Queens Boulevard where they changed for the trolley to Maspeth. Why they had been going to Maspeth he couldn't now remember.

He arrived at the church just as the cortege was going in the front door, which faced not west but southwest—close enough he supposed. As the funeral Mass ended, he stepped out of the pew and for the first and only time in his life mounted the pulpit. "I want to thank you all for coming, and to tell you that my mother died up in St. Luke's just at the time when further down Broadway people were pouring out of the theaters. I think that was appropriate, for the bright lights of Broadway were for my mother the light of eternity."

Then at the grave: That they may face the rising sun (and not the Long Island Expressway flyover). Catherine: the name that would be carved on the gravestone he would never revisit—for New Yorkers were not like the Genoveses, they did not like going to cemeteries on Sunday afternoons to sit on the graves and eat picnic lunches. It was the same story as watching her die and not going to the wake at Conway's (where God only knew, Girlie Doran might show up in the flesh).

Yet again as usual at the top of the heap.

The double-decker grave (bunk beds: he and his little brother had slept in them for years with David in the bed across the room and his desk in the corner as if on a long-distance train ride such as the one Big Jim had taken across the country to a conference in Seattle—to which the eldest son five years later would move for life (ironies: New York, etc.) and from which life Catherine would spend inordinate years trying to extract him, entirely against his will, widening an already gaping breach obviously caused by the events of the late '30s coupled with her own father's outright condemnation and brutal rejection of his only child.

Well, in his play *Endgame*, Samuel Beckett had stuck his *oulwans* in those two notorious garbage pails. In any case, Author might imagine a replay of the wakes, done as a single one, like a version of a popular play of his youth, *The Four-poster*, and remembering that as a child, in a period when her transgressions had played themselves out and his had yet to be seriously undertaken, he tried to listen to their low-voiced conversations.

In their four-tiered graves—their doubly ironic postmortem on the repeat wake, the doubleheader that had finally come about, if only on the page of a transgressive memoir, hardly an example of filial piety on the hoof.

The grave yawns wide because it is bored to absolute tears. On the Great Gettin'-Up Morning the last shall be first.

. . .

In all the fever of nostalgia suffered while riding back from his younger brother's house in Baldwin on the LIRR after the burial, he remembers the train trip (in the other direction) detailed in his third book *Time Remaining*—fiction always the great consolation for the terrible sorrow of remembering, and his memorable character Odette O'Doyle's perorations delivered between the stations on the way out to Bridgehampton.

Then Jones Beach and the causeway to Cap Tree State Park, the westernmost point on Fire Island (named for the fire signals to ships warning them of the shallows). Trip to Cap Tree with his mother and his new friend Lorcan Gallagher, a blow-in to the parish (who at that very time, unbeknownst to Author, had also been sharing the favors of his beloved Fintan). They had gone to Cap Tree from Jones Beach from time to time, always making him long for the rumored and unreachable Cherry Grove. What he tells Lorcan: that he is bound and determined to be talked about there one day in the not-too-distant future the way he was talked about in Northport, Vision Beach, Riis Park (where he wandered away from the blanket to go to the men's changing rooms and stood naked in the showers watching them watching him. Although the straights outnumbered the queers easily ten to one, there were never any remarks. The great majority of the men, young, middle aged, geriatric, were Jews who would never torment homosexuals, on humanitarian grounds, and also as he was told later in perhaps unknowing solidarity with the *Schwuler Männer* and the gypsies who perished in the death camps along with the Jews, although the *Schwuler Männer*, tagged with pink triangle, were all shot and hung up on barbed wire fences as symbols of the Weimar Republic degeneracy the Nazis claimed to have extirpated from German society root and branch).

Thus did the first voices appear from outside Author's mind—literary device or borderline schizophrenic access—a chorus as it were of birds from the "bird circuit" of queer bars on the East Side: the Blue Parrot, etc., migrated like swallows to Capistrano, back for the summer months to Cherry Grove—also known as "Chirpy Grave"—commentators to further the narration of the story of his life put forward by James Francis John McCourt, flamer and clown, once tormentor, now tormented—his comeuppance, on the prevailing winds from what was then the early immediate future in that same world, and is now the very distant past of an antediluvian age before the tidal wave and bursting flood gates of the homosexual revolution opened sending as much water to drown the old culture and break through the barrier of oppression as following the bursting of the banks of the one great lake upstate had created the raging flow of the Hudson that broke through the moraine as it ran across from Bay Ridge in Brooklyn to Staten Island and the north New Jersey shore at Keansburg to create the natural harbor which would make New York the great maritime metropolis it is, drawing to it the greatest world migration of steerage passengers ever known ("Give me your tired, your poor, your huddled masses, etc." by the well-named Emma Lazarus).

Tell everything.

The year 1957 would see his "coming out" at Cherry Grove and his first attempts at serious writing in diary and commonplace book form (as if he had all the time in the world, which from the present view he had), though Cherry Grove, with all the mouthy, affluent amazing queers and their attendant fucked-up boy losers, augmented with a platoon of hapless fag hags and an army of lesbians, butch and femme, plus the great poet W. H. Auden, all swarmed around Duffy's and the Sea Shack, was no common place always full of rude wit and shapeless elegance: ephemeral cartoon dialogue in hot air balloons, slipping from their grasp and floating out to sea (". . . because nobody remembers anything at the Grove").

"His sufferings have been chronic-acute, with no end in sight. His fear and his emotional loss are valid and deserve to be acknowledged and expressed in order to heal and transform the sacrifice. Any woman who fails to see it fails in compassion."

"What was that he said on the way out, about the vacuum cleaner?"

"He said he would have used the vacuum cleaner at home only that the thought of the suction pulling his dick off terrified him as much as the sound of the machine terrified the dog and the cat."

"Dana and Glen are the right men for the job."

"For the job the right men are Dana and Glen."

"*Ils ont le beguin pour lui*, they feel strongly about him."

"That's what I said bub—you know that the compulsion to rhyme is one of the less serious pathologies, but pathology it is."

"To me the story's more than a little pat—"

"'If a Harris pat —'"

"In which the heady scents of invention waft in the air."

"'Means a Paris hat, I may.'"

"Everybody carries his own baggage, dear."

"Not if I find a nice big burly black redcap, darling."

"I didn't notice Junior—the kid that is—toting any Mark Cross overnighter—as far as I can make out he came in a bathing suit under chinos and a Paul Stuart powder blue short-sleeved summer shirt and carrying two changes of smalls and socks—and maybe a toothbrush."

"No cosmetics—no razor."

"He's been going to Italian movies at the Corona Theater in—"

"Don't tell us, Corona."

"Actually the Corona Theater is on the Jackson Heights side of Junction Boulevard, the color line."

"Well, that changes everything."

"Gnarly."

"He did mention *Ossessione*—the Italian version of *The Postman Always Rings Twice*, directed by Luchino Visconti who made Maria Callas shove a tapeworm up her ass to lose all that weight and get a nose job and an abortion and put her into the *Scala Traviata*, which sealed her reputation."

"Excuse me, but the Meneghini's reputation was sealed by the Covent Garden *Norma*s."

"Paul Stuart is always the sign of—something."

"Dana and Glen want to dress him for the Belvedere ceremony of his official coming out—he needs a good old-fashioned seeing to."

"Which will either seal his reputation or settle his hash."

"I didn't catch his name, dear, was it Gigi?"

"I understand he's written a quantity of poetry—has anybody seen any of it?"

"Yes."

"And?"

"The general consensus seems to be that while it may not be death-less verse, it's a good deal better than Burma Shave."

"A perfectly wonderful young man to add to our circle of love and caring."

"Excuse me, I'll be back in a few minutes—there's something I must do."

"Throw up."

"Exactly—to step away somewhat from the comfort of a circle of love and caring into the dark night and take the—what was it, heady air of inspiration?"

"Scent—the heady scent on him."

"Amyl from the Meat Rack?"

"Yardley—I recognized it."

"Dana and Glen bought it for him—made him throw away the Mennen. What they'll slap on his face tomorrow night at the Belvedere is anyone's guess."

"My Sin."

"He will be taught how to love, and to lie still while the winner of the lottery, the chosen one, pops his cherry."

"In Cherry Grove—but not this year."

"He will belong to us all, of whom the chosen is but one—we shall teach him how to love deeply, as we do—well and widely, forever or for tonight, whichever lasts longer."

2

Nonetheless, to be fair, he must relate that he was born.

So long as they could remain assured they were living in eidetic reality, Americans doted on fiction—holding the one-way mirror up to nature, but now that they know they are arbitrary figures, fish in a barrel, in post-modern fiction, having nothing whatever to say about what they'll get up to, they have rejected literary fiction as the great betrayal it in fact is, have turned viciously against it, and since they can readily get their masochistic rocks off watching television, becoming enslaved to pornography on the Internet and blogging themselves into mindless states. Truth is stranger than fiction and what they know about themselves now is that they are strangers all, to others and to themselves. They are as the world turns pathetic failures, which state the Japanese find noble. *Who* won the war?

His eyes focused inward, intent upon a different time and place—what have we here? (Keeping an eye on the grounds is something worth pursuing several times a day.) And the voices whispering, conspirators all, *don't . . . stop . . . don't . . . stop . . . don't stop!*

Controlled experiments have indicated—four of his favorite words, we know—that the direction in which a subject is looking is a clear indication of the part of the brain being put to use. Looking down and to the left—which makes him prone to those cricks in the neck—indicates the determined recollection of memories.

It's a fearsome struggle, and you can't send in the Gurkhas.

To begin a life with the beginning of a life is an inconclusive beginning, what with what's known, has been known since the beginning: that there is no beginning, that the measuring of time from the six days of creation on is only now and ever was—what will be being categorically immeasurable—a palliative fiction. If time is the measure of change and outcome, the unconscious, tolerating neither of these things, is timeless and bent on betrayal.

The cock crew thrice.

And when looking up and to the right one supposes he's trying to imagine a coherent future—dangerous that: brings on stroke.

In the first place the Netflix pictures—to accompany the powdered-sugar donut dunked in the Vienna roast coffee—summon not only the year, but often the very day in the very season when something happened in them relative to events in his life just then, to as the Irish say the day that's in it, and relentlessly, and in the second place the memories as they come into consciousness, the *equipage*, do so in the very form of the motion picture itself—in overwhelming silent majesty, in master shot, two-shot, close-up, fade-out/fade-in, dialectical montage vs. *mise en scene*, the *sortilege* of silver nitrate, and despite the demotion in the talkies from the outright to the merely existential, the shock of recognition in film noir, the lush scores of the great romantic epics, wide-angle Cinemascope, visionary Technicolor, stereophonic sound and the money shot.

The mayfly and the June bug. Fly on the wall. ("Little fly upon the wall, ain't'cha got no home at all?" Etc.)

"The type of child that pulls the wings off flies." (At Vision Beach on the Jersey shore he started catching them on the kitchen table under a water glass and watching them crawl up and fall back until they suffocated.)

"Your fly's open." (Sometimes "You open for business?")

Flying so high with some guy in the sky—for instance with Rock Hudson and Bob Stack in Douglas Sirk's movie *Battle Hymn*. (He is caught singing it to his image in the mirror.) Flyboys—the Air Force.

A fly-by-night. Flying the flag and the pledge of allegiance (hand on heart in those days, but no "under God," which was exactly when the rot set in, making way for the snake-handling Christers, the End Times catatonics and the unconstitutional trespass of the Church of Rome on the affairs of state).

Flying the flag at halfmast; flag always lowered at sundown. "Up in the air junior birdmen, up in the air upside down."

The strange dreams of flying all over the room and looking down on everybody. ("And who is that one, I'd like to know, to be looking down on anybody.") Laws are made for men, not men for laws; the rules will be challenged, time and time again.

The flight into Egypt.

"I want to tell you I went with guys in those days that I wouldn't fly over today."

"Ain't no flies on that little operator." (Dialing O, he has learned the voice: "*Op*erator.")

"There's more things in that head than could be got out with a comb." Fly in the ointment; flies in amber. The Amber Lantern on 25A, summer pit stop on the drive out to Northport.

Black jazz musicians call something good, or "cool," "fly."

"Birds fly over the rainbow." (Judy and the Queer anthem.)

"Flying fuck." ("I don't give a flying fuck about the Church—never did.")

The fly-over zone—makes him angry to hear it called that when he's been back and forth and up and down all the early and middle part of his life, by bus and train, talking to people, telling them that no, he isn't English, that his accent was his father's, and his father's father's and John Barrymore's—you know, Drew Barrymore's great-grandfather? Did a nice line in *Hamlet*—no Mel Gibson, of course, but something remarkable for his day. Famous profile. Yes, I do, don't I, or at least one taken notice of. The fact is he began charming his way around the country in 1951, listening to adults just as he'd done as a child in Northport and Lavalette, Vision Beach and Windham, and continued for decades, his chief ability that of drawing people of every region out, never arguing, evincing real interest in every low-church Christian cult in the Bible Belt, not to mention the high-church Episcopalians, Lutherans, Methodist-Episcopalians, Methodists and every shade of Baptist, drawing the line only in Salt Lake City, taking one long look up that hill at the Mormon Tabernacle with the angel Moroni atop the spire, looking east, grabbing a quick lunch at the drugstore and boarding the next Greyhound bus to Reno and the Mapes hotel, the people on the street in broad daylight had frightened him so.

Harold Bloom, decades later, was able to handle them, not so he.

Making a "flying asshole" with the fingers. Join forefinger and thumb to make a circle. Hold the other three fingers out like a wing and flutter as you wave the arm around in dive bomber information. He learned to do it at the age of seven on Johnny Zilch's stoop, was seen doing it at home, but nobody but his big brother David had any idea what it was, and so another strand in the bond between them was formed.

But it seemed an ass was also a donkey, as in the children's party game of Pin the Tail On.

He was regent in the kingdom, nothing more; he might not last a season, neither that of mists nor of snows nor of rains nor of blossoms. ("*La rosa, sin porque florisce, porque florisce.*")

Catch the drift? For no reason, the flower flowers, because the flower flowers.*

Go take a walk. We ourselves have but one life to live, until they take it off the air, and not one spare second of it to spend meditating on our insignificance in the face of some distant spew in the sky.

Is the fault ours that terrible childhoods have turned the lot of you into depressives? God did not put men on this earth to feel like shit. Put that in your pipes and smoke it while you sit mesmerized taking in the last scene of Joe Gage's porn movie *Campus Pizza* while waiting on a delivery of same from Adriana on Third Avenue, and dreaming of a delicious antipasto, of tongue probing the hairless anal aperture of that ultimate manned-up proletarian offbeat-gorgeous Prince of Steamy Bottoms.

---

* Jorge Luis Borges, quoting Silesius.

Now get out—we have serious work to finish before morning and must first refresh our spirits with singing. And another thing now the room is empty (not only might you as well talk to the wall, but in nearly every case the conversation will prove of greater consequence by far since the wall bounces the sound back where it belongs), what you ought to be wrapping your minds around is eternity. God never closes the one whimpering door but he opens . . . for every shutdown there's a new big bang. Go thou in peace, and sin no more the sick sin of spite . . .

This conversation has been moved to the trash.

And this in memory of every heroic whacked-out fatso, every driven queen on crystal, every epileptic and every cocaine freak who ever dropped dead on a Karaoke floor anywhere on the planet Nevermore. It wasn't, however, long afterward that the dawn of liberation did so. What began to be said in those bright days was: the homosexual, fallen man, fallen woman, neither hungers nor thirsts after plea-bargain justice, nor after the inheritance of the earth, but to bear away by violence the King-dom of Heaven and bury it in the depths of the sea and get away with it, pleading double jeopardy: for being born in the first place into the ter-rible family of man, and simultaneously into the despised and greatly feared family next door.

. . .

We must now digest our complots in some form. Dissertation, then go out and hire that hall again.

Take his own life, the first four years of it anatomized anon, distant from abandonment, nigh on seven decades since. Does he get to run for a second term, and win? Is it in the cards after all?

(Many things not covered in the policy.)

And by extension did he ever try literally to take his own life—was looping a dishtowel around the towel rack in the kitchen, standing on chair and kicking it away, only to fall and break the towel rack and be discovered by his grandfather, rushing out from his room in the back, looking bewildered down on his canetta on the kitchen floor—and this at the age, not long before the church's designated age of the use of reason—any class of serious attempt at that against which the Almighty had fixed His canon? Or just a game? Surely in those years a consummation more devoutly to be wished would have been that of his favorite candy bar, "Forever Yours."

. . .

His mother used to say of a woman who lightened her hair at home that she was a suicide blonde—she did it herself. As to all-but-overwhelming suicidal impulses subsequent to the kitchen towel rack incident, there's really no knowing. Hindsight is easier, on the nerves in particular, unless one has the foresight to be clairvoyant, which can be, and so often is, simply shattering. And ignorance is a delicate and exotic fruit that finds its bloom, when touched, quite gone. (He told them all for years and years he did not like to be touched, a lie of lies; he burned for it.)

One might well wonder is he truly descended from the industrious Irish merchant class on the rise in the nineteenth century, or from a gang of visionary, schizophrenic snake handlers from Appalachia.

After all, every story told in every saloon in New York is told to cover some tracks.

He too has felt the sweaty allure of slow heat in a Texas town, and many were the steadies fellated by him in Lafayette Park and other queer haunts of the capital.

But the tracks on the High Line have been pulled up.

"Oh moon of Alabama, none too soon do we say goodbye; we miss not a bit our dear old mama, and if we don't have whiskey we surely will die!"

The man in the moon is a lady.

It's only a paper moon.

Is there a profile face in the man in the half moon, or is it just another

Venetian fancy? Both full and gibbous moons have distinct faces, and vary significantly, while the full moon man in the moon is seemingly so sure of lasting, the tragic gibbous moon man in stricken and in despair, saying always, "I'm going, and I don't know if I shall ever be coming back." He knows he never can and never will be ruler of the sky, and fears the worst.

Ring any bells? Bell ringing has been popular since about 1500.

One of those bells, one of those things, the bells weren't ringing for him and his guys, not back then. Pick up the bells and ring them during the consecration when the host is raised, *Hoc est enim corpus meum*, this is my very body.

What exactly, in detail, was the harrowing of Hell?

Department of Lost Wisdom: why did everybody once upon a time, when brewing pots of coffee, put eggshells in the coffee grounds? And which is it, does history repeat itself or is it incessantly repeated, eternally returning with no end to time, no end of change of which time is from the ages, for the ages the measure, by those doomed whose failing minds—advertising, television, every scrap of the known posted on the Internet, blogging, texting, twittering, checking the weather report—read every scrap?

His friend the painter Darragh Park, gone on Marcel Proust, had named his lurcher bitch Oriane. He himself went back to *In Search of Lost Time* looking for the paragraphs about "the little phrase" of the imaginary composer Vinteuil—not because he cared particularly what it might have been in actuality—Fauré, César Franck, Saint-Saëns—but, because he had a phrase of his own, from the music of Elliott Carter. (Author himself was drawn not to the clammy Duchesse de Guermantes, but most passionately to the fabulous courtesan Odette de Crécy. For years he kept seeing Simone Signoret from Jacques Clouzot's movie *Diabolique*, dressed not in the dingy *schmattas* they put her in, but in all the finery of the *Belle Époque*. And as Marcel of course he'd cast himself—he too was accused of name dropping—*and* place-dropping. He had become expert at the art of pattern recognition; his scent was Echelon.

Then along came Catherine Deneuve in the part and became to Odette de Crécy what Bette Davis is to Margot Channing, the real thing, *la vraie souche*.)

. . .

So to sit and look through windows of old times and in the manner of the motion picture camera—ah, yes, cinematic technique: wide . . . tight . . . wide . . . tight . . . wide . . . tight—until the whole thing starts mattering—or remembering his nights in Central Park, lolling in hansom cabs, singing Cole Porter tunes to bewildered youths who just didn't get it (but who put out all the same: this is New York), rock climbing in the Ramble and running the gauntlet along the paths behind the Central Park West high stone wall, in the manner of the forensic totality of a crime scene constructed itself incrementally in the mind, as if the complete effect was in memory too stark, too terrible to absorb as a single accomplishment, a one fell swoop done thing. And the compassionate lesson of pain is something out of a Trappist monastery: Gethsemane, for example, down there in Kentucky, where in the '70s the monks were fucking in the bushes like rabbits—celebrating the body electric. Was a stop ever put to it? The tissue paper may be tissues of lies, but the objects in the box are genuine. In any case, it simply can't have been as terrible as all that.

There was always music—there is still. All art aspires to the condition of it. Only through music is it possible to approach the disparate sublimity of the spires at Chartres. One has never understood people who say they dislike music. They dislike music—yet the reason is quite simple after all: they find in it the source of too many unanticipated sensations.

Tastes vary. Yes, the *Archduke Trio* is divine, and all the rest of Beethoven. And Haydn and Mozart, and Schubert and Schumann and Berlioz and Debussy and Elliott Carter—but somehow they all pale beside the countless times over the years he's fallen back on the silken pillows in a veritable swoon, eyes brimming with ecstatic tears, over the "Meditation" from *Thaïs*—secure in the resolve that no future meditation of his own, no peace of mind or repose of soul would ever be disturbed by the sound of shots fired in anger. Not to mention the Second Movement of the Barber Violin Concerto, "Marietta's Lied" from Korngold's *Die Tote Stadt*, or risen up and pacing the floor, moaning low with the desperate Amneris in the Judgment Scene from Verdi's *Aida*: "*E in poter di costoro io stessa lo gettai . . . io stessa . . . io stessa*" (He is now in their power, his sentence I have sealed)—or with Lady Macbeth—"*Una macchia!*" A spot!

Or with Violetta in the "*Sempre libera!*" liberty forever, or with *La Principessa Turandot* in "*In questa reggia,*" that sentimental little ditty, and of course—and what an interpretation—but then he did goon on Ljuba Welitsch—Salome in the final scene ("Kill that woman!").

In addition, Spike Jones's "Cocktails for Two" and Sheldon Harnack's "The Boston Beguine" were important formative influences on the "zany" subterfuge and his obsessive attraction to chaos and pillage.

His brief is not to entertain, but to instruct—so kindly wipe that grin off your face and pay heed. There will be gags sufficient en route but each will have a strangely uncanny aura, such as his mother's famous "Meet me there on the corner at three o'clock. If you get there first make a mark on the sidewalk, if I get there first I'll rub it out."

. . .

And what of death? Will he have his ashes scattered on the waters of the little rivulet in the Ramble that, sprung from some recess under the rocks, exonerates itself into the Boat Lake, where in his grandfather's day real gondolas and *gondolieri* imported from Venice did abound? The very word (*gondolieri*) speaks of yesterday (and the Gilbert and Sullivan operetta *The Gondoliers*), and as these were imported directly from Venice and joined the Italian community (never very happy for the length of their stay, these citizens of *La Serenissima*, among the lower-order Neapolitans and the Sicilians, few of whom spoke the high Italian, and none of whom could make head nor tail out of *Veneziano*). The air rang out with song, in voices surpassing in sweetness and in power any but the first line of male star singers at the Metropolitan Opera who used to come up to Central Park on Sunday afternoons to listen to them, or so his grandfather said (and in some cases to pay for lessons).

The leprous grotesqueries of human folly are surely a subject of comedic as well as tragic, recognition—given to arousing feelings of scorn and hilarity right alongside ones of terror and pity—a long day at the theater—but that is of course the point, one was at the theater all morning, an experience replicated in the American theater of the last century only by O'Neill's *Strange Interlude*, a sadly undervalued masterpiece quite on the level of O'Neill's other great plays, *The Iceman Cometh*, *Mourning Becomes Electra* and *Long Day's Journey into Night*.

And yet to batten on them, concluding that the lost Aristotelian treatise on comedy showed the representation of hubris in the only authentic political light, as a subject to be enacted by the clowns and that was in no tragedy, only melodrama raising its voice to, yes, hilarious pitches, to promulgate such desolate ideas is to lose one's soul little by little with each expostulation—which is why it is of the greatest importance to distance such antics from the exuberant celebration of certain failures that is true Camp, and of the sublimities, every bit as wanton as those of tragedy, comedy and Euripidean melodrama called High Camp. High Camp arrives at the very point in the most complex culture the world has ever known, at which Schopenhauer's *The World as Will and Idea* and Nietzsche's *The Will to Power* succeed one another in the long drawn out and triumphant campaign by Batman and Robin to pulverize Enlightenment presumption.

The philosopher Wittgenstein would have been impossible but for having arisen out of the milieu of that most febrile instance of sociopolitical and religious ferment, the Austro-Hungarian Empire. And what Beethoven's *Fidelio* was to Vienna and to Europe in the nineteenth century, so was Berg's opera *Lulu* to the twentieth. In darkened places sentimental he: off to take a ditto journey, disguised of course. (Mae West as the Empress of Russia to her maid in *Catherine Was Great* "Oh, Var-*vara*, *hahnd* me my traveling case and my peasant disguise.")

A good part of the time in spiritual drag as Margaret, Duchess of Argyll, the great liberated woman of postwar Britain ("Always a poodle! That, and three strands of pearls!"), detailing his checkered formal and informal education. Through thickets of briar and branch, of great felled oak and whispering hemlock. A 14-inch chain saw will at all times do the necessary, so do bring along a woodsman (not tin).

Only connect, and you can get away with just about anything; and if the action of your brain's synapses are getting slower and slower, try Effexor, or perhaps Cymbalta.

THREE

1

To begin his life with the beginning of his life: the facts are these.

Born at nine a.m. on July 4, 1941, a rainy summer Friday (a First Friday, breaking along with his mother's water the last of the chain of nine consecutive First Friday devotions to the Sacred Heart in commemoration of the vision granted St. Margaret Mary Alacoque in the middle of the seventeenth century. His mother always used to say, "I take from the Sacred Heart"), in Flushing Hospital, the morning star invisible in the downpour, but up there somewhere. The morning and the evening star—also known as the folding or enfolding star in relation to the Good Shepherd meaning that it hovers over the crib at the start of each day and returns to check on the progress in the evening. Venereal *métier* all connected with desire, with Eros pushing up against Thanatos: the organism's assertions, also known as *thriving*, all in avoidance of crib death.

That he was born anomalous wasn't ratified for sixty-five years.

Born into the worldview held from July 4 to December 7, 1941, after which The United States of America comes to define and dictate the story of the world in the second half of the twentieth century.

One can't possibly imagine, one knows only what one can do oneself—kill them.

And so two years and some months later, he wanted desperately to kill his baby brother.

Bramwell was inclined to be a surly child.

His name isn't Bramwell.

Some names have been changed to protect one from the innocent.

—

The odd thing was, of the three necessities in the commission of a transgression, motive, means and opportunity, the motive and the means, which should have been, or so it would seem, the more important, disjunct from opportunity, had shrunk in significance to nothing; opportunity had become the all of it—became a particular thing in itself rather than simply a kind of thing: a thing demanding tribute, "I will do such things, I know not what they are, but they shall be the terrors of the earth!" (*King Lear*). And no other tribute than the matter at hand, as if to say, "If you want to stay alive . . . ask for nothing. It will not respond to mendicant address, and it will not come knocking at the door selling encyclopedias, but it in its own time and on its own terms pays off."

In the not unbidden years to come the zany performance worked like a charm—reminded people of the fascination they felt at the death-defying leaps of the child's imagination—wondering what the fight-or-flight response must feel like in an air battle—and they were just that, defying deaths with fairy tales of happily ever after on earth and happy forever with Himself in heaven. No fairy would have been able to hear "happy forever with *herself*," not even after she'd been promoted in the ranks to official Queen of Heaven, sitting body and soul on her own gay throne close to the throne of God, a two seater, with a perch at the top for the dove.

. . .

High New York romance, *Manhattan Tower* quality. Passages in the writing up of aspiring by way of the Paterian dictate to the sublime piano music of Debussy (*Estampes, Images*) finding themselves trapped in the clutches of that of Scriabin (*Poem of Fire, Poem of Ecstasy*) and later of the orgiastic sublime in the *Visions de l'Amen* of the seraphic Olivier Messiaen, leading in turn to television celebrity, newspaper celebrity, book celebrity, a thoroughly futile whirlwind excursion to Los Angeles to address the question of the picture deal, and a thrilling, melodramatic, headlong slide down the skids to the gutter.

—

In the classroom, passive, going into defensive trances, as if careful not to be detected.

It wasn't he who found the four-leaf clover, never once.

It was a *cul-de-sac* lined with yew trees, unpopulated at the end.

And like that—like what? Nothing else, *Shazam*—and with the sunrise at his back, Redemption.

Dear Life,
I'm holding on.
Love,
Me

(Oh, brother.)

"Hello?" he called out into the soughing wind.

(Oh, *brother*!)

He did have two—still does in fact. How did it come to this?

We shall go no further than part way at present—what Freud calls the manifest content of dreams, and particularly of the definitive but elusive elements colliding in the hypnagogic state, in no way constituting fiction. What good is it?

As always in such extreme cases of special pleading the good of it is but an evaluation of the *utility* of it. The guy says the horse can do. *Si, la speranza chi delude sempre,* hope deludes us ever—and Jesus wept, how one was known for singing the whole of *In questa reggia*, in this royal palace, and *gli enigmi a capella* and how the firmly supported but unearthly sound would rise through the canyons of midtown until one actually became known as some demented town crier letting the town know much discord was afoot, so stay where you are, be careful of midnight guests and keep the pearl-handled .38 within reach, but not on the mantelpiece where someone else may find it.

Remember what Martha Graham, that high priestess of modern dance, said. "You are in competition with nobody but yourself"—

certainly not with such writers as William Cullen Bryant, Fitz James O'Brien, Horace Greeley, Horatio Alger, O. Henry, Stephen Crane, or F. Scott Fitzgerald, nor with Maxwell Bodenheim, Dawn Powell, Joseph Mitchell, John O'Hara, J. D. Salinger, John Rechy, or even your buddy Buddy Brodkey (though he was strangely fascinated and generous enough in his acerbic and ironic way to say he thought you were good—proclaiming as you stood together at the bottom of the spiral staircase in the old offices of *The New Yorker*, "You realize, this guy knows *Bette Davis*!" His way of acknowledging your loyalty to him).

Baudelaire called us the self-terrifiers, *seautontimoremenos.*

Either alter melancholy and nostalgia and the knowledge of *das Geheimnis des Todes*, the mystery of death—Bobby Otto from down the block made the horror comics come true by getting his shoe caught in a Long Island Railroad tie during a ridiculous game of chicken, and as a consequence meeting a hideous death under the approaching train, his head rolling down the embankment in plain view of all the boys present—with a digression of compounds, a long and deep study of the alchemy of finance, the consolation of philosophy, interminable psychoanalysis, or snap out of it, pull yourself together, pull your socks up and haul your spirit by the red worsted man-ropes Providence has provided all striving boys into life, to live it, to best it, to enlist, and join the men who faced the foe at Marathon. After all, were you in on that game of chicken at the Elmhurst station or were you home either jerking off in front of the hall mirror or practicing those Chopin *Études*—or is it in some freakish way worse that you weren't, and were?

And what the commentators fail to understand is, Narcissus was a very nice boy.

Yet murmuring voices in empty rooms are not his idea of instruction or amusement.

One's memory is faulty. *You don't mean to say so.*

The clues multiply and with them the questions. As the Dublin dinner party hostess assured a most inquisitive guest, "Sure there's no time now to be giving more than the gist. We'll be *in communicado* in the morning and I'll give you the whole syllabus then, plus repercussions and commentary—but it's to die with you—because you see it was to die with me."

What a kick in the head, to realize that none of his specimen days had ever been run up as a sample of life's garment, loose or otherwise to be paraded down the catwalk with the fall line, but only left hanging in the storeroom behind the showroom.

Consider the crack in the unlocked cubicle door—"I suffer from claustrophobia, officer"—through which he spied on the men at the urinals (terrified all the while of being caught and ending up on the wrong end of a strong fist—or worse: Johnny Zilch said there were guys who shoved their clenched fists up faggots' asses), like the partial view seats, the score desks in the Dress Circle at the Metropolitan, which allowed him to hear the opera and glimpse the prompter's box and the string section of the orchestra, read the drama but see next to nothing of it unfolding on the stage, the silent pictures' closing fadeout technique, came to stand for the narrow aperture through which it seemed to him his obsessive malady allowed him to view the world itself.

They do say the paperwork is the most onerous part.

Pile it up in the corner.

. . .

There may or may not have been a beginning, no matter. Avoiding comparison, invidious or not, to a certain rogue classic of English literature, our boy, unlike the infant Tristram Shandy, does in fact manage to get himself born, and raised to the critical age of four, at which in life, ask any competent psychoanalyst, the personality is fixed for life, and if there are to be multiple initiatives kicking over to get the same story rolling, it'll be as if on an empty stage four principal actors—chief spokesmen of the chorus rather than protagonist or antagonist players—and in a story in which nearly everybody is, his or her worst enemy, what bizarre rapier dancing. *Lights!*

"Who made the world?"

"God made the world."
(And later, "And who made you?"
Nobody made me, father, I wanted to.
"God made me, father.")

One can hear it—one can see it: lips parted in that fetching little buttoned smile.

"There is no female equivalent of James," he told them.

"You'll do," they said.

Since the world began, a talent to amuse. Man up, won't you? A talent to amuse is nothing to be sneezed at.

God made the world as such, not enough of it and not enough time for tragic souls, but it was men who made cities, worlds within a cosmos both far too vast and far too insufficient for the crucial necessities of civilized life, without which self slaughter is the only correct answer to the riddle, and fuck the Almighty, his canon, the four horsemen he got to ride in at the end, *his* works, *his* pomps, *his* fakements, *his* mother's telephone number and all the rest of it.

Apart from the Trinity—Me, Myself and I—the Pleroma, the Garden of Paradise—expulsion from—and perhaps Norma's moon, one can see no real value in religious ideas other than that they induce *preoccupations*, which lead to spiritual questions and dusty answers in the vain pursuit of certainties in this our life that comes to dust—offset by ceremonies, celebrations, decoration and of course first and foremost music frozen in stone. What good is Chartres, or the rose windows or Palestrina or even Bach? Oh do not ask what is it, or what they are. For a good time go play miniature golf.

The days of messages scribbled on toilet stalls, personal correspondence slipped under the steel partition and sometimes even through the mail slot at the correct address, but one couldn't have . . . one just might have been followed back to the brownstone in the East 50s and—but there it was, the slender parcel, containing the note wrapped around the smart Mark Cross wallet.

Perhaps you don't remember me from last night, the muscatel was flowing and the room was dimly lit—but what of it, I'm not ashamed to say that like the cat that sees best in the dark, I only had eyes for you—such a sweet sight to see you, an artist, at work.

Although I know your name, mine wouldn't mean anything to you. It's in the lap of the gods whether or not we meet again on the rocky road to love on another day's march closer home, but I wish you safe journey and a peaceful ending of the fever of life.

An Admirer.

They never did meet, which seemed odd; there were so many familiar faces and serial one night stands replayed at sometimes wide and distant intervals in the melee, but he did ever after keep a closer check on his wallet.

Pink baths are probably the easiest and most considerate all told (but for the love of God don't make a hash of it: slice *down*, not across the artery—down from the crook in the arm all the way to the wrist), to allay for all eternity the veiled answer to the desperate plea—for instance in his case the terrible metaphysical question, unquestionably freighted with emblematic and perhaps definitive meaning, why did bright hot summer sunshine put Sunny Jim in the hospital, in witch-hazel gauze wraps head to toe, out of ambulatory condition for a week each time ending up in his later years being the spectator from the front porch, the lonely queer under the shade tree "thinking out loud" as his mother had done walking through the rooms at 37-13 94th Street, accomplishing things, but always to the drone of a woman talking to herself like Mary Tyrone at the end of *Long Day's Journey into Night*, discouraging interruption—and you can have the radio on the whole way tuned to the Bach B-Minor Mass and an ice cold jeroboam of champagne in an ice bucket within easy reach. But you must stick to it—the Bach—you must *not reach up to change the station to show tunes*, because as sure as God made the little green apple on the apple tree that was the start of the pith of the argument, the first of his innumerable and incessant tricks, that radio will fall in the bright pink bathtub and *zzzt, zzzt*, no telling what might happen, anything from a blackout in the hotel to a blazing inferno, but certainly the end of the affair, a suicide to match Bellini's Norma's—but Norma was never his role: his role was Amneris—*atroce gelosia*, horrible jealousy. And lying prostrate on the lid of the tomb begging for peace—*pace . . . pace . . . pace.*

(Can I get you anything, Jim? Catherine would ask at the end of the meal. "Peace and quiet, Catherine, peace and quiet," Big Jim would say.)

And later as you get ever more romantic, Gluck's *Orfeo ed Euridice*, Debussy's *Pelléas et Mélisande*, yes, Saint-Saëns's *Samson et Dalila*. "*Se pourrait-il que sur son coeur l'amour eût perdue sa puissance? La nuit est sombre et sans lueur . . . Rien ne peut trahir sa présence. Hélas! il ne vient pas!*" (Could it be that love has lost its power over his heart? The night is dark, without any light, nothing can betray his presence—alas! He is not coming!)

And always and forever Butterfly's great renunciation in Act III, "*Sotto il gran ponte del cielo, non v'è donna di voi più felice…Siatele sempre, non v'attritate per me.*" (Under the great bridge of heaven no woman is happier than you. Always be happy . . . don't feel sad for me.)

Until that is you went and created your own fabulous diva—clever way to placate—the salvific Mawrdew Czgowchwz, who augmented her vocal range in midcareer from falcon contralto to *oltrano*, and as life follows art back into art, your role then became writing *Mawrdew Czgowchwz*, and you played it to the hilt in the only theater with the capacity to accommodate your innumerable fans: the Theater of Your Mind, where your legend lives, in the upstairs apartment like Belasco's. And of course they published it and made you strangely famous.

Or consider the strange progress of a specimen session on the terrifying psychoanalytic couch.

"What comes to mind?" "What doesn't?" Disappeared things more than anything—things that in his father's expression "There's not the call for it there was."

Household words that were like one's friends—suddenly gone like political dissidents in totalitarian states. Forever Yours, Sanka, Oxydol and Oxydol's own Ma Perkins on the radio, Ben-Gay, Old Dutch cleanser, Kirkman's soap, Fels Naptha. (It was the Fels of Fels Naptha who commissioned Samuel Barber's Violin Concerto for his son, who proclaimed it unplayable. Silly boy.) Ipana toothpaste, the Hudson—the car not the river. "Step down into the new Hudson."

Strangely evocative of baptism; dream material. Bringing to mind ("What comes to mind?") that in certain places off rotting piers you could for years step down into the river. Drag queens would be baptized by high priestesses in solemn ceremonies and take on their drag queen names, so that part of the river had ben renamed "the Jordan."

The Packard, the Oldsmobile, the Pontiac, the Edsel, the New York, New Haven and Hartford, the New York Central, the Erie Lackawanna, the Pennsylvania, the Atchison, Topeka and Santa Fe, Dugan's donuts, Bulova watches, Buster Brown shoes, Thom McAn shoes, knickerbockers, Jantzen bathing suits.

Then take the case of "Take *Air-Wick* for example. It used to have a *wick*. You pulled the wick up out of the disinfectant liquid in the bottle and it disinfected the air in the room. Now the product comes in spray can, like other room deodorizers, no wick, and yet it's still called *Air-Wick*. Why? You used to explain the whole design of the thing to a kid, what do you tell him now? Tell me."

I suppose you might say that *air-wick* is an expression—and that the names of things tend to cling to them. And after all what harm could those enemas have really done, whether he needed them or not? Mae West swore by them.

Let them understand if they will he is not setting down the official authorized biography of his family or of the city they inhabited—they didn't last, the city did, and does—he is bringing them to life to tell the story of themselves, creating when bursting on the scene all at once out of nowhere a nimbus of white light, the components of which, invisible at the outset, may be discovered singly and in primary-secondary combination by the prism of the reader's consciousness patiently employed.

The fact is that it was an unusual family in that nobody in it seemed to be in love with the situation, having discovered elsewhere, places, times and ongoing scenarios in which they were sure of being romanced more memorably—and therefore not for the wish to abjure the company of the others as such at 37-13, but out of a compelling desire to be left alone among their souvenirs, except at the family's famous parties.

Perhaps the best that can be said is that out of necessity they gave it a fair shot.

I wish I could forget all about them, I really do—except for my brother David, known to his fraternity brothers as "Mac."

Star light, star bright, his wish is for two of the man—he wants twin big brothers. If as Unamuno would have it poets and philosophers are twin brothers, they must be identical ones. The philosopher also writes that it is only by going deeply into ourselves that we find our brothers, but speculation on the proposition has been rife and had yielded strong evidence of the truth's being felt and found in the reverse maneuver. This revelation is the secret of sacred incest not to mention frenetic adolescent masturbation in front of the hall mirror.

To do so you must write it out and move on.

The moving finger writes—*MENE, MENE TEKEL UPHARSIN*—the writing on the wall, "Ye have been tried in the balance and found wanting"—and having writ, moves on. No great surprise in that, it is the *métier* of the public scold. But move on to what—the life of the world to come? All this time-to-move-on shit is just that—shit.

Beckett knew: life is a gift from an Indian giver. Socrates knew at the beginning of it all, and Freud most belatedly reiterated the truth of it: formal adherence to any religious, philosophical or psychological system, including psychoanalysis when thought of as a religion, indeed the modern age's greatest manifestation of what Harold Bloom has called mankind's religion-making genius, is to sing along with a crazy cartoonist, following his bouncing balls across the color screen.

And Freud's were made of brass and his song is to the Song of Solomon as is "Smoke Gets in Your Eyes" to "Wanting You." And now get out ("I'm sorry, the hour is up." *The Immortal Hour*).

How beautiful they are, the Lordly Ones. Yes.

Terrible thing to turn it in for however many minutes of fame.

Time, change over time, over eons and the fascination with the origins of place *ab urbe condita*, founding myths of world cities from Nineveh to Los Angeles. In the study of geography in his elementary school it was said that every city has a particular trade or privilege in the industrial world, thus New York's two principal industries were book publishing and the garment industry (long before the running up was outsourced to Asia). That the city's privilege it was to be the center of the first serious go at world government, the hub of all American investment save in commodities such as hog and soybean futures—that privilege was Chicago's—and the nation's capital of the legitimate theater as well as of modern art, did not seem to warrant inclusion in the roll call of industry as such.

Confusion reigns, but need not govern. Nostalgia is not nor ever was the pain of past events as they may have been recorded as it were on hundreds of thousands of sound-equipped surveillance cameras, it is the pain felt exactly in the moment for a past that has nothing better to tell than haunted and fantastical stories. Heisenberg's Principle of Uncertainty applies with certainty to the empirical impossibility of determining both the position and the valence of any particle of information at the same time.

The parlor game of the story the ending of which when put side by side with the beginning is incomprehensible. Thus the talking book, the book of the told tale, largely dispensing with that seldom subtle and ultimately spurious device of relaxation and casual reader comfort, the propelling governance of a narrating intelligence summoned to spark insight, interpretation and conclusion.

And terrible books in which the hero eases out of bed and pads—yes, *pads*—across the bedroom floor to the bathroom.

His ambition was cast in the mold of the story his grandfather told him of the night on the radio when Orson Welles on his *Mercury Theatre on the Air* had H. G. Wells's *War of the Worlds*—this was in 1939, the year of the World's Fair out in Flushing Meadows, just before the real war, the one they were in, the Second World War that started in Europe when Hitler invaded Poland. He liked to think of all the people in Northport running around like chickens without heads yelling the sky is falling in—but how could Chicken Little run around screaming that the sky was falling in if she had no head? They probably got that story wrong, his grandfather said, it was probably the rooster. Anyway he learned a new word that day: hoax.

Never so much reason for laughter as now, never so many fools blowing the coals of contention to set fire to the world—affectation, bombast, false sentiment, frigid conceits, folly, pretense, meanness and vainglory, all at high tide.

The horror—the *horror*!

Get over it. No point in shooting up over it however—getting drunk was cheaper and more socially acceptable—whether or not you chose to get with the program—and you did want to be accepted someplace besides Max's Kansas City and the opera line. You wanted to travel the world with a diva—and you did. Right there in the grand salon of the Ritz in Madrid.

Victoria de los Angeles told the company, "Jimmy can go anywhere." And no less than the Mexican ambassadress—she was as gorgeous as Maria Monte as the Cobra Woman, swathed in gold lamé and dripping with Mexican jade—thought you were one hot tamale and said so, *¡Ay, Caramba!* in less than strictly diplomatic parlance—and all that ran through your mind was *that which we have in us to portray we have in us* *to become, but that which we have become we can very seldom portray.* The portrait of Dorian Gray, hah-hah, suspended for all time in the golden aura of the Immortal Hour.

Meanwhile, stay vigilant and pray for the swift return of what wits one had. Fish gotta swim, sometimes upstream, the salmon for example, the emblem fish of wisdom in Irish lore, reputed to be, the ones never caught, the repositories of all knowledge, both practical and metaphysical.

An optimist is a pessimist with *yutz*, brass neck and bottle.

. . .

In and among the general population of that other country the Past are the prophets not honored, and they are doubly vexed because they know us for what we are and know we are not permitted to let them know whether or not their prophecies came true. People were different then.

No, sweetheart, the people you mean are different now—they're dead.

Remember what Bette Davis said about Joan Crawford—just because you're dead doesn't mean you've changed.

Bette was a philosopher.

I still wish I could rid myself of them all—all except for Mac—and chuck you overboard to finish the job.

"Back off Sherlock, I'm on it," Moriarty said. "You know as well as I do how you need me, how you always have since you grew out of that stuffed panda. You call this a memoir, but I call it what it is, a *catalogue raisonée* of a controversial New York gallery exhibit (from these lips to God's ears), of which your servant has appointed himself curator, because face it, Delphic, you couldn't unassisted organize a boiled egg, I speak metaphorically, my metaphor is drawn from ovaries and the oldest question on earth: which came first . . ."

Accrued through such processes of random access, the facts are these. And as for them, where else, in the beginning at least, would the candy—and later the cigarettes—the Lucky Strikes—and the hooch have come from, considering the warnings, for instance, the extracted solemn promises never to dip into a stranger's pockets for supply— orders that didn't stick, but at least you were never kidnapped. But life is risk. Those who go with strange men risk losing their lives, those who don't will never have lives to risk. And yet it seemed no risk for him, shamming—*Jimmying*—the way you jimmy a lock to break and enter—his way between and around an army of fascinated bruisers with that lopsided grin he took from Tony Perkins in the stage version of Thomas Wolfe's *Look Homeward, Angel* and later in *Greenwillow*— never, never would he marry, born to wander till—puss-head barbarians who might have taken him apart limb from limb in a hot second, but that he somehow reminded them of their kid brothers, or their kid sisters, or both at once, which flummoxed them—and still snagging the odd swell, still agog over T. S. Eliot and amazed at his grasp of the work.

And in that amphibian life of resolute disobedience, what did he discover? That Balkan Sobranie cigarettes tasted like what he imagined dried horseshit must have, treated with vintage horse piss stored lovingly in wooden casques like Château Margaux. And Gauloises like a *routier's* armpit and Gitanes like a Frenchman's asshole—and you could get good long sniffs of either any night of the week in any *pissoir* in the *Jardin du Luxembourg* without spending a *sou*, simply for the price of being called *pede*, faggot, which in those days was nothing next to being called *Gaulliste*—on the Left Bank *pissoir* circuit at any rate.

And what of cousin Thomas the "juvenile delinquent" who had come to live with the family when Author was seven? Did he drop his pants and show our hero his hairy cock and low hangers and make his little cousin go down on him while he fantasized about fucking a big star, Ava Gardner?

He never did any of those things. He was a really sweet, nice guy, if troubled. The drunken father, the mother who, in my mother's famous saying, died in self-defense, the broken home. He didn't have a lot of trust in people. My father called him doubting Thomas and Grampa never trusted him because he used to go and hang out at the pool hall down under the El on Roosevelt Avenue. And the fact that he went to Newton High made him different. He liked the kid brother better than he liked me, but I couldn't really blame him, I saw the point: he was a likeable kid. So was he himself.

Aren't they all, the troubled. The troubled are trouble, too often big trouble. One may be sure he proved just that to the delight of the transient population on Riker's Island.

I never heard anything about him getting into trouble. He took us to See Uncle Don.

Who, I presume you know, was thrown off the air for being heard to say, when he thought the microphones were turned off, "That ought to hold the little bastards."

A notorious, if apocryphal, story—and the way adults really feel about children if you think about it.

Pluck your magic twanger, Froggie—I mean, seriously now, what gave? But they had that demonstration and you got to hear what your voice sounded like on the radio.

What a shock—but it brought a certain understanding of things, such as the way people hear you—understand you. I told Thomas and he agreed completely. So did my mother years later when we all sat around the kitchen table listening to one of her prerecorded radio programs on WWRL, the local radio station in Woodside. It was the only thing I ever told Thomas that I didn't tell David too. For some reason, maybe because Thomas was an outcast, and I had a foreboding—very corny, I admit. So I told Thomas that the fact of the matter was—is— that only you know what you *really* sound like and only you know what you really mean—except to others. You can never really know what you mean to others; stands to reason since people are always changing their minds.

The only mean thing he ever said to me was about my going to the pool hall with him and teaching me some shots. "No can do, pal; in the first place you have to be sixteen and in the second place you're as cock-eyed as your mother." Well, I drew myself up to my full five feet and said, "Thomas, do me a favor, O.K.? If you have anything nasty to say about me, have the decency to say it behind my back." He roared with laughter. I'd heard it at a party, of course.

Right after cousin Thomas Newman's stay with the family—he disappeared one night for good, leaving no note, no forwarding address; it was thought he'd joined the Navy—which immediately revived Author's earlier little-boy idea of joining the Navy like Eugene O'Flaherty—greatly reinforced by the enchantment of Rodgers and Hammerstein's *South Pacific*.

Although he'd been advised by his older brother that walking around the house singing "I'm going to wash that man right out of my hair" would not play as well as "Pistol Packin' Mama" had. Years later, the phantom cousin Thomas showed up one night at a party at the Bronx McCourts on Loring Place, in the company of his more knockout-blonde brother Kevin, whom Author had never met, shocking him as he stood in line in the bathroom gazing fixedly at both their cocks as they shared a low-class fraternal moment, seldom witnessed in real life by genteel people, but memorably dramatized in Joe Gage's realistic down home feature *Jock Park*—Thomas's member as swarthy as the rest of him and long as a line from the base of his palm to the tip of the middle finger he had raised so often at the world, Kevin's shorter, thicker, whiter, with a patch of blonde public hair sticking out of his boxer shorts and covering the base. (Trimmed to be neat?) Thomas seemed a ghost—another ghost, rather, because in those days, feeling isolated even in the family ("You're with your own." Who haven't a clue) he, Author, would team up with the ghost of his cousin Claire, who died as a young teenager.

The idea had come to him sitting there at the O'Keefes once over at East 188th Street, right off the Grand Concourse, down the block from the Loew's Paradise and Krumm's Kandy Kitchen, listening to his Aunt May talking about the lost girl, dead of meningitis in her early teens. What it in fact was, the idea, was that they could get up to mischief just like everybody else. There was still mischief in paradise, although no longer of the lethal kind. Innocent merriment, like the three little maids from school in *The Mikado*—and by the way, since when did ladies go into the seminary except as cooks and skivvies?

And so at the Christmas parties at the Bronx McCourts' on Loring Place, when everybody else was gathered around the upright singing carols—"Silent Night," "O Holy Night" (he hated missing it, it was his favorite and he'd learned to sing it in the original French—"*Peuple, à genoux! Attends ta déliverance!*" Fall on your knees, and hear . . .), "It Came Upon a Midnight Clear," "O Little Town of Bethlehem"—he would go into the back room, here Betty and Florrie slept, and pleading sinus headache, lie down on Florrie's bed and summon his dead cousin in heaven.

His dead cousin Claire's ghost appeared to him at parties on Loring Place and spurred him on to mischief (she who was such a saint in life). John, Kathleen, Miriam and Martello seem more interesting than he and his brothers—is that because they have a dead sister? May, Jimmy, John, Betty and Florrie all seem more interesting because they have a dead brother who was no good and a dead sister who was long-suffering.

Maybe if the kid (his little brother) died—a natural death, like pneumonia or a rheumatic heart like the kid over on 92nd Street who was playing touch football in the afternoon. Came home to supper with a fever, went straight to bed and was dead by midnight. He'd be in heaven with his cousin Claire and *they* and he would get all kinds of sympathy—and there he was, aching to sympathize with somebody, but walking around with that chip on his bony shoulder big as a two-by-four from the lumber yard up on Northern Boulevard and an expression that tried to be tough, masking all the sickening feelings of unrequited love he felt for the kid.

Which is really off the wall: how could you expect your kid brother to love you or look up to you when you were a son of a bitch (and so far as he was concerned their mother *was* an embarrassment, that was for sure) and later revealed to the whole neighborhood as a faggot hypocrite looking so pious up there on the altar with your fellow server Tommy O'Hara, who was straight as an arrow, and the nicest guy in the neighborhood, and you a hypocrite faggot who probably went home at night to dream of sucking his companion acolyte's cock, but Tommy wouldn't have a thing to do with you, although he was such a decent, regular guy he treated the hypocrite faggot as an equal, even with respect on account of his intelligence and scholarly abilities when not another boy in the neighborhood except for Lorcan Gallagher and of course, when he felt like getting his "benefits," Fintan, would even look at you.

So there Author was in the company of the mischievous ghost of his saintly cousin Claire—same name as the girl he was about to start going steady with at such a young age—in the back bedroom down the long hall at Loring Place, going through the bureau in the back bedroom shared by his aunts Betty and Florrie, where they find in the bottom drawer the picture of their uncle Tom (whom he has already decided was queer and beaten to death as a gay knock, and therefore more fascinating than ever).

The parties on Loring Place (1912, a few blocks south of the strange, sepulchral New York University Hall of Fame), after his grandmother and great Aunt Lizzie were as his mother would say "out of the picture," were rousing but those at 37-13 something more . . .

David's college graduation party in 1952 at 37-13. Whisky, beer, women and song—and gorgeous college men. As May Bark, in another much later context, running into Author and his mother lunching in public at the best of the neighborhood spaghetti joints, *Il Grotto Azzuro* (The Blue Grotto), memorably said, "Oh, Catherine, wasn't that a great party? I'm not back from that party yet."

By that time in his life, the effect over a four-year span on an eleven-year-old homosexual of sweaty growing male bodies smelling of man musk and alcohol when some of them would climb in with him in the bunk beds because there was enough room was very pronounced. Mac's new friends were college men, they called themselves that and they were as different from the former David's neighborhood friends at the Oakwood could be, not only in the same college, but in the same *fraternity*, in which there had been secret ceremonies somewhere along Spittoon Deauville Creek (Spittoon Deauville meaning the devil's tail), so Author had become more unnerved than ever, for in addition to wanting badly to grow up, he felt that no fraternity would ever accept him, no matter if his brother had been a brother. And that was another thing: Mac drank his beer from a white beer mug with the fraternity's Greek name, Phi Kappa, inscribed on it. A whole new plethora of brothers had taken over Mac's life; what need was there any longer for him? But the fraternity brothers of Phi Kappa certainly were nice to him, and also made him go weak in the legs and masturbate to dry orgasm when they would sleep over and one or the other of them inevitably would share his bunk bed, teasing him in the morning about his *stertorous* snoring.

Is he in mourning for his life? The bereaved should never be left alone, lest they succumb to the more extreme forms of physical culture. (One look at a Charles Atlas on the back page of an *Archie* comic—sand kicked by bullies in the face of a 98-pound weakling—can ruin a life.)

. . .

A writer as drawn-in as a long December night, looking over the broad surface of his sturdy oaken desk, captivated by a natural love of maps and chirographical delights, by the love of genealogy and family legend, of incidents curving along innumerable intersecting trajectories, in which nothing approaching the whole figuration of a single one can be contained within the compass of the narrative of that life's first four years. What we do know is he got the drop on them so early on, they coalesced without thinking—the men. Then his brother David disengaged from them in this one vital area—he had gotten the drop on the kid; vital because children want to be bested, the more they can learn how it's done, but only by someone they can admire, love and trust.

Special, evident and hidden arguments, testimonies, illustrations, and these not in brief. The problematic of writing was already situated as such, bound to the irreducible structure of *deferral*—every return diminishes likelihood, stick with the story you've got: print the legend—in its relations to consciousness. (Is there a Prince of Denmark in the roaring crowd? Hardly: men descend to meet, as that lofty windbag Emerson declared, and since the day that flights of angels sang him to his rest, Western Civilization's most notorious and sexually compelling starveling narcissist can no longer find the company on the ramparts of Elsinore up to snuff for serious discourse beyond the subjects of sex and the dead.)

No, he must for the life of him stay safe and warm among the shades, sung there by those angels (of the order of Thrones) if not quite at rest, at least at peace with the knowledge that there never was an answer, nor never will be one—for the fall, or the descent, of man was there always, precisely for the asking, presence, history and the disappearance or delay of the origin. In the last analysis the whimper may have signaled the beginning.

Were any of the fallen angels save Lucifer gifted with *l'esprit d'escalier* (or falling sickness)—or for that matter was Johanna Schopenhauer? There may or may not have been a beginning—no matter. A stab at art defined in terms of its conformity to the condition of music—and that music in which seemingly innumerable scales of tones, overtones, fractal and semitones related only to one another in ways they and they alone determine, to be employed when placed in the uncertain Author's hands in their original forms, or inverted, or retrograde, or retrograde inverted. The composition of such a work must be of such an order as to seem nonexistent. And watch your language, or you can go sit in the corner saving up spit.

So far as that other country his own past, his visionary lands of Nod and Counterpane, he will not have a barren acre in all its territories, not so much as the tops of mountains: wherever nature fails all will be had by art. Lakes and rivers will not be left desolate, all highways, bridges, aqueducts, canals and reservoirs, all public works most curiously maintained.

. . .

The city in the middle nineteenth century: McCourt stone cutters, artisans and builders, arrive from County Tyrone in Ireland. The late nineteenth century: David Matthew Moore, scion of a family of Dublin and Philadelphia, posthumous son of Matthew Moore, "broken" Civil War veteran, wounded in the Wilderness and brought up to the Washington hospital (enter Walt Whitman and the boys' calling cards) and afflicted for ten years with a morphine addiction that finally killed him. David Matthew, grammar school classmate of Al Smith, goes to work in 1891 as a hod carrier on the site of Carnegie Hall; then out to Chicago for the Columbian Exhibition, then back to New York as a "skyboy" ("negroes" on the work force and "danger money").

In later years he came to wonder: had Walt Whitman ever lain with his great-grandfather raging with fever, suffering terrible nightmares of the Wilderness, and touched him immodestly, bringing him the one great uplifting joy that even an old man's hand can bring: fist pussy? It suited him to think so, so he did, nothing easier, once again following the bouncing balls of heroes.

As Renaissance Rome was built on the broken stones of the decline and fall, so do new visionary conceptual structures form themselves from the debris of exploded nineteenth century rhetorical exertions, in prose and verse, in fiction and in fact. Thus "What exactly do you mean?" once a blistering birch-rod taunt, has become nothing but a limp weeping willow branch waving aimlessly at the essential existential question first voiced by infants at the outset of their wondering, *Why . . . why because . . . because why?* So don't be an ass, Freddy, how can I know what I mean until I see what I say? If I knew what I meant, or thought I did, I'd be in Parliament—or actually in Congress—or in a pulpit (soap boxes having gone the way of all flash). One of the ways in which life is an affront to the spirit is made manifest in its expert way of palming off its clients with sneaky feints and parries, allowing that some things may in fact be inevitable, playing to their grandiosity far more insidiously than Satan tempted Christ on the mountain by implying the existence of things that may not be. What then—small flavor to the fare, without the word of the lie, so help you, or "*Se non è vero, dovrebbe essere?*" If it's not true, it should be. Closely associated to the question is the pursuit of that excellence of writing called amplification, in which writer or plaintiff, whose theme admits of many successive starting points and pauses, enlarges on one impressive point after another in ascending scale. Throw away that truss, and good luck to you. Socrates gets Gorgias to agree that when addressing a sellout audience a rhetorician is more effective than an expert because mastery of the tools of persuasion makes a man more convincing than presentation of the facts—like Hitler for example. And in any and all cases, including the process of pleading for sympathy in the case through one's wrenching revelations the rhetorical question remains what it has always been, the question to which the answer is long since known, or at least credited ("so what?"). Memoirs, personal histories involving family and the city the way it used to be (taking care as Flaubert said about his novel *L'Éducation sentimentale* lest the background devour the foreground) must be rendered in a measured tone of voice. (Act only according to that maxim by which you can at the same time will that it should become a universal law independent of all references to empirical contingent factors, and you'll get nowhere fast, although it must be admitted the exhilaration of feeling almighty and breaking the speed limit is worth the stiff fine, not to mention the fine stiff private part sprung by the surreptitious gander at the toothsome hunk of chiseled beefcake writing you up, possibly unaware of your appraisal.)

Those were the days; they are not still. And not until the narrator was as the Japanese say already dead—meaning the surrender by his memory of everything read and reread, leaving him empty, culpable, filled with remorse and adrift in the doldrums of life's tempestuous sea will the never-ending story be suspended. "Don't ever tell anybody anything. If you do, you start missing everybody." And be assured, nothing will ever come to take their place. Moreover the armature, never to be discarded, never to be covered in a plain wrapper, is mere neither in the sense that it is a trivial paucity nor in the sense that it is the swollen entirety. The story is the telling of the story, the lapping flow of yakkety-yak. The gift of gab is dandy, but the gift of listening is the thing. What they'll all say is telling this story this way is not the right way to tell the story—the story should be told the way stories are told, front to back, not slantwise.

Only if you're desperate to convince somebody it all actually happened—and anyway nothing happens front to back, absolutely nothing; that's just premeditated compensation for the fluctuations of memory.

Suppose a happy family decides, sitting around the dinner table one Christmas, to tell its happy history. Do they divide the story up among themselves so that the first speaker tells the earliest beginnings, the next recites the lineage, the next the social background, etc. No, they all talk at once, scarcely able to contain their happiness, rather samey though it be.

. . .

Old half-forgotten, half-remembered moompix in the mail and the anatomy of nostalgia. Late '40s "problem pictures" and the problem child— an explosive match. A walk on the High Line—once the last leg on the journey of the freight cars that carried to the Bell Laboratories (reincarnated decades later as Westbeth, the artists' gulag) the components that made up the first atomic bombs, the one tested at White Sands and those dropped on Hiroshima and Nagasaki. They walked only twenty feet above the ground below, an improvement on the old Camp high wire act. Moriarty never walked on the high wire with him, nor handled the trapeze, so in mid-air switch act (Moriarty said, "swish act") as always partnered by a stranger, on whose kindness he could only now and then depend. Moriarty must always have a front-row seat in the audience below. While the crowd ooh-ahed and gasped, he sat stonily silent muttering only occasionally, *Stupid faggot makes himself a laughing stock, a buffoon.* On the High Line they tore up the tracks; his own are rusted and covered over.

A cold, foggy January night of nearly unprecedented sadness. (Does he contradict himself? Very well, he contradicts himself. Revisionary whatsis, the Heisenberg principle of Literature.) Conversation punctuated by foghorns. Sherlock Homo, far from the comforts of hearth and home, out in the world searching out clues. Ghosts favor dense fog and will appear in it. Anyway, winter weather is changeable.

Author, berated, turns the tables on the adversary.

"And just where do you think we're sitting, on the ramparts at Elsinore, you beset by a disconnect between strategic thinking and operational action? All that is over—Hamlet is extinct and the world is occupied in the invention of the post-human. Hazmats. Nevertheless, you have a point—my mother, so the story goes, might have married my Uncle Tom if he hadn't stood her up—"

Ah, the sinuous narrative.

"You could stand up to Kitty," Florrie said, "but you couldn't stand her up—not more than once"—and had his father not been sitting quietly at the kitchen table doing his Latin homework and invited her out for an ice-cream soda . . .

Hamlet. Very like a whale. Manhattan as drawn by the Dutch as *Manatus*, oriented west and in the distinct shape of a right whale; Manhattan memorably thought of as a great ocean liner moored in captivity to Queens, Brooklyn, Weehawken, Hoboken and Jersey City. The ship and the whale it would see off Nantucket, if like the great liners moored to docks along the North River, it could ever sail the North Atlantic, two in one, like everybody. (Have you ever seen them together?)

The two of them, hardly a pair, but together then and there, he no Hamlet, the other no Horatio, walking the boat deck of Leo Lerman's great ship, the S.S. (or S.O.S.) *Manhattan*, in permanent opposition.

That he had a voracious hunger for something big and white called Dick, prefixed with any given name, goes without saying—and an even bigger one for big black samples in the same line. Remember the 4th Street Baths in Atlanta? Even his name, Emory Renoir.

One despises racial prejudice.

So it says here in small print, right under "He detests cheap sentiment." Said preference—for black cock, for the musky scent of the black man before he showers, for the astonishing sheen of the blue-black men of the Georgia highland.

And all the while an East Side Celestial Line (he was thinking of Nathaniel Hawthorne's Celestial Railway on a bright summer afternoon—his birthday in fact, shared with Hawthorne, fireworks all set up to go off that night down in Coney Island) running high over East End Avenue from 79th Street to 92nd Street, passing over Yorkville and the erstwhile dwellings of the Moores and the McCourts, Carl Schurz Park and the deserted Gracie Mansion. The Celestial Railway was the place from which he covered the waterfront in memory, including all the great liners, voyages out and returns, not to mention the trucks, the meat packing district, as well as his father's "other woman." The Celestial Railway is the place to ride in comfort, talk about their East Side home life— and about the poignant turn the ambulance took when Kitty Moore was being moved from the NYU Rehabilitation Center, west across town leaving Astoria behind forever.

"What's it all about?"

"*About?* You're asking for a parable; *about* is a parable—parables are all about—"

"Whatever they're about—in succinct form. (Joe always gets his guy to shoot on the officer's badge)."

"You should know better than to ask a stupid question, especially as one is incapable of giving a stupid answer," Moriarty said. "It's a trial to be with me I know—a trial with you in the witness box, but until the day the boy on the Maine monument comes up to you as you sit alone in Columbus Circle, takes your hand and leads first over the rainbow bridge into the Ramble and then up the beanstalk to heaven in the shape of the Rainbow Room where that night you are the principal attraction they've been talking up in the columns, and Decca is interested . . . you're stuck with yours fucking truly."

Not so much a trial, as a strain—truthfully, a strain.

And as for him, at the end of two full years of focused hot flash recall, for his is the type that stays up late and digs deep—activity analogous to blasting quarries as did his ancestors, in which veins of significant detail are buried in the great dense rock of the compacted past—then finally sitting down on a rainy afternoon to open a crate containing every single splinter of the true cross—including the one under glass he's been kissing that's since gone missing—for him to glue together—many of them of course blood-stained, which presents its own set of problems, for example the extremely complicated x-ray procedures used to determine which of the shards contain the true blood of the Redeemer and which the blood from the fetid gums of the many Renaissance popes and cardinals and their catamites, pet *castrati*, favored painters—Caravaggio for example—whores, mistresses and frolicsome bastard children who used the sacred splinters as toothpicks at state banquets and after-theater suppers—the resulting construction to become the sensation of sensations in the long history of sensations at the planned third and greatest of all New York World's Fairs.

Or a box containing all the pieces of Jackson Pollock's huge painting, "Lavender Mist"—assuming he could fit them together—how many viewers can read "Lavender Mist"? Offer it up for the love of God, the remission of sins and the souls in Purgatory.

"Who may or may not be able is none of one's business; one's never pried."

"What an incorrigible liar you are."

"This too is true."

"So give it a whirl—who were they—or who might they have been?"

And fuck the begrudgers.

. . .

The McCourts of Dungannon in the county Tyrone in the province of Ulster and the Moores of Aungier Street in Dublin's fair city and any other rag-tag collaterals you could name—he couldn't, apart from the Goodbodys, millers from Kildare, later stockbrokers in Dublin, later ditto in New York, and Quakers.

Kitty Moore on the McCourts:

"The Moores were distinguished. The McCourts were *distinctive*— no doubt about it—but *distinguished*?"

"Well, at least they weren't shipped off to Australia like some."

"No—well, there's no record of it, anyway."

(Shipping and the waterfront in both families, eventually.)

"He was raised well—quite well brought up, was he not?"

"Indeed he was—until the rope broke."

Great Musick Hall. Fishamble Street, Dublin. 1742. He'd be having none of it that afternoon. (Dean Swift: who supervised the choristers of Christ Church rehearsing Handel's *Messiah* and repairing to the Black Bull thereafter.) Yet the work was admirable (and the composer a match for him, it was widely reported, in irascibility).

"The divine does surely dote upon his boys."

"His *milly cherry-bini in coro*, so."

"*No be a cainnte* with them allegations on the poor fella."

"Whatever of the boys, there's a fearful dearth of the altos—not a daysent singan' capon to be recruited in the city."

"No such Romish abominations are to be tolerated in Protestant Ireland."

"Whatever of that, to proceed to the matter at hand, here's one specifies himself an alto, and a man of parts—and him all of fourteen years of age."

"Would he have a name, this manly part singer?"

"He would—one Tobias Moore off Aungier Street."

"That's *of* Aungier Street, surely."

"There's many off the streets that make a sound—and more at the crossroads."

"Sure there must be a family of Moores in Aungier Street."

"Be assured there's more in the Coombe."

"Is this Tobias an imposter, so, and *off* a slip of the pen that uncovers him?"

"He's a Dublin boy, that's certain; there's no Moores among the Irish beyond the limits of the paved streets of the metropolis, and as to the mother's people, sure they're all blow-ins from Mullingar or someplace."

"Moore will be revealed."

"And less relieved, saith the Angel of the Lord."

A propos: The Old Testament Account of Tobias and the Archangel, who helped the boy collect a debt.

(Unnamed in Torah, but identified as Raphael, patron of physicians.)

"I know the garsoon, a lazy article, given to sitting down on the quays tying nautical knots and singing old ballads in the native tongue. The voice is indeed remarkable and gathers crowds."

Roll 'em! Toby Moore singing "I Know That My Redeemer Liveth" in a voice sweeter than that of Count John McCormack singing at the crossroads in Athlone 150 years later.

And before you declare it never happened, were you there to hear him not warble his song?

Handel wants to take him back to London and put him in his operas—*Tamerlano* would suit him right down to the ground once he gets his growth, but Tobias's father forbids it.

Kitty Moore at the age of sixteen started going down across the dividing line of 86th with Elizabeth McCourt (Elizabeth Josepha as previously noted, she having been born on March 19, the feast of St. Joseph, patron saint of a happy death) to the McCourt's large and rather bustling household on 83rd Street, in socially preferable lower Yorkville, and commenced walking out with the eldest (and fair-haired boy) son Tom, and heard talk even then of Tom Senior's plans to set up a family business and strike it rich in the coming big boom—nothing shady like the Teapot Dome Scandal, and nothing maritime like the poor Moores, but in good solid Florida land, *terra firma* as he put it. Solid ground!

Then, in the spring of 1923, with Warren Harding in the White House, Tom, junior, without prior notice, stood Kitty up.

In days of old, when knights were bold
And ladies not particular,
They stood them up against the wall
And screwed 'em perpendicular.

Dilating on the incident in later years—the metaphor, a good one, of the iris dilating, the pupil widening even as the eye narrows—which is however a matter of the eyelid and not of the pupil, meant to convey both displeasure and resolve. ("Do that to me once, shame on you, do it twice, shame on me.") In short, something called a temperament.

A Moore relation had been a signer. Sometime during the Second World War Kitty Moore was given the opportunity of making her own Declaration of Independence, one with a single signer. Having been informed by letter from The Daughters of the American Revolution in Washington that according to their records of the Moores' residence in Philadelphia in the year 1776 and of the fact that a near relation had been a signer of the Declaration of Independence, she had long been eligible for membership in that august sorority, the distaff equivalent of the Sons of Cincinnatus, but due to an unaccountable oversight had apparently never been formally apprised of her privileged status as an original American, an omission the Daughters would be happy to correct by enlisting her in the rolls were she to arrive in Washington for the ceremony. She had promptly replied, saying she would be glad to give the summons serious consideration on the day after the Daughters invited Marian Anderson, the black singer, to sing at Constitution Hall.

Which was the source of another crux, a vital one the substance of which only came out in articulate fullness sixty years later at the Kateri Residence on West 87th Street and West End Avenue. This one particular day, Author had gone up from East 22nd Street to look in on his mother, only to find her in a particularly snarky mood, a thing that could be tricky to deal with, but was in fact far more interesting, the energy behind it always preferable to the lethargy she would fall into simply by flinging in the towel (actually regrouping her forces, always aware there would always be fresh towels).

"Mrs. *McCawt*! Mrs. *McCawt*! Mrs. *McCawt*!"

He was just beginning to get an inkling. "I'm just beginning to get an inkling—elucidate some more: *Splayn* me."

The clear blue eyes narrowed again as of old.

"Your father . . . David . . . Brendan . . . *you* . . . all very lovely of course . . ."

"Aha! I think I get it. For almost fifty-two years, from November 1929 to April 1982 you were indeed Mrs. McCourt. But before November 1929 and since April 1982 you were again and have been Kitty Moore."

"*Exactly.*"

"Dead right—and fine by me. To tell the truth I've always found Kitty Moore more interesting."

The two identities had always clashed in her professional life—she was Mrs. McCourt when she taught the sixth grade at St. Francis Xavier on 16th Street in Manhattan and Miss Moore when she did the student musical shows in high schools, blithely ignoring any reservations the IRS might come to have on the arrangement. And in visits to Loring Place she'd always be greeted as Kitty Moore by her mother-in-law. "Come in Kitty Moore, and bring your children in with you." "You have lovely legs Kitty Moore, for a stout woman." And in the end, when it came to it, there was no way on earth she was going to be buried with them. And anyway, Big Jim was with the Moores already.

Matthew Moore, veteran of the Battle of the Wilderness in the Civil War, became a casualty, psychological as well as physical—in the Soldiers' Hospital in Washington, raving in his delirium about how his people were maritime purveyors and how did he get into the Army of the Republic under the command of a drunken bastard like Ulysses S. Grant (all the while being given morphine in large doses and taking comfort in Whitman's generous dispensing of the very corn mash moonshine Union soldiers had found distilling away in isolated patches of the sacred soil of the South: the copper kettles, the copper coils—you could lay there by the juniper/while the moon is bright/watch them jugs a-fillin'/in the pale moonlight while downing your fill to sleep a dreamless sleep before getting up with the sunrise and the bugle call to go out into some clearing in the woods, some small Virginia meadow, to be slaughtered while the birds fled as fast as bullets from the trees). And before you say it isn't true, were you there to note his absence?

The white lightning elixir was to be found readily available in the nation's capital so that it shouldn't be a total loss.

. . .

Then forward again to David Matthew Moore telling his grandson he should never, once he was grown up, shun an old duffer on a park bench anywhere. There was one such who had been in the 1880s in the habit of the lunch hour from his job as a clerk at the Customs House, sitting on the bench down by the river telling anybody who cared to listen the story of a boy who loved his father more than anyone else in the world and would sit with him for hours on end watching the boats coming down from the trading posts along the Hudson and with cargo offloaded from the barges on the Erie Canal, and thrilling at each appearance of the great three-masted ships coming into the harbor from the old mother country and Caribes. Then how the father, a man possessed of too great a soul to thrive in commerce, lost everything, went mad and died in a delirium just as David Matthew said his sister Katie told him on Grand Street some time in the 1880s their father had in 1882. "There are Moores all over the place, don't-cha-know."

"Like Flossie and Charlie in Northport—they're Moores; and your favorite singer, Grace Moore on the radio from the Metropolitan Opera."

. . .

Concerning Dave Moore and Carnegie Hall (he pronounced it "Car-*nay*-gie" as did the benefactor—"I built Car-*nay*-gie Hall, don't-cha-know, then I went in to listen to the music"). He watched as the hero of the hour "Pete" Tchaikovsky each night mounted a carriage with a fellow hod carrier who was mortified, because of course all the boys were Irish and he hadn't come down in the last hail storm, or in the great blizzard of 1888 either.

. . .

The McCourts: their story. An 1830 Sperrin Mountains Ulster stone cutter scenario: ferrying cut stone across Lough Neagh (created when Finn Macool ripped a chunk of turf and hurled it into the Irish Sea, forming the Isle of Man) to Belfast for the building of mansions for the Protestants of New York at the beginning of the boom—two brothers, bachelors both, see the ships at anchor, waiting to cross the Irish Sea to Liverpool, cash in and instead of recrossing Lough Neagh to bring their wages home, book passage to Liverpool in England and from there to New York, never to be heard of again in Dungannon, County Tyrone, Ireland.

Cut to Author's great-grandfather McCourt carving away while the archbishop looks up in true and humble Catholic American approval—scene hardly equivalent to Michelangelo up on a Vatican scaffold in agony and ecstasy, urged on from below by Julius II, grandiose, sanctimonious slave-driving sodomite Bishop of Rome—but worth the detour, as was the quarry at Hastings-on-the-Hudson. (Author once quipped to the writer Susannah Lessard, Stanford White's great-granddaughter, author of *The Architect of Desire*, that in all likelihood his great grandfather had sold stone to hers and may even have decorated the cladding on a number of his buildings—the second Madison Square Garden for example, on the roof of which the great architect, profligate and despoiler of virgins, was shot dead by Harry K. Thaw in 1906.)

2

The Goodbodys: an incursion.

The Goodbodys: Quaker millers of oats and subsequently stockbrokers in Dublin and New York. Brought up in conversation by his father, whose mother and Aunt Lizzie were Goodbodys born but of a Catholic mother.

"The Goodbodys are Quakers, they came to do good and stayed to do well." The two oat cereals the boy ate: Cheerios in the summer and Quaker Oats in the winter. Also the horses in Central Park and of the mounted police had bags of oats tied to their bridles from which they chomped at will, why horseshit smelled like hay, fragrant almost, although his grandfather said it was full of tuberculosis germs, spores that together with the unpasteurized milk that the horse-drawn milk wagons delivered in steel cans, from which pails of milk were filled for customers, which had killed half the children on the Lower East Side before pasteurization was finally brought in. (In Windham the milk was brought to Munson House from the farm right across the road every morning, unpasteurized, and the boy wondered about that, concluding the obvious: that since there were no horse wagons in the picture, there were no germs from horseshit.)

He remembers that when he went to see Garbo in the movie *Camille* on a comeback Tuesday at the Polk, Garbo goes to the country to recuperate from her latest attack of consumption and the country air and food is supposed to help cure her, but there she is sitting up in bed—this absolutely gorgeous and sophisticated woman demonstrating the greater humanity of a woman of the *demi-monde* brought up to the ways of the country—*drinking a whole bowl of unpasteurized milk.*

The Quakers and the Shakers. The main thing is that Quakers don't go to church, they go to "meeting"—clearly the meaning of "Sunday go-to-meeting clothes." At meetings they sit silent (something he can't imagine outside of a place like Creedmoor, the infamous mental institution which in the *Life* magazine exposure showed rows of people all drugged up or electroshocked up or lobotomized or in insulin shock sitting naked on steel benches, their eyes the eyes of the characters in the horror flick *I Walked with a Zombie* or standing in an empty hall being hosed down with cold water, and where his mother used to say they'd all drive her to one day) until the spirit descends and one after another of the Quakers speaks out of a vision. He of course had visions, but told nobody about them. Andy was only a stuffed panda, after all, but as close as he feels to his big brother, he can't bring himself to tell him, and he knows his mother would just fly off the handle (an expression). He could probably tell his Aunt Betty: she was supposed to have had them too, around the time she made that prophecy at his christening party. He especially wanted to know if she was having a good one that afternoon she put him in the hospital with second-degree burns from lying out asleep in the sun in Northport.

In any event, said tangent ends in the money loop, the fact that the Goodbodys were millionaires many times over and the McCourts had lost everything they ever had, and maybe this was because Quakers didn't drink and ate a goddam apple every day. So what was better, an amusing life, parties, theaters, the opera, dancing, singing and his father's astonishing prowess at the racetrack (though the bookies, whose great respect he had, did wonder about an inside track), lots of new clothes, signet rings, signet cufflinks, watches and more watches, the best seats in the house on Broadway, easily had from scalpers and an outrageous allowance of ten, then fifteen, then twenty dollars a week when everybody else was getting five at the very most . . . or the life of frugality, probity, scrupulous honesty and truth telling (whatever kind of Irish could the Goodbodys ever be?) and sitting around on hard benches waiting for somebody to be moved by the Spirit to speak. (He'd have liked to see them try that one up on Loring Place.)

"If they'd been less prejudiced the Goodbodys might have stopped that conniving bastard who sold papa a chunk of the Everglades."

Tippy Toes was the Gershwin musical about the Florida Land Bust. People have been taking about the Moores and the McCourts for so long now and it has become impossible to disentangle the dried hemp strands of tall tale telling and officially signed, sealed and delivered timeline fact.

One thing however is true beyond dispute: never mind what names she was called, Catherine Anita should never have raced down the hill on that winter's day in Carl Schurz Park and banged into the mayor's sled. It was a far worse thing than turning Republican in 1940 and voting for Wendell Willkie and Tom Dewey, and Vincent Impelleteri for mayor and Rockefeller for governor and God help them Richard Nixon for president, but their close friend state senator Tom Duffy (Helen Fisher, Kitty Moore's oldest friend from across the alley on East 88th Street, had married him), a good Irish-American Democrat and a moderate social drinker, had never held it against them.

They were impossible up at 1912 Loring Place, listening on the radio to the odious anti-Semite Father Coughlin until Dave Moore, up there on a visit, banged so loud on the dining room table they turned the radio off. Don't start in denigrating the Jewish people around *him*.

3

Returning to New York as such, the most existential city on the face of the earth.

Origin of "Gotham:" City of Goats. Separate the goats from the sheep—their cloven hoofs. Thus considered traditionally to be the home of various occult rites, including the alchemy attached to finance and capitalism, at last finding a way to turn lead and almost everything else into gold. Also tragedy *tragos oidos*, Greek for *goat song*.

Gotham the City of Goats. The three billy goats and the troll—the three billy goats were obviously on their way home to Gotham, when they met the troll, representative of all that is primitive nature and unsettled places.

Origin of the Rialto (high river) in Venice, the proto New York of the West, as independent of Italy as New York is of the U.S.A.

If the polar ice cap melts in the twenty-first century and the tides rise to engulf New York, what a life will swim before its eyes.

Neither his theatrical ambitions nor his glancing foray into Comparative Literature—Petrarch, Ariosto, Shakespeare, Milton, Herrick, Schiller, Kleist, Baudelaire, Rimbaud, Claudel, Beckett—succeeded in becoming anything other than strategies—the word was getting to be the hot term in criticism—for his own "self-dramatization" as an outlaw faggot, a queer who belonged in his heart in Times Square on the Deuce (John Rechy's *City of Night* had come out and caused a seismic shift in the glittery queer schist of the Naked City). Thus while acting the part of a serious close reader of Verlaine's *Villes I & II*, his personal scenario was to act the part of a Verlaine falling in with a guttersnipe—nothing easier in the environs of Washington Square—down to Little Italy, across to the West Village and up into tough-guy territory, to Second Avenue to Slugger Ann's (ballsy little Jackie Curtis, Slugger's grandson, working illegally behind the bar) but avoiding Stanley's—unmannerly heterosexuals all full of shit and with short fuses. Over to Tompkins Square for Irish, Polish and Ukrainian trade, no questions asked and never a hint of a gay knock, and always to the gay bars where white trash boys right off the bus at the new Port Authority terminal at 42d and Eighth (and never were bus station and location/situation better matched; it was easier than Chinese take-out).

To turn Manhattan into an isle of joy. A Prospero, from Shakespeare's *Tempest*, might manage it for a day and a night. During the war sailors used to do it on shore leave, or so the stories went at the Stage Door Canteen—Kit Cornell, a major star, slinging hash among other attractions and cooing the balcony scene from *Romeo and Juliet* with some impossible perfect American boy bound for the North Atlantic.

. . .

The perfectly correct diagramed sentence has become the secret weapon of nice people. What a thing he could make of it telling nothing but the truth, securely moored within the radius of the reader's convenience, but the truth isn't the half of it. "What is truth?" said jesting Pilate, washing his hands, and we must assume that when Homer nods, he dreams as Zeus would dream, which is called enthusiasm.

The seeker after it, the so-called true story, may send out as many all-points bulletins as he likes, as in the progression of effective emblems his chances at that of tracking it, of bringing it to book, are slim to nil.

Take cars for example: the old '30s Ford in Jo Normoyle's victory garden in Greenlawn; bumper cars in the amusement parks: Rockaway, Coney Island, Rye Beach, Seaside Heights. Drive-ins up in Windham (and the make-outs in adjoining cars).

"Drive-in dinner, drive-in movie, then we went for a drive."

And the menacing phrase, "As needs must when the devil drives."

Or umbrellas.

Rainy days.

Umbrellas in the South on sunny hot days—poor black old ladies carrying black ones, all the young blacks undaunted by the sun—white women carrying white parasols, white men wearing wide brimmed Panama hats. Married white women called "Miss" by acquaintances. (Short for *Missus*.)

Bad luck to open an umbrella indoors—but what about the *umbrellino* in the processions in church?

Clearly and of necessity the perfect map of that other country where they do things differently would, when unrolled, be exactly commensurate with the area of the country itself. When given the choice between this impossibly unwieldy representation of the world as everything that is the case and the driven will behind it and the legend of suspect classification, print the legend and live with it.

In which case the thing's a hoax—no great tragedy really.

If there's no meaning, nobody will care at all about it. Cause of deriving insufficient profit from the trouble of its perusal.

One won't let them find out there's not; it's not hard.

Are we talking about a supremely headstrong visionary activity blindly undertaken at great personal cost, or about a work whose coming-into-being—should existence so permit (existence precedes essence, the existentialists claimed, remember?)—is a spontaneous process independent of intention, precept, even consciousness—something in the way of a shall we say *seizure*?

One hasn't decided yet.

Still one wonders—will anyone believe a single word of it?

Darling, don't let's ask for the moon, we'll have the money—who gives a rat's ass if they buy it once they've bought it, all sales final? Nobody we know. And so it's come to this—how did it go?—We shall in what ensues go but a fraction of the way.

. . .

Apart from the self-styled truths outlandishly held in the American Declaration of Independence (that notorious example of Enlightenment wish-fulfillment) to be self-evident (on grounds somewhat less secure than St. Anselm of Canterbury's ontological proof of the existence of God (a perfect being must exist)—an old favorite—and therefore in a scientific sense also less stable than that found at the junctures of the earth's ever-shifting tectonic plates), all valued in terms of good Protestant money, although it must be admitted that outside the world of myth and of the Christian mystery of the Incarnation, all neonates delivered by evolution into the world who are equal to the trauma are delivered more or less equally helpless. When applied to the regulation of blind instinct, society as a governing principle, and in the light of modern psychoanalysis, its noble failure to hold the center illustrates perfectly Robert Burton's contention that all governments founded on the basis of Utopian parity are governments to be wished for rather than effected. On the other hand Churchill's more humane dictum holds that democracy is the worst form of government with the obvious exception of all the others.

Then came the day—a refrain repeated so often it came to stand for the same thing as the first four notes of Beethoven's Fifth Symphony (the knocking on the door of fate), probably the most often played four notes in all music.

Terror can become a kind of beauty too.

When two fellows stand up to it together.

The silence of Ajax in the Book 11 of the *Odyssey* is more eloquent and forceful than anything he might have said, but although he had read the *Odyssey*, the silence of Ajax had not moved him—indeed not much not having to do with Telemachus had. In fact if you asked him a question about Ajax, in order to hide his burgeoning erudition, he would chant, "Ajax, the foaming cleanser, foams the dirt right down the drain."

A boy like Jack Horner, sent to sit in the corner, excluded from stickball games, blackballed from adolescent sex clubs, thrown down in the street and stepped on, disgraced in plain view of idle curious passersby (boys will be boys, so let them be: it wasn't as if it was a bad neighborhood full of juvenile delinquents; in all likelihood all the boys in the tussle went to Blessed Sacrament School). Children trapped in themselves yearn to be publicized, according to their own designs, and as they grow older focus on it entirely as the most effective form of revenge. Do you know he said that when he was growing up the only time he was never told to go peddle his papers elsewhere was the brief interval during which he had a paper route delivering the *Long Island Star Journal*?

He sat there at the Wurlitzer spinet—eighty-eight keys—banging out "Unchained Melody" between Chopin nocturnes. I'll be coming home, wait for me, when all the while he was home and they were already waiting for him to come to the dinner table. Or, when the mind descends to the gutter from which he is in the company of other guttersnipes so disposed looking at the stars, imbued with the spirit of—enthused by— the famous British Music Hall ditty "If I had it all to do over, I'd do it all over you," he thinks he does and so makes the attempt. The unwary reader is best counseled to emulate the audience at adult cinemas and, as it were, wear a raincoat.

"Wherein," asks Longinus, "lies the force of a rhetorical image?"

Doubtless in adding energy and passion in a hundred different ways to a speech, but especially in this, "when it is mingled with the practical, argumentative parts of an oration it does not merely convince the reader, it enthralls him."

Catherine McCourt and her two boys met her friend May Purse while Christmas shopping on the Avenue—they called Junction Boulevard the Avenue. "Oh, Catherine," said she, looking down at the kid brother, "what a beautiful child—I could eat him up." Author, far from any sort of man, cut in with "Good idea, I'll carve." The kid started in bawling his ass off—worse than when Author gave him a giraffe animal cracker snapped in two at the bottom of the neck. "I want a fixed cookie!" "Eat it you little worm, or I'll do the same to you."

Just as 1001 nights is more enthralling than 1000 nights, signaling as it does an endless store of tales, so is the use of the hendecasyllable in syllable-stress, variable-foot verse (dubbed by Author in a treatment of prosody all his own the Hephaestion) periodically more enthralling than is the relentless use of the iambic decasyllable, but the revered cartographer of the celestial plane that had represented from time immemorial that quantity called the sublime seldom gets it wrong.

Zip—and what must follow as the night the day?

Hostile takeover by death—you feed smart cues.

Charmingly put, the reply—how is it that the worst news, when conveyed in charming fashion gives the listener the greatest delight.

Ask the entertainment business.

The simple fact that the charm is viewed as one against the awful truth—doesn't always work: for instance that time you sat down in the middle of the street outside Max's Kansas City, the place to be in the Warhol years, drunk as two skunks, mumbling incoherently about the rigors of the requisite course of study, then breaking out in a wail about the hell of being Schopenhauer's excluded middle. Not cute. And before this lark goes any further one must absolutely disallow any comparison with Robert Schumann's Florestan and Eusebius.

Done.

4

Memory enkindled by way of spirited conversations importantly including for satirical purposes those of autodidacts, constructed "on the wing" in dialogue—since few have the *yutz* to construct a coherent story and deliver it in the space of an hour without arousing the suspicion common among police interrogators—is always more a living thing, and therefore more "reliable" (an illusion, but one which has from time immemorial soothed the anxieties of the hearers of told tales—"some snowy night in front of the fire"), than the elaborations cut out of whole cloth (no matter how rich the fabric, how exquisite the workmanship and how *soignée* or well-tended the destined wearer, by a needlewoman working alone in an ill-lit room). Also the element of instruction—the moral of the story— including such vital activities as modern psychoanalysis—his analyst's analyst was analyzed by Freud, so kiss his ass—reinforcement in the act of coming out, liberation theology and demonstrating animal husbandry for later twentieth century American male homosexuality. What a thing he could make of it, still telling nothing but the truth—in the first place were he so constrained and secondly were there any such thing.

As to the entertainment business. The Church, the motion picture industry, the opera, the Broadway theater, the Sunday funny papers and comic books. The epistles and the gospels and the sermons at Mass then home to the funnies, *Dick Tracy, Bringing Up Father*, familiarly known as Jiggs and Maggie, *Gasoline Alley, The Katzenjammer Kids, L'il Abner, Barney Google and Snuffy Smith*, Major Hoople in *Our Boarding House, Prince Valiant, Tim Tyler's Luck* (his first blonde love, prefiguring the one he calls Fintan), *Mark Trail, Nancy, The Sad Sack, Mandrake the Magician, The Phantom,* etc., novenas, solemn benediction, High Mass, funeral Masses on Saturday (*Dies irae, dies illa*), then home to *Make Believe Ballroom* and the Saturday afternoon Metropolitan Opera broadcast—followed by confession: did it again father, all week long. Saint Aloysius Gonzaga, *aiutaci!* ("Help me!")

Baseball games on the radio, the Yankees, the Giants, the Dodgers. Dizzy Dean, Gladys Gooding and "The Star Spangled Banner." The seventh-inning stretch.

Radio and later television: Jack Benny, Fred Allen, George and Gracie.

All the children in the EC horror comic books were going to go to hell; readers of them had a very good chance of following them straight there.

Previews of coming attractions.

Washington, D.C., the men's room of the Mayflower Hotel, February 1952.

"Take a look, boy, take a *good look*. This here's Mr. Johnson—no white man you're ever gonna meet is ever gonna have one like him."

Thus to progress in high school dramatic society—from young romantic second lead in *You Can't Take It with You* to lead in *Nothing But the Truth*, an old Richard Bennett (Joan and Connie's father) vehicle from his Broadway matinee idol days, rival to Osgood Perkins (Tony's father), all the while relegated, for want of the ability to find in the character the truth (as specified by the great Stanislavski), as had Tony Perkins playing Eugene Gant in *Look Homeward, Angel* on Broadway, to a walk-on in the aching melodrama of his own life. Hence on stage in the high school auditorium, in front of an audience jammed to the rafters, kissing Maureen McGilligan with a chaste kiss with the same lips that earlier that same day, sometime in the middle of the afternoon, in the murky light of that darkened doleful changeless place, one of so many in the city, terrified all the while of being caught and ending up on the wrong end of a strong fist—or worse: Fintan had said there were cops who stuck their billy clubs up faggots' assholes—lips he'd had wrapped around any number of *menbri virili* male members pushed through the sizeable hole in the wall of a partition in the labyrinthine Canal Street Station—emblematic of what would become his lifelong locked-in penchant for disreputable venues, the most notoriously frenetic, depraved, and both because of its twists and turns and its proximity to Chinatown, enabled to become an extremely lucrative annex and pit stop in the thriving business of police graft in that neighborhood, in fact the most famous pit stop in the entire New York City Transit System—many of whose proud and manly owners, to go by the perfect shines on their costly English wing-tip shoes, must be, when industriously engaged aboveground, executives, junior and senior, of innumerable prestigious Wall Street firms.

The term *glory hole* and its eerie "Black Mass" relationship to the confessional—and later the knowledge of the seducer priests. Originally a small locker at the stern of a boat or between the decks of a ship. (Wouldn't it have something to do with sailors.)

Think of the goings on in such tight spaces between the Promenade Deck and the Boat Deck on the *Île de France*, the *Flandre*, the *Andrea Doria*, the *Michelangelo*, the *Raffaello*, the *Vulcania*, the *Stockholm*, the *Nieuw Amsterdam*, the *Queen Mary*, the *Queen Elizabeth*.

They were like the confined states of the magic closet in the hall at 37-13 stuck between the real and the imaginary floors of the McCourts' apartment until the doors, released at will, opened onto the floor of wonders, wonders not visible in the rolling terrain of the Land of Counterpane. The game of the Land of Counterpane entered Author's dream life by way of a picture book illustrating the topography and settlement of Manhattan Island before the Dutch landed and bought it from the Lenape for twenty-four dollars worth of beads. The Lenape were a division of the Algonquin Federation. The Algonquin Round Table. King Arthur and Lancelot. He dreams of fires, floods and hurricanes.

Did they have them (glory holes) on the Circle Line? On the Staten Island Ferry? On the boat to Rye Beach, especially for the return trip?

Was there one on the *General Slocum* on June 15, 1904, right next to the boiler room, where perhaps two bosuns—probably not, probably deck hands—were locked together like two dogs in the street moanin' low and having the greatest sex of their young lives at the very moment the boiler exploded and they were blown to smithereens right there in the Hellcat Strait. Find time for an act of perfect contrition in that one, you can run for pope.

His subway career: maps, alternate route journeys: trips to Grand Central, Times Square, Astoria, Flushing and Woodlawn, and later to The Met, Fordham Road, Van Cortlandt Park (Manhattan College, my father's and brother's college, which became mine), Bay Ridge, Canarsie, Red Hook, Coney Island, Brooklyn Heights. The St. George Hotel swimming pool; later still, tea-rooms and the "stations" . . .

The ground rules established long ago—*fado, fado* (fate, fate)—on the filthy floor of some primeval shithouse of the ages. More grunts to be heard on any given afternoon than found drilling in the trenches of Camp Lejeune—"and you don't have to buy them orchid corsages to pin on."

"I tried to push his head away, but he would have none of it, so soon enough he had all of it."

"I said to the woman, 'Woman, don't just stand there posing for animal crackers, hoping to attract the real animal—it won't work. Standing on ceremony may get you the bride's bouquet, but if you call that luck you're in a bad way. Get a move on—every day is Sadie Hawkins Day for fags.'"

"The pissed-up old bag, she hasn't had a really good time since Petronius's suicide banquet." (In the *Satyricon*, on which *The Great Gatsby* was modeled.)

"The witch is older than Ancient Agnes and dirt combined."

"Shrieking in hysterics, she just couldn't stop."

"Couldn't? Wouldn't."

"Whether she couldn't or wouldn't, she didn't—the point is she *frightened* them *away*. Imagine—two officers of the law, both fled."

"I was there, it was a triumph."

"I'm sure it was. Do you know what it's like in here—the zoo: specifically the seal pen, the monkey house and the lions and tigers and the hippopotamus pool. The *noise . . .* and the people! Fish gotta swim, but sometimes it's just hell on earth."

". . . for instance calling the pyramids unnecessary."

"*Unnecessary?*"

"Unnecessary. Dig it. Lethal woman—Queen of the Philistine Pig People."

"I told him, you gotta come, baby—no come no gum."

"Sorry, darling, not tonight, I have simply the most killing headache."

"Promise?"

"Promise."

"Swear to God and hope to die?"

"If you insist, yes—there, are you satisfied?"

"As never before in my life, because you see I hope you die too, I hope you die soon—I'll be *waitin'* for you to die."

"Oh, Mary, the girl walked right into that one."

"Shoots from the hip and clusters the impacts—quite a woman."

(Pistol Packin' Momma, lay that pistol down. The Pistol Club: drink till midnight, piss 'til dawn.)

"My momma told me not to come—she said, 'That ain't no way to have fun, son.'"

"Mothers will stop at nothing to enslave us."

"Or watch over us in our times of trouble."

"At the cross her station keeping . . ."

"Eighth Street, the BMT, uptown side—known as the Snake Pit."

"Her life is an open book, but one contents oneself with reading the jacket flaps."

"Last night I dreamed I went to Mandalay."

"Did you hear that? Pure Freud, the screened expression of her deepest, dearest wish—to go to a man and get laid."

"I wouldn't give her the satisfaction."

"What satisfaction? She'd lose."

"Yes, she'd loose—badly—and then slink back to that den of losers she practically lives in and be crowned Queen of the Losers. I wouldn't, I won't give her the satisfaction—call me withholding if you like, but I simply won't."

Nobody on the other side of the partition, no whisperer through a glory hole, had as yet treated him to any cordial invitation—as yet in this game he had remained strictly a utensil. Must have been the white bucks. If you were standing up being sucked off by a kid, you might legitimately claim ignorance of the sucker's age, but if you were caught down on your knees sucking off a kid in white bucks, kiss the world *arrivederci*, so long, you were going away for a long time.

Then one fine day the thank-you note passed under the stall at Canal Street.

> *Dear* —————
>
> *You're a good kid, you make a lot of people happy—are you wearing a bib?*

Wouldn't that old Dorothy Day be surprised—she'd get a large charge out of that one. Many novenas would ensue; special intention.

Thus began a literary exercise, of sitting right down and writing himself a letter, one that went on for years, intensified as his education progressed and he shifted the venue of his ministrations to better toilets, such as the one adjacent to the Charleston Gardens restaurant in B. Altman's department store and the one on the uptown side of the IRT 59th Street local directly under the perfume counter at Bloomingdale's. Among his many reflections sitting in the latter was the fact that there was once an insane asylum called Bloomingdale.

> *Whoever you are and whatever age, education and social stratum— your scent would suggest youth, manliness and perhaps a predilection for the sea, and your tongue, across which suspicions of indescribable flavors*

parade in wanton disregard for oral hygiene, a lust for cock that must in time become insatiable—each venous web on each rigid shaft a map of another river system to explore in your mind as you cover the waterfront and hang round down around the Hudson. Old Spice means quality said the captain to the bosun—and indeed it well might, but not by itself. And what with these accommodating apertures the size of the portholes on the Queen Mary*; I myself have seen hunks of meat put through that would fill a decent sized dinner plate. Most lives in these grim places are mercifully shrouded, but why should yours be among them. Were you not so shy—or perhaps you have a slight case of acne? 'T'will pass—you could stick your head through and give us a gander at your pretty face which I put strong odds on is not just another. And you last and last, don't you—are you* Tantric? *Of boys like you it may be said either that you take longest or that you last longest—and by the choice of words of the speaker much is learned—of him, while you remain a mystery.*

I think you can have never been sick with nerves before an important first date, barring of course the double date during which you have been obliged to maintain an agonizing custody of the eyes and refrain from casting adoring glances at him *the whole while, especially during the feature you couldn't begin to describe for the life of you next day. Eyes straight ahead, sailor.*

You are the happy owner of impressive skills and a genuine aptitude—a yutz—*in a highly competitive arena, in which boys with empty pasts gain peopled futures along the immense thoroughfare of life (well, we must call it something), sometimes but not necessarily always saturated in a violet aura of sadness, to which on the evidence of the rabid exuberance with which you feast on sin, one cannot think you have as yet succumbed, doubtless having already in your time here below kissed many an unsuspecting cheek, many tops of blissfully innocent children's heads, many of the sacred relics of Christendom under Plexiglas, not to mention the rings of holy prelates, with lips that often and for some time in blandishment obscene—tenebrous rites unspoken of, such as the* osculum infandum, *the devil's kiss, and the* vademecum, *the devil's guidebook—have* been employed, here and in any number of such precipitations—stolen moments are all we have together—peopled not alone, alas, by such gorgeous alluring stuff such as we, but also with sundry monstrosities of the deep, emblematic of the black rot and mephitic sludge lodged in the heart of every human animal who has ever walked the earth, excluding only Our Savior and his Blessed Mother and possibly the Beloved Disciple. Not to mention a perversely compelling fractured composure and the flop sweat that stains the walls and mirrors of each and every similar refuge in the city with filthy streaks of accusation, guilt sadistic triumph, anger, evasion, threat and fear.

Fear not! Expunge the feeling that there are bigger sprats to catch and swim with determination into the net. Try to remember it is not enough to be spoken of with fondness as the good time that was had by all—you can do better—much—than a dime a throw. He takes you off his income tax and what do you get? A Tootsie Roll.

And take care to steer clear of sloppy sentimental love songs of earlier generations—"How Deep Is the Ocean" for example. You don't need to know—you don't have to try to find out. As to how many roses are sprinkled, that depends on the rose garden and your moment in it.

Why do I feel you are a boisterous hoyden cursed with an honest heart? Call Regent 4-3134 evenings Monday through Thursday; one is generally at home sitting in front of the fire in word hell correcting freshman compositions. I must confess I am no fusilladier—but no gentleman is.

Carpe diem, kiddo—we all lose our charms in the end.

Yours sincerely,
Occupant of Neighboring Stall (but you knew that)

He may have been a good English teacher, but how could a boy be a hoyden? (Has one forgotten Eddie Midwinter, the has-been actor, one's first Shakespeare teacher, at Moore's Hotel in Northport and later at Munson House in Windham? "God save the mark," Eddie would say, and Author would ask, "What mark?" "I suppose the mark of 'Mark me well.'"

In Windham in 1948, the big election year, in which Dewey was the announced winner yet Truman edged him out in the small hours of the morning, Author said, "There's was nobody for him to play with up here," which to tell the truth was a relief, because he no longer saw any sense in playing. He'd played with Marsha and Butch O'Sullivan in Northport and got them to take off their clothes and be examined for the army.

"My mother says Marsha O'Sullivan was a hoyden. Am I a hoyden, Eddie?"

"A hoyden is a tomboy—a boy can't be a tomboy."

"Unless that's his name—Tom—but then I guess he'd be called Boy Tom not Tom Boy. So a hoyden can act like a boy, but she can't really be one, right?"

"Not unless it's Shakespeare."

"Because she hasn't got a penis, right? You mean the girls in Shakespeare have *penises*?"

"Well, you see they're not really girls, they're boys pretending to be girls."

"Oh?" He remembered how it was done—one of the older boys, he better not say who, had shown him. You tucked your penis out of the way behind between your legs and you put on lipstick—which Marie Sherman had done to him in Northport on his fourth birthday. He hadn't really liked the effect, except that he could make a sad face looking like a girl, then pop his penis out and make a happy face as a boy. Johnny Zilch said a girl could play the same trick by turning her back and strapping on a rubber cock—called a dildo—then turn around again and say, "Who wants to give a guy a blow job?"

"Who wants to get fucked?"

(But it was stupid you couldn't tell a girl, except maybe Marsha O'Sullivan; an ordinary girl could run right home and tell her mother, and that Mary Ann Fingerhut caper had been enough.)

What he's waiting for in every toilet stall, through every glory, glory hole-a-luyia, is the beautiful blonde man whose picture was turned face-down in his Aunt Florrie's bottom bureau drawer—or rather a facsimile. Sucking the cock of a man whose head was bashed in with a crowbar in a bar fight in Rochester—well, really, talk about a cover story for a gay knock: once-gorgeous closeted faggot gets shitfaced, makes pass at wrong customer, probably throws in some really nasty sarcasm—this faggot is *begging* for it—is the stuff of the EC horror comics pornographic imitation, the grim version of the pornographic *Archie* comic passed around on Johnny Zilch's stoop in which Archie fucks Jughead, Big Moose fucks Reggie, Mr. Wetherbee sucks Miss Grundy and Betty and Veronica are down on the floor eating out each other's cunts.

. . .

And all the while, a peculiar sort of Jughead to be in love with Archie Andrews (and tormented after seeing Johnny Zilch's pornographic *Archie* comic) but in somersaulting love with athletic Tiernan McMenniman (who also had red hair) his best high school buddy, dreaming of rescuing him from death in dire straits or some fate worse—although how that was to be managed when he himself had been consigned . . . perhaps St. Aloysius Gonzaga, the patron saint of boys (and purity) could save him first, then he could get on with the job. His father's middle name was Aloysius, so that might be an in. Saint Aloysius Gonzaga *aiutime, e sia lodato Gesucristo, figlio di Dio, il Dio dell'amore*, help me, and may Jesus Christ be praised, the son of God, the God of love.

But meanwhile if they went to see *Calamity Jane* on two successive weekends and listened to Doris Day sing "Secret Love"—Well, you couldn't pray to a movie star, but as the rumors were rife that "Dodo" was a lesbian, you might weep silently with her, even if she was pulling down more spondooliks in a week than you'd ever get to see in the next ten years.

And even after they went to see James Dean in *East of Eden*, with the scene set in the traveling carnival stopping in Salinas, and in *Rebel Without a Cause*, with the scene set in the planetarium in Griffith Park in fabulous Los Angeles, to be aroused by James Dean and Richard Davalos, by James Dean and Sal Mineo, he remained faithful in his dreams to Tiernan. He dreamed nightly, having forsworn nightly masturbation, of taking his beloved friend to the carnival which by then had stopped coming to the lots behind Blessed Sacrament School, of winning him a kewpie doll, which he could find hilarious, of them both making up stories about where the workmen and the roustabouts had come from, and lastly, holding on and holding on, tighter and tighter, sometimes actually until the clock radio came on with the last numbers in the all-night jazz show, of getting him under the trucks where every night they'd find used Trojans, and kissing him and rolling all over him until they both came melting into one another. Marthe Mödl and Ramon Vinay in Wagner's opera *Tristan und Isolde* had brought it all about, and the ghost of Jeanne Eagles in the performance given by Kim Novak in *The Jeanne Eagles Story* as the doomed star, the greatest actress anybody ever saw on the American stage.

But life goes on, and through all four years at Manhattan College, even while sitting down from time to time to write himself that letter, making believe it came from somebody as elegant as his Shakespeare and Renaissance literature professor Harry Blair (whose telephone exchange was Regent-something), but strapping, too, like Rock Hudson in *Written on the Wind*, Author was desperately in love with Turlough O'Shea (a ringer forty years in advance of glory for a strapping, gorgeous Joe Gage porn superstar), built like a brick shithouse, right down to the dimpled chin and the curved to the left erected cock, who shot a mean game of pool in the dormitory rec room and next sat down and ripped out a Bach fugue the like to make you think of Glenn Gould on speed at Carnegie Hall; whose favorite singer of all time was the tenor Jussi Björling. Fell for him like a ton of hot bricks, enough to build a second fucking Carnegie Hall, on the night of all the freshmen's arrival, in the communal swim at the pool in the gymnasium up on the hill—and was in his Junior year suborned by him into the caper of the theft and desecration of the big chapel bell, for while Tiernan was a model Christian Brothers boy, Turlough was an outright apostate—but *puta madre*, holy motherfucker, could that boy make magic on those bongos. The only awful thing was he'd joined a fraternity. Our hero said, "Well, what can you do, you clearly have a deep seated need to be hero-worshiped by dimwit heterosexual hooligans?" (His brother David had been a brother in the same fraternity a decade earlier, and he'd hated them calling one another brothers—they weren't wearing any goddam monks' robes, were they? And David—known to his frat brothers as Mac—was *his* brother for better or for worse, not theirs, and no stupid Greek letters were going to change that. They could give it as much of the old college try as they wanted, it was never going to be true—as God was his witness he'd see to that. A melodrama of melodramas.)

One disremembers the dimple.

Turlough was nicknamed "Locky" and "Lock," which the longing lover, grasping at anything thicker than straws, took to be a sign from heaven, in that "lock" was in the Bronx a term of highest praise—"Yer a lock, yer a dollar three-eighty."

With whom was he more in love, Tiernan McMenniman or Turlough O'Shea? Put it this way, looking back, and realizing that all along Tiernan had remained a good Catholic Christian Brothers boy, realizing his Irish Catholic dream in four children and eight grandchildren and returning to the fiftieth reunion of their graduating class in 1958 looking so much the same fellow in the alumni magazine that Author, who had not been able to attend (*"Impossible venir. Mensonge suit."* Unable to attend. Lie follows) fell in love again with his goodness and with decency, his Dream of Olwen still to have been positioned between the two, Tiernan the good man and Turlough the rogue, Lucky Pierre down on all fours *à la chienne*, doggy-style, while they took turns front and rear. Then he flips over on his back, his legs wrapped around one of their necks, being fucked like a screaming virgin Catholic bride in the missionary position, while the other has made himself comfortably at home squat on his heart pal's face, the heart pal's hot, wet, delectable tongue diving into the tunnel of love, dreaming of it and dreaming of it, but didn't the dream invariably turn nightmare as the double dream of spring turned rough and nasty, hurling terms of abuse at him to his face and rear end and laughing between themselves like the sadistic neighborhood boys who'd turned on him, turned on a dime, and made his life a hell on earth until his father called in the police, and he found himself sitting miserably in Doctor Parrish's office on Central Park South, he of the charming, ribald welcome—"Get in here you old whore. What have you been up to now? Florence has just brought—your records and I declare there's more men been up that ass than's been up the Statue of Liberty and the Empire State Building combined!"—with a double dose of the clap, front and rear, and thanking a loving, merciful and all-forgiving God, who never had so much as a cold sore, for penicillin.

Liebkranker Mann. Lovesick Man. (*Velia*, Lehár.)

And in the end it was of course the teeth—prominent two (or four) front teeth = killer smiles = total capitulation—same effect as Gene Tierney's malocclusion had on the heterosexual males in the audience of the movie melodrama *Leave Her to Heaven.*

Why would one fall in love with teeth? Why would a sixty-nine-year-old homosexual (naughty number, magical age) writer hang on his bedroom workplace door by way of mounting his escutcheon, a yard-long red bath towel, with the heraldic image of Bugs Bunny rampant, holding a half eaten carrot and asking the question of all questions ("What's up, Doc?") for which he has become immortal? See Freud on the phenomenon of phallic substitution and Stella Adler on building a character ("When all else fails, substitute").

The Shadow knows and may well tell the world.

. . .

Author on stage in the Theater of Memory (the Adonis Theater, formerly the Tivoli, on 52nd Street—love beckoned, then spat in your face when you got too close—and Eighth Avenue, *the* queer porn theater of action in the bad old days). Men shuffling back and forth up and down the aisles horning up for the next feature, for which they may have to wait until midnight, or for as long as he can hold the stage. All the others (they know who they are, and so does he, sitting in the dark so that he can only see the first several rows of the orchestra and some faces in the front rows of each of the tiers above, up to the second balcony—his famous second balcony sincerity in play). Starter's orders.

What to do but a monologue? Narrating a documentary—for the play has turned into a motion picture, one like *Gone with the Wind* on several counts: a cast of thousands, the majority of them nameless undressed dress extras. Two sides, good and bad, the bad ever so much more gallant and more glamorous in all that gold braid, both as to the cast and to the civil war within, the war between the states of being.

And last but not least the burning of the glamorous gold braid's city represented in his morbid and ineradicable fear of atomic attack.

As has been mentioned, his sufferings were chronic-acute, with no end in sight. He had once been Sunny Jim, called that by one who brought him books, but once interrupted by them, and burned too often by the sun that gives the earth its light and life yet still became the enemy, he fell into the realization that the world is vain, conceited, careless and stupid, and came to cherish the rain. (He had after all been born in it, but born indoors.)

What in years to come old Eddie Midwinter, actor, member of the Blackfriars, Papal Count (Pius XI) and rumored pederast, said on their walk around Windham Mountain was true, talking of the boy Puck who used to stand on the banner logo of the *New York Journal-American*, rendered in stone on the pediment of the Puck Building on the southeast corner of Houston and Lafayette Streets, and who was also called Robin Goodfellow and was in the bargain a character in Shakespeare's *A Midsummer Night's Dream*—a sort of Robin to the Batman of Oberon, King of the Fairies. His most famous line, emblazoned on that logo was "Lord what fools these mortals be!" And it was true.

"Nobody was driving officer, we were all in the back seat."

. . .

Nature is never not pictured as imperious, dwarfing the human observer ("I am nature," declared the painter Jackson Pollock, meaning every word, three in sum), the natural experience in scale of the small child "sublime in expectation." Also thunder and lightning. Also the redwoods in Hitchcock's *Vertigo.* The motif of the sublime thus employed in English literature of the eighteenth and nineteenth centuries was first introduced to Author on his own ancestral ground, Manhattan, his grandfather—pointing to skyscraper after skyscraper saying, "I built that, I built that," and in further excursions in childhood and adolescence up the left wall of the great Pangaea's teeming immemorial cunt to Niagara Falls, various limestone caverns and finally, in the mode of the European travelogues crossing the Alps, in the trips through the Rockies and the Painted Desert (first encountered by Author onscreen in John Ford's repeated use of Monument Valley in Utah as an emblem of overweening fate and implacable landscape: an indication of the adult stance Author took regarding nature as best viewed from a safe vantage—the Hudson from the club car of the 20th Century Limited to Chicago, then of the Great Plains and the Rockies from the observation car of the Super Chief to Los Angeles, or all of it from the wide windows of a Greyhound Scenicruiser, the Alps from the dining car of the trans-European express from Paris to Rome, or down the Rhine from Düsseldorf to Cologne on a full-moon night, etc.).

Freud was everywhere back then. He'd said that by the age of four, the traits of personality were locked in, the temperament cast, the destiny simultaneously open and constrained. His apothegms having in a few short decades effectively replaced Shakespeare's, the threnody was on every pair of avaricious, treacherous, innocent and hot-to-trot lips in the city ("Hello, suckers!") and much was made of such matters as the connection between the sublime and Freudian sublimation in latency. Every time a sublime (or epileptic) rush occurs, latency is suspended, the boy masturbates to orgasm without ejaculation, then becomes quiescent again; the stimulus thus discharged, the boy lapses into the equivalent of quiet postcoital depression coming only with ejaculation and dependent on the quotient of remorse entailed either by guilt or manic-depressive—bipolar—symptomology, an idea unfortunately not sufficiently road tested to satisfy the great majority of dealerships.

And if anybody's looking for his motivation, it fell down behind the back seat.

Nobody was driving officer . . .

. . .

The only way to control the capricious mechanisms of memory is to restyle them—and stick to your stories, always remembering to vary them a little at each telling, a thing one learns from reading detective novels: guilty suspects never vary their stories. One must learn to rein in the headlong gallop of random and unbridled recollection or go stark raving mad. One knows not what fairyland Shakespeare lived in but he himself had experienced, unaided by the products of better living through chemistry, while since sitting in a victory garden in Greenlawn, Long Island, at the age of four, a single session of sweet, silent thought . . . you can hardly be called pissed to the gills on Scotch or hidden like some errant Olympian in a hashish cloud, enveloped in the abstract, said to be the new bling—nor can it be so serene when in the first place you have to jerk off to get your heart started, then pop a Dexamyl to remember the name of the wretch it was, still is, the memory of whom got your fist so sloppy and smelling like Clorox. Perhaps what they say about modern life in the big city is true after all: Only the combination of liquor and Xanax can produce a modicum of serenity, however brief.

Keep away from heroin.

. . .

Nostalgia is the polar opposite of the sublime, as can be demonstrated by returning after decades to a house we remember as grand and spacious and seems for the first few minutes shockingly small and cramped. Microscopic representation is never sublime.

. . .

Forever ago . . . ante time. The altercation between the Writer and his Other—he and him. *Je est un autre* (Rimbaud). First person: the vertical; third person: the horizontal. Panegyric the vertical, pathos the horizontal. Orators who excel at the one usually fail at the other, hence the necessary split.

The falsity (and the art) in all such reminiscence lies in the arrangement for the reader of *a sequence of memories*, keying such a sequence into the more-or-less attested and authenticated historical narration through which it is generally held he comes to grips with the saga. To begin a life with the beginning of a life is an inconclusive beginning, what with what's known, has been known since the beginning: that there is no beginning, that the measuring of time from the six days of creation on is only now and ever was a palliative fiction. If time is the measure of change and outcome, the unconscious, tolerating neither of these things, is timeless.

We let ourselves down when we allow ourselves to be born. Our waking thoughts, the first we hear of them, come out of a sleep—"*Oh! quand je dors, viens auprès de ma couche*"—or slumber (the nicety of the distinction the first of innumerable such swerves). After the voices (mixed chorus and parent pillow talk) and of course hours and hours of stertorous snoring heard *in utero*, the perceptual complexity and imperfect differentiation in the first year of life between and among the voices of the family, the people downstairs, the people across the alley (the stubborn silence of the people on the other side of the dividing wall, like all subsequent subtractions, becoming apparent only by degrees, against prolonged and rugged resistance to the harsh terms of unconditional surrender).

The voices on the radio: baseball play-by-play, war news, Roosevelt, Churchill, Hitler, *Rinso white . . . Wadda-my-bid, wadda-my-bid . . . sooowld American. . . Don't touch that dial, it's time for Blondie! . . . It's Make Believe Ballroom time. . . The Bickersons.* (He knows Blondie—Debbie Harry—"Heart of Glass." Another whole life later. Don't touch that dial!)

The Saturday afternoon broadcasts from the Metropolitan Opera, then later in the aftermath of the war and the widespread elation of the interval between 1945 and 1947 the idea of listening over the short-wave headset to the uncomplaining voices of the newscasters all clothed in the rhetoric of triumph like Roman generals in procession wearing rouge. The truth is our lives are measureless—as is the cosmos.

Were it not for the fact he has bad dreams, petit mal seizures, alcoholism, rheumatoid arthritis (*fibromyalgia rheumatica*), chronic acute dysthymic depression, he might get out more, but illness of any kind is hardly a thing to be encouraged by others, and home is where the (sound) heart is, so please do not call Regent 4-3134. Try your luck on the Internet. (Oh do not ask what is it.)

5

All right, all right, what's it going to be, the High Line on a moonlit night, or the Land of Counterpane on a rainy one.

Sounds to the Grand Jury like the Land of Counterpane, with the High Line located somewhere in the folds, as in the brain. But do not ask which is it—visiting hours are lately restricted on the ward: there have been incidents of an untoward nature sufficient to utterly ruin any story.

Then also the George Washington Bridge to New Jersey. The Hudson was called the Rhine of America, and so later at the opera *Das Rheingold*, the rainbow bridge to Valhalla, a cemetery in Westchester.

"Yes, we built that thing, a city in itself, in under a year . . ." On trips with his grandfather to the city he stood at the window at the front of the first car of the IRT as it got closer and closer to the great skyline (sharing, as he would somewhat facetiously declare decades later, those qualities Longinus prescribes for written sublime, majesty and elevation of structure), wondering why his grandfather had said the Moores were well raised until the rope broke when he'd said they'd been rich ship's chandlers—he thought he said, "chandeliers"—but his grandfather was probably joking unless there were black sheep, which wouldn't be surprising either . . . and wondering what it feels like to be hanged by the neck until you are dead—but his grandfather also told him that a lot of men back then had strong necks. There was an Irish expression, "he's got the brass neck to such-and-such"—and that in those days there was a rule that if you were hanged and the rope broke and you didn't die, you were set free. Most of the men hanged were highwaymen, condemned to the gallows for highway robbery (which was what his mother said Joe

O'Neill, who ran the delicatessen on Polk Avenue between 94th and 95th Streets and made great potato salad and macaroni salad and cole slaw and gave them credit until the end of the month, was getting away with).

No doubt could remain the boy was irredeemably queer. When the pain of impossible love came to rule the day and at the end of a four-year pursuit next to which the most comprehensive education in the history of Western civilization, in history itself, in art, in literature, in music and in philosophy, seemed a walk in Paradise Gardens (a pleonasm), came down to rolling around on the floor in a muck sweat with Turlough O'Shea.

And at exactly the same time a D in moral theology got him hauled before the school chaplain. (A bit foolish, a bit grandiose to write on the final exam in response to a question on the Jansenists and the Jesuits, "As for France itself, the eldest daughter of the Church and by far the most obstreperous, it has become impossible to track down every heresy, but the latest is the declaration by a student of higher mathematics at the Sorbonne that the number of angels dancing on the head of a pin is, according to a close examination of the esoteric writings of the great Pascal, in every case a finite calculable prime." Typical undergraduate guff, one blushes to recall it.)

Bruno Tausig, the first priest so summoned since Author was caught playing gynecologist with Mary Ann Fingerhut, was a worldly, sophisticated European Jesuit with the original Picasso "View from a Window at St. Raphael" on his wall who put him to the question because of his midterm essay airing the proposition that while everything that was the will of God happens, not everything that happens is the will of God (citing O'Casey's *Juno and the Paycock*: "Ah, what can God do agen the stupidity o' men?" And O'Casey was a Protestant). Tausig smoothed the thing over, reconciling for the moment the apparent clash between Roman Catholic dogma and a liberal education. Nevertheless the rumor that he had been called a formal heretic on top of the fact that he was known to be an as yet unmasked homosexual kept him out of Pen & Sword, the senior class honor society.

And in the same neighborhood with Turlough O'Shea and Ray Manning, off to the Half Note, the Five Spot, the Vanguard and Bird-land in the greatest jazz period that ever has been. Monk, Miles, Trane, Ornette.

Then to the carousel where he would get on and David Moore would watch him ride. Then over to the Maine Monument where he would explain the ridiculous Spanish-American War drummed up by William Randolph Hearst and how Teddy Roosevelt never rode up San Juan Hill leading the Rough Riders at all, and Author because of this would have nothing to do with any Teddy bear—Grampa said Teddy had been some-thing of a bluff in the Spanish-American War—San Juan Hill and all that malarkey, although he did get the national parks set up, and in addi-tion to his getting the bear named after him as a symbol of all that, they wrote a song about the color of his daughter Alice's dress—"My Alice Blue Gown." And later when she was the widow of House Speaker Long-worth she would walk up to people at parties and say, "If you haven't got anything nice to say about anybody . . . come sit next to me." She also got famous for saying about the disgraced president Warren Gamaliel Harding, "He wasn't a bad man, really, only a slob."

So instead he had Andy Panda, which his grandfather bought at Rumplemayer's on Central Park South in the St. Moritz hotel after he had his tea with saccharine tablets in it and he'd smoked his pipe and the boy had his ice cream soda. Author loved Andy and carried him until he grew out of him, but the image of the boy on the Maine Monument would haunt him all his days.

.   .   .

Breaking and entering the House of Mirth—casing the joint; they're all asleep, proceed by stealth and in silence, one sneaking back from exile. He sneaks up the back stairs—the back door is never locked—and walks down to the magic elevator closet, steps in, pushes the button he drew on the wall and descends to the floor between floors and steps out into a big party, the party of parties at 37-13.

The evocation of pagan moods in the dithyramb honoring Dionysus, in opposition to the Apollonian paean.

"The ancient Athenians counted among the special qualities of the dithyramb its special rhythm, its highly wrought vocabulary, its commanding narrative content and its originally antistrophic character." There had certainly been more sedate parties, more elegant parties in which adults danced the two-step to music from the Victrola. With songs and laughter—his mother's fortieth birthday party for instance, on November 13, 1947, when he was just finishing up in the first grade at Blessed Sacrament. He had always helped set them up . . . the gold pop-up cigarette canister with each individual cigarette stuck in its own tubular holder, as unique in his experience down to the present day as the flat disc onyx Bakelite calendar (a fascinating object he'd never seen replicated anywhere: Each face bore the image of a hemisphere, the continents raised in gold relief, in the middle of which a little cut-out window showed a number from 1 to 31—representing the simplest casting of the date: no day, no month, no year, only a number—and when the disc was turned from Eastern to Western Hemisphere, forward or backward, the number in the window changed accordingly), which he would be sure to turn at midnight, his officially designated bedtime on party nights, honored as his father would remark, more in the breach than in the observance.

And then the days of the full kegs of beer hauled up the back stairs and set up and tapped in the kitchen by Tappa Kegga Day, the universal undergraduate fraternity, Manhattan College's Phi Beta Kappa chapter. Saying at the fortieth birthday party: "Life begins at forty—and ends at forty-one." (What did that mean?) Then his mother, at the prompting of the guests, all but his Aunt Betty (always called Elizabeth by Big Jim, as he was always called Jimmy by his two sisters), plays and sings "Smoke Gets in Your Eyes." Everybody remarks how beautifully she sings it, better than Irene Dunne in *Roberta* on the screen, then somebody asks was it Kitty and Jim's song and somebody else says it couldn't have been, it came out in the '30s a few years after they were married, and anyway their song as she remembers it was "Only Make Believe" from *Show Boat*—also with Irene Dunne and the gorgeous Alan Jones. "Same composer, though." Then, picking up on Elizabeth's sullen mood, she plays and sings *her* song, "Stardust" (significantly a lonely song, not about a broken love affair, but about having no love affairs at all—a nun could sing it, a Sister of Charity); everybody laughs.

"Bette Davis says it's her favorite song too."

"I rest my case."

Last of all she plays for her father his and her mother's song, "Vilja" from *The Merry Widow* which gets the best reception of all. Then in comes David and they rip through some Gilbert and Sullivan numbers because she has played Ralph Rackstraw in *H.M.S. Pinafore*, with the Brooklyn Diocesan Choir as chorus members. Everybody joins in on "Carefully on Tiptoe Stealing."

"Oh goodness me, Oh what was that?"

"Certainly it was the cat."

"It was indeed the cat."

"Certainly it was the cat."

From that very night and for decades Author decided that the real story, the story of November 1929—the Crash, his parents' wedding, to 1941, his birth, Pearl Harbor, was the real story (he had entirely forgotten or suppressed Hiroshima), and to get it he would have to set about the investigation like Mr. Keene, Tracer of Lost Persons, on the radio. Something lay behind those songs that wasn't only music and lyrics. In coming years he would be enlightened in the investigation by the knowledge that early sound pictures—particularly from Warner Brothers— really dealt in true-life stories.

1941. The Warsaw Ghetto/The Yankees/Joe DiMaggio, and finally in December, five months after his birth, the Day of Infamy, the sneak attack by the Japanese on Pearl Harbor, America's entry into the war, and the lights went out all over the world—except of course in Gotham. As one New York cabbie (whose name really was John, and whose friends all called him Johnny, said to him decades later, "Real live nephew of your Uncle Sam, eh? 1941—you must be close to seventy—I must say you don't look it; you're very well preserved.

"Y'know my old man was killed in that war—the 'good war,' at Anzio. Not so old, either, only twenty-five, but it all happened in the last century; they were kids and kids today don't give a shit about anything that happened before they were born—imagine. Only a few years back everybody was jumping up and down, and it was all over the television and in the papers and there were memorials and honors paid to the living veterans and to the dead, like my father—remember? 'The Greatest Generation.' They even got around to putting up a monument down in Washington. Now the whole four years of it—six counting the two years before Pearl Harbor—is a goddam computer game. Some world. My old man and all the others gave their lives for, huh?"

For Americans, never invaded, part identity crisis ("people spoke of nothing else"), part radio and newsreel, theater entertainment, part jitterbug.

Was the substitution of his arrival on the ninth First Friday to be viewed as a fulfillment or as bad luck? His Aunt and godmother, Elizabeth (Josepha) McCourt, his mother's classmate at St. Lawrence Academy in Manhattan and in those wartime days given to visions and prophecy, delivered some class of oracular pronouncement predicting greatness for the infant—or at least some definite advancement—admixed with great misfortune, for he would be both tormentor and tormented. (That hit the nail on the head.)

Two weeks later removed to 37-13 94th Street, Jackson Heights, the top floor of a two-family asphalt-shingled (fake red brick) dwelling on a tree-lined street half a block south of the corner at which Elmhurst Avenue (main artery of the formerly affluent village of Elmhurst characterized by the great trees forming green archway across it) merged with 37th (Polk) Avenue.

Jackson Heights was not known for having either hill nor dale, nor had it at any time belonged to any family called Jackson, unlike the Bronx, an old Dutch patroon family, but named for the Hero of New Orleans, the low-class ruffian seventh president of the United States.

"There's not a single rise or retaining wall to be seen from Woodside to Corona," said his grandfather, installed in the family in the pivotal role he'd played since the Depression, merging his sizeable pension with the rest of the family exchequer. However as every exception proves the rule, there did exist a single genuine hill within its borders, on 94th Street, two blocks north of 37-13, directly behind Blessed Sacrament School at 94th and 35th (Hayes) Avenue (that Republican bum who stole the 1876 election in plain view from Samuel Tilden), its northwesterly slope descending to Northern Boulevard, and from which on a clear day a clear view could be had of the majestic Manhattan skyline.

When he was a child, and until his brother David left for Korea, his parents slept behind a hardly soundproof draw curtain in the alcove —providing easy access to the real or fantasized primal scene. (Somebody had read Freud, or had heard about him anyway: "So you read Freud, Miss West?" "Well, not exactly—I have him read t'me; I find it relaxin'").

. . .

Who had lived there before them? His brother claimed to have heard ghosts (like the ghost of Christmas Past: "That was no ghost," his father said, "that was the Flahertys"). Also that there was probably the body of a deformed child, victim of a mercy killing, stashed in the wall.

When decades later he went off the rails—lost it on an ill-prescribed cocktail of Dexamyl and Compazine, he didn't tell them he was the Sacred Heart, but he thought of it. Always having been interested in the events leading up to his birth, and the myth of descent from high places (to wit from bardic realms and the halls of merchant princes), he would compare what had been going on in the world at the time of the birth of Christ in Bethlehem to what was going on in the world at his own birth—the complications being two: that exact comprehensive knowledge of the world and its doings was attributed to the divine infant in the manger, and that the actual date of Christ's birth was at the time being reckoned as between 3 and 6 B.C. The Christ born before the birth of Christ, a situation perfectly congruent with Church Father Tertullian's immortal declaration *"Credo quia absurdam est,"* I believe that which is impossible, leading to the Pauline or Roman triumph over the Jerusalem Church of James the Less, the Christ's kid brother (James, whose older brother David was named after the king from whom the Christ was reputedly descended—who's on first?) to the Epiphany the arrival of the magi on January 6 while celebrating a reputably subsequent historical event, the slaughter by Herod Antipas of the Holy Innocents (a move dictated by the fact that the three kings of Orient that were in the Christmas carol, urged by the angel of the Lord, returned to their lands beyond the Tigris and Euphrates not through Jerusalem but by way of the *périphérique* and out on the low road to Galilee, thus failing to give the information Herod sought more than a week earlier on December 28).

Therefore had Author, perhaps the Second Coming of the Sacred Heart after all, been born on Friday, July 4, 1941.

The doctrine of the Holy Trinity, the lead-off proposition of the mandatory Nicene Creed, is reflected in the Holy Family and in the essential reality of the primary triad (the triangle being, along with the circle a world-originating geometric figure: the connection by a third line of any two intersecting lines forming one) in which each developing child, irrespective of siblings until the age of two and a half to three, in which the brain achieves its all but full neurological development (a second and more or less final spurt occurring, as it were, out of the blue at age eleven produces as A, B and C the child (of either sex, with variously calibrated temperamental charges) for whom the melodrama of the vicissitudes felt as unique and unaffected by any other.

So it says here in small print.

An elaboration of these events in the melodrama of the child comes about because the parents then become as caught up in what became the reality of the naked singularity, which is why the child, to whatever degree disaffected, already thinks he can become unique by outwitting the firstborn (Esau and Jacob—and Jacob is the Hebrew for James) and using those same purloined skills to render his contributions to the family's validity and prestige made by the younger siblings null and void). Therefore the essential and eternal melodrama of Trinity, the foundation and principal hierarchal element of the Christian faith, the logical and indispensable antecedent in the Nicene Creed recited at every Mass to the birth, death and resurrection of the Second Person, the Son? And such matters were discussed around the dinner table, for Catherine, having in her years of expiation become a daily communicant, had taken up in place of any extreme of piety (which would not have suited her temperament at all and which moreover would have read as phony as a three-dollar bill) a bracing and methodical study of the not very difficult doxology of the family religion, which since the Baltimore Catechism seemed to Author a primer written for simpletons, and he being a naturally inquisitive and studious child, a subject of such great fascination that early expectations of a vocation to the priesthood itself were rather easily, although never in any sense forcibly, impressed upon his mind so that for some years in his latency he dreamed of rising to the purple. *Naturalment.*

And later on, when the circus (the Barnum and Bailey world, just as phony as it could be), after too many visits, turned boring, the rough-and-tumble rodeo took over. (Marie and Lee Sherman, show-biz friends visiting Northport from Los Angeles, had told him there was a street in Beverly Hills called Rodeo Drive; he imagined a street of rodeo rough riders every day but Sunday, and maybe even at night under lights, and the top-floor apartment in Jackson Heights as an Algonquin long house: "So if you gave me back to the Indians I'd live in the same kind of set-up as this?") On the High Line corkscrew thinking strikes again, thus to uncork: The Algonquin long house, the Algonquin Round Table. King

Arthur's Round Table at Camelot. Algonquins in ceremonial headdresses around their Round Table. Present for the occasion as chosen maiden in the upcoming human sacrificial rites, Kateri Tekawitha ("Kitty, take them with you"), the Mohawk saint (Mohawks were one of the five Algonquin nations). King Arthur and the Algonquin chief exchange gifts. King Arthur sits wearing an Algonquin feather headdress (inspired by Big Jim's surefire party-turn, the Indian chief and the Italian waiting-for-the-train fortune-telling scale joke, to be elaborated upon in a future installment, and the Algonquin chief is given leave to spend the night with Queen Guinevere, wearing Sir Lancelot's scalp hanging off his ceremonial buffalo hide and bear's tooth belt.

(During the French and Indian War, the Algonquins tore their British captives guts out and wrapped the long intestines around trees, leaving the men to die in agony while buzzards circled overhead.)

6

He found the circus wagon endowed with a magic hall closet next to the telephone on the telephone table, the magic, theretofore kept from him, that the closet could function as an elevator once you found the button ("Button, button, who's got the button"), no trouble at all for him. In the elevator he could descend half a floor—of the two-story house—into the middle world, a world of his own. (Explaining this decades later out in Cherry Grove, he attracted the laughter of the chorus of heinous old fairies.)

"Early recognition, darling, in the very marrow of his bones."

Visionary prescience of the precocious homosexual child—*Ander als die Andern*, as the Germans say. *Schwul*, queer. When you're in the closet, *everything* is pretend, and you, my dear, were in the closet in the Land of Oz and would only come out for Dorothy, the Scarecrow, the Cowardly Lion and your favorite, the Tin Woodman. Seems the Tin Woodman is the favorite of all homosexuals. They're doing a study—they suspect the absence of a real heart so all feeling is simulated almost from birth. Pathological narcissism rampant in the homosexual population. Extreme measures taken to correct—electroshock, insulin shock, exorcism—cruel, and futile. Makes sense to mother.

Further evidence of the obsessional surfaces in a diary entry from August 27, 1955, his brother David's wedding day in Tacoma, Washington.

All these entries are half cocked, each one including something unspoken. Guns half cocked and cocks sawed off. Fintan says Chaz told my enemies down the cellar that the Algonquin sucked their British prisoners cocks stiff as pokers, then took their own hunting knives and sliced off the heads and a good portion of the shafts, leaving in many cases—the drummer boys' in particular—nothing but nubs for them to piss through.

So what I say is that when Dorothy Parker, finally given back to the Indians, the Algonquin, was sent in to do the same to the Round Table with no weapon but her teeth (reckoning that is her teeth were as sharp as the rest of her mouth . . .), instead of mutilating the tall, dark and handsome monarch, sat up all night with him making wisecracks and telling him what a despicable little toad Alexander Woollcott was, and what a terrible actress Helen Hayes, until he called in Merlin and Morgan le Fey for a few rubbers of bridge. Morgan, offering Dottie the privilege of the opening bid, mewed "Age before beauty," whereupon Dottie, bidding a spade, countered, "And pearls before swine." The two sat playing rubber after rubber, looking across at one another from time to time, venom pouring out of their eyes, daggers drawn until dawn.

. . .

There is in the end movement of a child continuousness without continuity—the old expression, no farther than the end of his nose— the only condition under which he can rightly be called innocent. The first appearance of the continuity of motive enlists the child in the Company of the Sons of Eve of which the uniform, seldom worn lightly, is forthright aggression in summer, his season, the season of vacations he soon comes to realize is emblematic of liberty (equality will elude him forever, and fraternity for a very long time) and as the need for protection grows toward winter by the leaps and bounds of which his body is as yet incapable of response, increased resentment and rage at his inability to dictate the motives of others. Freud calls him His Majesty the Baby, perhaps having had in mind the simpleton Edward VIII, later and for decades too long, Duke of Windsor, companioned by his ludicrous wife. ("Curtsey to Wallis Windsor? I'd sooner suffer double amputation!")

. . .

The history of every childhood is a record of coping, either more successfully or less, with cardinal numbers, ordinal numbers, the part and whole relation, situations having state-of-affairs reference points, semicolons, the simultaneous coexistence of the gross quantities of what is accrued and what is lost, retention and protension, utterances of the occasional, the fevered emergence of the *noema* and its fabricated correlates (pitiful compensation for the virtual omniscience lost in the Fall), recognition of the addition to general meaning of the relevant context of utterance (if any) and any number of other facets of that tuition required for participation in whatever vicissitudes that lie in wait out there, and on top of these the anxiety and disillusionment of postexpulsion, left-in-the-*lurch*, troubled and uncertain times (expressed more colloquially as the breaks of the game), and most significant of all the fact that the experiencing subject at any time, in the light of his impressionistic experiences of the actual world, considers that world but a peculiar case in the vast array of possible worlds ("Stick it in the wall socket, Doctor Pangloss"), each of which corresponds to the other possible courses of experience and action, and not a clue in any of it of anything called a foregone conclusion.

The mystery of crib death becomes less opaque at each forensic turn. Failure to thrive: why not just get it over with while still being pampered like a pet cocker spaniel puppy?

We are told first to teach the children the forms of things—good and bad—that later the substance of them will make itself known according to what they have been taught to recognize—but this child seemed to understand the substance beforehand. It was as if they'd put him in front of a mirror for the first time and said, "That's Jimmy. That's you," and he'd looked back up at them in mock wonder, as if to ask, "What was your first clue?"

. . .

". . . and the dish ran away with the spoon." His favorite. (She was a gold-rimmed Rosenthal porcelain dish, he a Black, Starr and Gorham

sterling spoon. The families were beside themselves, but they were undeterred. And the Knight of Spoons, one night in June, married them and
very soon they went upon their thrill-of-China honeymoon.)

Things might well have stayed that way, but nothing is sustained.

Katie had a baby,
They called him Sunny Jim;
She put him in the bassinet
To see if he could swim.
He swam around the basinet
Just like a little fish,
She fed him milk and honey—
Wasn't that a dainty dish.
Then Katie did a wicked thing—
She went and had another,
Then said to happy Sunny Jim,
"Here's your darling baby brother."
Jimmy didn't know what to do—
To kiss the thing to please his mother
Or put a pillow over its pretty face
And watch it quickly smother.

The remainder of the story is very sad indeed,
For unlucky Jim on torrent rage did ravenously feed.
The sun went down, the night fell fast,
He made a plan: the die was cast.
This outrage must not, would not last.

(A plan which, if taken as a mirror of Author's self-annihilation wish,
or if fending off same, flip-side, obverse to reverse, the skidding path
to the myth of descent from a high place, an exhilarating belief, or to
the terror instilled by old wives' tales of the fairies and their changeling
tricks.)

A few years later, his brother David told him, came the episode of the building blocks.

"He was sitting in the living room playing with building blocks and you came through reading a book and walked right into what he had built so far, into the porch and sat down. He started again, making good progress until in the front porch you closed the book—so when it happened again there appeared to be no excuse—and walked out into the living room and again through the kid's blocks—just kept walking like a sleepwalker or a zombie to the back of the house. The kid sat there looking down at the scattered blocks and said, 'Jesus Christ!'"

(Diagnosis revised six decades later from the enigmatic "Three sheets to the wind" to epileptic petit mal absence brain seizure—so far as the young block builder would have been concerned, however, so the fuck what, who gives a rat's ass, etc.)

Speculation on reasons for Author's behavior over the years had long gone past its sell-by date.

When they told him to say what he had to say, what they were telling him was, say what you have a right to say—but the day would come when he would say what he needn't necessarily ought to have said and for that be called a liar.

. . .

Fortified by the best in food and drink, their determined assumptions of gaiety, undeterred by varieties of individual anguish, although strenuous, were undeniably effective, recognized as such by family and friends, who visited often; they'd gotten through both the Depression and the War (to which Big Jim, at thirty-six, was never summoned). For years on end they continued giving the best parties around, and yet sorrow, bitterness and remorse lurked always beneath the surface. To say they lived like hypocrites would be terribly unjust; they lived like all conflicted souls do, simultaneously adamant and fundamentally uncertain. Decades later he would judge them redeemed by the struggle—and only one of them found it apt to thank him without sarcasm for what value

he placed upon the verdict of acquittal, value for his own sake as much
as for anybody else's. This brother was also happy to be told of the petit
mal diagnosis, wishing it had been made earlier so that they would have
understood him and not simply made allowances up to the point where
their patience gave out.

He himself was the only one still caught up in the story of the
infant congenitally hampered in bonding with the mother (the him
he never recognized, had never even heard of) and with anybody, false
without special instruction—striving in his own dark world, where
lights had hardly come on, but as Augustine says we learn everything
we learn mimetically. He was able at least in the dim glow to observe
the *form* of the thing from the way each of the others in the house
bonded (loosely) with one another, the men chiefly over baseball talk,
the woman with herself, "thinking out loud," and to the greatest extent
with her firstborn (if constant tension and loud argument can be both
wounding and bonding—they say it can), and the minute he began to
talk—he longed from birth to be included—which so far as they were
concerned he had been since birth, and they were in truth delighted
with him, something he could never really believe, hampered as he was
in feeling the embrace as ever in the satisfaction of the strength of the
simulated clutch.

Meanwhile Catherine, without her mother, completely rejected by
her father, a situation made worse by his presence in the household and
his hold on her eldest son, whom she herself had neglected, her attempts
at restitution tried in earnest—den mother in the Cub Scouts, an ill-
conceived and finally aborted attempt at refining his deportment by
enrolling him in Madame Argotti's dancing school where, after the fadeout of the "Smoke Gets in Your Eyes" affair, she had taken the job of pia-
nist—at last drove her out of the home, into music teaching in schools
in the Archdiocese of New York, later combined with full-time comprehensive teaching at the sixth-grade level, and most importantly into
parish activity and the politics of parish club work, unusual intimacy
with many of the faculty of Blessed Sacrament School, the order of the

Grey Nuns of the Sacred Heart (replicating her status as favorite among the Sisters of Charity at St. Lawrence Academy), and culminating in great success in the founding of the all-female parish dramatic society, the Genesians, all of whose shows sold out.

. . .

The crack of the starting pistol (called the report, yes) is the first slap at birth (reiterated when the bishop slaps the boy's face at his Confirmation) and it begins: the dreadful competitive race (personal best, his ass) to the extreme limits of the possible. No child is ever reconciled to this unforeseen and unwanted disruption. Every ambition to entertain the world is imposed, beginning with pretending. (Others find peace of mind, why not he?) And the energy expanded in compliance to the express commands of the elders is nothing other than a desperately aggressive compensatory compulsion, repeated until the moment of death, to achieve the impossible: satisfactory reparation for the tragedy of expulsion from a paradise forever lost, the mourning for which— *lacrimae rerum*, the tears in things—expressed in the strangest of all ways, the non-ejaculatory orgasm, lasting through infancy, suspended during the period of latency (for those who undergo one), only to recur with mounting anxiety and distracting delight until the first ejaculation, the trumpeted formal entrance into adolescence. The paradox becomes the greatest and most sustaining comfort to be had in the course of a contemplative life.

Information concerning the infantile orgasm and/or the postorgasmic bliss satisfying for the moment the drive toward quietus the "little death" of the Elizabethans, and for Freud the chief manifestation of the death instinct (*Beyond the Pleasure Principle*), was of necessity inferential and speculative. Few parents in those days observed it, although the presence of the male infant erection and orgasm was in constant evidence in the bassinet, fewer still understood and nobody at all discussed it (for fear of admitting the failure of the renunciation by godparent proxy of the devil's works and pomps in the sacrament of Baptism to take hold), and for a Catholic (unlike a Scottish nanny) to assist in bringing such release about in order to soothe a restive child was literally unthinkable—it would never have entered her mind, or if it had, if it been heard of, could never be spoken of outside the confessional.

The self soothing nonejaculatory orgasm of infancy and latency leading to less soothing, more self-terrifying ejaculatory orgasm (alone or with others my child?" "With others, father"), addiction to which was at one time said to drive boys mad: they got that right after all.

. . .

Like all children, barring the destitute and the offspring of such sorry sufferers as dress in rags, play blackjack in smokey back rooms and drink themselves into oblivion, he had his stuffed toy, Andy the panda, a confidante replaced in later years (to his eternal regret) by Moriarty, already familiar to readers from earlier herein, who unlike the sweet and loving panda talked back, promising endless increase, of more from where what there already was enough of had come from.

More devil himself than devil's advocate, he held out the promise of invincibility empowered by the splendor of the life to come on earth; we did after all win the war.

. . .

A child's language explodes between the ages of two and four; four year olds are able to talk about experiences they have been through (the war from 1941 to 1945 as reported on the radio) with a modicum of outside coaching.

Two languages were to be heard in church, Latin and an English strangely different from the normal everyday, spoken from the parochial pulpit in sermons, to which his mother seemed to be listening with half an ear and which seemed to be putting his father to sleep, although he supposed not really: Big Jim's eyes were closed, but he wasn't snoring, and he was famous for his snoring when asleep ("Roll over, Jim"). He discovered years later that the children of the moneyed never heard their parents snore—only their Scottish nannies in the afternoon, waking them from their naps—or doing anything else in the bedroom either, except using swear words while tying black bow tie and laughing while putting on jewelry and perfume.

The language of the prayers said in church in wartime, unlike that on the radio urging commitment to victory, reprisal and total annihilation of the diabolical enemy, even while admonishing the congregation to hate only the enemy's actions, to forestall in prayer all hatred of the enemy himself, but in the words of the pastor of the parish, Father (later Monsignor) James McMahon, to leave him to heaven—which seemed strange since the Japanese were doing unspeakable evil led on by the devil—they were devils and the wicked who did evil were on the way to hell unless they made a last- minute perfect act of contrition, which the Japanese not being Catholic could never do (only his brother David said some, in fact, were, converted by the Jesuit Saint Francis Xavier hundreds of years earlier; they lived mostly in the seaport city of Nagasaki (the second city atomic bombed, on August 9, 1945), which is also where Madame Butterfly lived, only she converted to the Methodist Church and not to Catholicism. Had she converted to Catholicism she would never have been allowed to commit suicide, and there would go the opera out the window).

The language heard in the wooden church also differed markedly from that heard around the dinner table and from the everyday language of the neighborhood. It was, Father O'Pray explained on the afternoon he came to Sunday dinner, elevated language, intending to rise above the terrible hatreds brought on by war, and as Longinus says (although the priest did not include the fact in his little homily spoken with grace before the meal), "the effect of elevated language on the audience is not persuasion but transport. At every time and in every way, imposing speech, with the spell it throws over us usually prevails over that which aims at persuasion and gratification. Our persuasions we can usually tame" (or as with uncontrollable homosexual feelings suppress) "but the influences of the sublime bring power and irresistible might to bear and reign supreme over every hearer."

Longinus. Longines watches. Huh?

. . .

The story of the growing child is a succession of stories, beginning with the stories read to him, the ones he hears on the radio and the ones he learns to read himself (laying the foundation for a double life), which become as much a part of his story as any he brings back from school or from up the street or any told of him from adult to adult, especially those he overhears.

Seasons on, how crestfallen to discover on the radio a woman called Fanny Brice. There she was on the cover of the sheet music for her song, "My Man."

His mother called it a torch song. "Why?"

"Because she's carrying a torch for a man."

"Does smoke get in her eyes?" Silence. "Why is she carrying the torch for him, why can't he carry it himself?"

"That's a good question." (Which meant he wasn't going to get an answer. There were two ways of knowing you'd get none: when they said, "Ask a silly question, you get a silly answer," and when they said, "That's a good question," so as his mother used to say you couldn't win for losing. He asked David. "What does it mean carrying a torch?"

"Well, it could mean a lot of things. The Nazis carried torches waving swastikas in torchlight parades: we saw them in the newsreels. When the Mob burns a guy's house down the cops say they torched it. The rebels torched the Wilderness to burn the Union soldiers to death.)

Englishmen call a flashlight a torch—you hear it in English movies— so if you were English and you went down to the cellar to change a fuse, or to show a frightened child there was no such thing as the Bogeyman (it was pronounced "boogie" as in that song he loved that the Andrews Sisters sang, "Boogie Woogie Bugle Boy," but it was spelled Bogey. Humphrey Bogart was called Bogey). You would ask them, the Bogeys, to hold the torch for you while you changed the fuse. If you knew how. Most things were ifs.

There was also, his brother explained, the torch of the Olympics, first carried by relay runners from Marathon to Athens in ancient Greece. Skipping then over centuries to the drama of the 1936 Munich Olympiad and of Jesse Owens, the black track star, tall as a tree and swift as an antelope, making mincemeat and a mockery of the Nazi's myth of the superman (who in this case looked like Joe Palooka and didn't even wear a blue cape).

"Also the English carried torches for Joan of Arc, but that was something else too."

"Oh."

And there she was on the radio, Fanny Brice, who according to his grandfather had been a great star of vaudeville, whatever vaudeville was anyway, and in the Ziegfeld Follies (ignorant people said "Ziegfield"), playing a character called Baby Snooks, companioned by another infant called Robespierre. Eerie fascination and jealousy as his family laughed on and on—his grandfather and his brother David in particular: wasn't *he* supposed to be the comedian? Did one have to be on the radio before anybody paid serious attention? In that respect peacetime was just like wartime, only a bit quieter. There were charades at parties, and plays put on out in the garage—although after the Mary Ann Fingerhut incident the garage went off limits—but obviously getting on the radio was the only real way to be somebody.

Boogies were things you picked out of your nose (if you ate them that was disgusting: put that one in your pipe, Publius Terentius Afer— the Roman playwright Terence to whom nothing human was alien—and give it a long draw) and also a dance, the Boogie-Woogie.

Also black men, Negroes, boogers, but it was wrong to say so, even though the jazz music and the dance called the "Boogie-Woogie" was obviously of African-American provenance—no white man could ever have invented either.

So—always wrong to say a thing that wasn't so, and often wrong to say a thing that was.

The family had a weekly helper whose name was Quiet Love, a follower of Father Divine (she reckoned if it was love the Lord wouldn't mind). Father Divine took some explanation, as did Andy Devine, St. John the Divine (although never, decades later, did *La Divina* or Divine, Maria Callas). "Hello, Quiet Love," he would say coming into the kitchen.

"Hello perfect child of God."

Johnny Zilch said, "I'll lay you ten to one Quiet Love isn't so quiet when Father Divine goes around the world with her."

Notes on the regression to the womb state in psychoanalysis: The male analyst's infrequent comments are the voice of the father as heard by the infant within. Having been informed by reliable genetic rumor whispering in every cell throughout the entire three trimesters in the womb—in his case one in which at least one if not two abrupt and premature expulsions had already occurred—mishaps in the realm of gestation, venereal melodramas in the world outside, but tragedies in the troubled soul of the woman, his mother the haunted tragedienne for whom no amount of abject contrition, no relief from fear of divine reprisals and no number of First Friday devotions to the Sacred Heart could get through to cancel either one or both, carriers as they had been of annihilation, of making of that womb a charnel house, an unsafe place from which he might or might not emerge alive. Small wonder that some part of every day of his life has been taken up with the serious contemplation of death.

The thousand and one white dots revealed decades later at the other end of life in the electroencephalogram are testimony of a thousand and one lightning storms, night and day. Lightning storms briefly illuminate the ground of experiences in such a way as to embed it indelibly in the hippocampus (memory). Longinus insists on the poet's "joining" with the sublime—via the possession by a spirit not one's own—enthusiasm—which is why there can be no active verb "to enthuse." The god cannot be injected like a drug, he must himself cathect on the ego's plane, first in the form of the maternal/paternal, single hermaphroditic introject. "The soul is filled with joy and vaunting, as if it had itself produced what it has heard," which is a logical reaction to the fact the first sounds are those heard in the womb and in the protracted interval of total narcissism from birth up to the beginnings of the realization of itself as a separate entity. "It is a law of nature that in all things there are certain constituent parts, coexistent with their substance."

It follows of necessity that one cause of sublimity is the choice of the most striking circumstances involved in whatever we are describing, and further, the power of afterwards combining them into one animate whole. Emerson concurs: The soul always hears an admonition in such an impulse to choose no matter what the ostensible subject may be.

For instance, Sappho, in dealing with the passionate manifestations of infatuation and of the frenzy attending blinded lovers, always chooses her strokes from the signs which she observes to be actually exhibited in such cases. Tall order.

And they didn't get that way—blinded by jerking off, wet or dry. (Dry comers who dig to jerk off dry are merely being efficient—and remember when you thought girls didn't—couldn't?) They came down with the thing like scarlet fever. The spirit of the poet mounts the chariot with his hero and accompanies the winged steeds as they lift off into the void and cavernous vault of the air.

> *Bring me my bow of gold burning:*
> *Bring me my arrows of desire:*
> *Bring me my spear: O clouds unfold!*
> *Bring me my chariot of fire!*
> —William Blake

. . .

The first awareness is of sound day and night, before the two are sep-
arable, different from the sound in the womb, which always includes
murmurs of the voices on the outside—and shouting, and singing
accompanied by rolling slide piano on the Wurlitzer spinet, not to mention the New York Philharmonic, the Metropolitan Opera and the *Make
Believe Ballroom* on the radio. And then the Christening party. The noise.
The people—their faces not yet distinguishable. What was the point of
being the center of attention, in the spotlight, when everyone else but
oneself is holding a glass in his/her hand and one can't see their faces,
not even the ones in the front row? Toothless and wailing as the pictures
show—forecast of the end at the very beginning? How could he then
have otherwise grown up than destined to work a room?

In life the first to come and last to go, the sounds, and the second
the outlines and contours of faces and inanimate objects—the rattle:
sound and shape in one. Sight outlines the contours of faces and inanimate objects—the rattle: sound and shape combined in one contin-
uous succession of scramble events in which the adults loom and the
events themselves pass in review like the gigantic balloons in the Macy's
Thanksgiving Day parade (and so far as giants go one does not bond
with them, one is swallowed up) perfectly exemplifying mobility without motive (as he was to put it years later)—had they known that at the
end of the parade they would be deflated, would they have agreed to join
it, allowed themselves to be filled with hot air, tied to ropes and hauled
down Broadway twenty feet above ground, merely to delight a festive
proletarian horde?

So that coming into the world of shapes was like a morning after the
blackout curtains had been pulled back, the bombers had stopped flying
low overhead on their way to Floyd Bennett Field in Bayside to be over-
hauled and refueled and the only noises now the cats in the alley and the
foghorns moaning in Flushing Bay and the recurring sounds of the El
trains running on regular schedules—local and express running at different speeds, sounding different pitches passing by over Roosevelt Avenue
on the way to Flushing, where he had been born, the more distant tracks

of the Long Island Rail Road running from Long Island City through Glendale, Maspeth and Woodside to Elmhurst, Corona and Flushing, Bayside, Little Neck, Great Neck and Plandome to Port Washington— and the sparrows on the wash line and the telephone wires out the back bedroom windows.

The *camera oscura* is the darkened mind before the use of reason.

The subject apprehended by the artist though a pinprick of light, projected upside down the way in the first moments after birth the artist might have seen the world had he not been born as all are blind to shapes.

In the beginning God said, "Let there be light," but what is not revealed is that the world, just born and held upside down, was terrified, as terrified as the neonate, expelled from a world of warmth and soft sounds that it seemed were beginning to make sense—into *this*.

When well enough is nowhere to be found in the equation, leaving it a moot point, best to dispatch it without delay to moot court and call it quits. Things might well have stayed that way, but nothing holds.

If however the infant decides to carry on, then after the rubber-nippled bottles and the jars of Gerber's baby food (which four decades later he found himself feeding to friends dying of one or more of the many complications of AIDS, the last of which, cytomegalovirus, brought on the terminal dementia), Quaker Oats, Cream of Wheat (a.k.a. Farina), and Ralston (the dark one made of barley) in winter, and in the warmer weather the Wheaties, Cheerios, Nabisco Shredded Wheat (picture of Niagara Falls on the back of the box. His brother David said millions of people went to Niagara Falls on their honeymoons for the thrill of going over them in a barrel), Post Toasties, Kellogg's Corn Flakes and his favorite, Kix.

. . .

Keep away from light sockets, from the Christmas tree—David had eaten a glass ball when he was a baby and Grampa had to make him eat a whole loaf of bread and drink a gallon of milk to get it to dissolve, then milk of magnesia to get the bread lumps with the glass in them to pass, then even so he had a sore throat and a sore rectum for the rest of the holiday.

But most of all at Christmas time keep out of the way of David's trains—big O gauge Lionel models running on tracks laid down by his grandfather all around the side walls, behind the couch and honking louder than the Long Island Rail Road trains off in the distance, so that when he was put to bed early and David stayed up running them, the trio of the El trains, the Long Island Rail Road and the foghorns in the bay became a foghorn quartet.

Keep away from them—if one hit you it would crush your body to a bloody pulp and your head would roll all over the living room rug like Bobby Otto's, spoiling everybody's Christmas and sending his mother to Creedmoor for sure and maybe forever.

He would go down into the cellar, once the bogeyman phase had passed—he'd equated it with the troll in the Three Billy Goats Gruff story his grandfather told them in the rocking chair—to hold the flashlight when his grandfather changed a fuse when part of the apartment had gone dark. His grandfather said, "You know the old story: It's easy to go down into the cellar, it's not always so easy to come back up, after you've seen the secrets."

Blowing a fuse meant losing your temper and shouting like crazy. Out in Northport they told him the linden tree produced white blossoms in late May that covered the lawn like a snowfall, but they never got there before late June and there were no linden trees in Jackson Heights, only oaks, maples and elms (Elmhurst Avenue ended at the corner of 94th Street, feeding into 37th Avenue). The avenues in ascending order from Roosevelt (over which ran the El to Flushing): Roosevelt, Polk (37th), Fillmore (35th), Hayes (34th), then Northern Boulevard, the neighborhood's northern dividing line. (What a lineup of losers, he decided years later—and why was there no 36th Avenue. Should he invent it? Unlucky, like 13 in an elevator. The last number on the roulette wheel, his brother David said.)

. . .

The infant is his own sole current event—in the face of 1941, the crawl: the exploration through thickets to clearings, the playpen and the leash: other children.

The conventions of the day were centered around the afternoon play periods when four mothers and their harnessed children would be put into one big playpen. Kitty McCourt, Marge Hartigan, Marian Talmadge and Virginia Lally. The seances rotated, and the family groups went to one another on foot—hence the halters and leashes—but were most often held at the Lallys—Virginia put out far and away the best spread and was an awfully nice woman who had to be forced into accepting the others' hospitality.

The children: James Francis and the baby brother, and a scattering of others on whom he is disinclined to bestow made-up names, given to choose between the oldest of the others, shied away from Brian Harrrigan, who looked too uncannily like his little brother, thinking that if they were to fight, he *would* find a way to kill him—getting him out of the crib enclosure and over to the wall socket for instance. . . . So he palled up with Penny Talmadge and they got to be friends as they grew older (He also introduced her to the ghost of the family saint, his dead and heaven-residing cousin Claire, but it's his secret since only he asked his Aunt May and she told him all about it. She was a saint, but she was fun too and if he prayed to her she'd get him out of "close calls"—scrapes.) Penny was a spunky redhead and he wanted to be like her—not a girl to be sure, but a redhead. The baby brothers seemed to get along, but Billy Hederman was moody and morose and Kenneth Lawrence sanguine and rambunctious, so he generally teamed up with Penny and Author, where the rule that three always turns into two against one seemed never to rear up, and they became known as the Three Musketeers. They told Brian he could be D'Artagnan, the fourth musketeer, who after all ran the whole show in the stories, but he seemed inconsolable and determined to isolate. (It was no wonder to Author a half-century on that standing in a dingy advertising company bar hangout on 40th Street Brian had a vision of Jesus Christ and thereafter became a devout evangelical—although never so far as Author was aware in the least a violent one, one who might murder a doctor who performed abortions or blow up an abortion clinic.)

In the game of Cowboys and Indians, the hero younger kids play the Indians, which they love because they get to wear feathers and carry tomahawks and because their mothers turn their faces red by smoothing light coatings of lipstick over them. So one afternoon Author tells Billy Hederman that the only way to get to an Indian so he doesn't scalp you or stretch you out pegged down over an anthill and leave you in the sun is to get him drunk—they have no guts and can't drink—and then stomp them to death. So it's out with the Coke, and poured into shot glasses, which the little kids drink avidly and playing the game fall down drunk and the older boys, crying "Fire water to the Navaho!" jump up and down on them. This is when Author has to be pulled off his little brother who has "spoiled" the game by bursting out into tears as his brother kicks him in the ribs.

Besides Fanny Brice as Baby Snooks there was on the radio an entire (and entirely other) world to be reckoned with, wider in scope and deeper in mystery than any he was able to conjure up by taking the elevator to the middle floor. The family gathered in the living room around the dark mahogany radio with the church door front, each member imagining the look of that world in a unique way that would stay in his memory in a way that could never be expunged.

Although the Green Hornet was a comic book character to begin with, he quickly became a radio serial hero equal to the Shadow. *The Shadow*, with Orson Welles doing Lamont Cranston with his female sidekick the very sophisticated Margo Lane, but his M.O. was to walk around invisible, whereas Britt Reid, played by Al Hodge with the sexiest voice on radio, had a houseboy named Kato of ambiguous Oriental origins, by turns Japanese, Filipino and Korean. Nobody seems to have come up with the idea of naming him after the Roman senator and stoic, Cato, pronounced the same way: Kay-toe.

Also because the Green Hornet and Kato would go from their apartment into another building where the Black Bomber (like the limousines that drove up to the opera on Monday nights) was garaged it fed into Author's fantasies of passages from one house to another, or of a passage from the cellar to a high cavern somewhere under New York's rock foundation.

The Green Hornet featured snippets from classical music scores: on it Author first heard Tchaikovsky's *Pathétique* symphony which he demanded to hear the whole of, and some time later was taken to Carnegie Hall to hear it under the direction of Dimitri Mitropolous.

Irony was the ticket at 37-13 (as for instance in Catherine McCourt's denomination of social engineers on the distaff side: Madame Fullcharge, Mrs. Yakkenfloster, Mrs. Uptheblock and Mrs. Hat) as indeed in the rest of the city, having been a hallmark of its discourse for at least a century before it was taken up by the rest of the nation, making him a true adept at Ciceronian oration (four salient points in each and every sentence—and fuck them if they can't follow the argument—in the citywide Forensic Society competitions. "*Quisquo tandem abutare nostra patientia O Catalina!*" How long will you try our patience, O Cataline?).

"Why?" "Because." "Because why?"
Why because, because why, those were the questions.
"Rise and shine."

7

Morning radio. Before his mother decided they would all be daily communicants, troop up to church and tie the dog to the railings, morning radio was a feature of the day. Mary Margaret McBride by preference, but occasionally a turn of the dial to Dorothy and Dick, etc. Years later, in the wake of the gossip columnist Dorothy Kilgallen's sudden and mysterious death, his (anonymous) parody would make the rounds.

"Good morning, darling."

"Good morning dear."

"And what did you do last night?"

"Oh, I worked late at the paper, then caught the second act of *I Remember Mama.*"

"Funny, I always think it ought to be *Life with Father*—incest is best. How many times is that now?"

"Oh, I've lost count, but I always cry. Then I dropped in at the M'Clintics. Kit was in her usual form, full to the brim with those honeyed tones and as always looking for a new script. And how was your evening down around the river? The moon is full."

"No soap, I'm afraid, so I hoofed it over to the USO. Picked up a sailor and took him to Toots Shor's to look at all the real men."

"You're such a fag,"

"Truer words were never spoken from the pulpit. Toots was a bit put out, but did his grin-and-bear it best. Wife Babe thought it was a hoot and made eyes at the boy as he stood there clutching his white sailor hat, making him blush to the roots of his blonde hair. I must say being married to an important and powerful newspaper woman—even if she has

no chin, is a falling-down flannel-mouth drunk, and is no Roz Russell—
has its distinct advantages."

"Bitch."

"And to know that as Catholics we can never divorce—nice."

"Cocksucker—where did you take him to perform the dread deed?"

"To Staten Island on the ferry—and back. In the wheelhouse, both
times, coming and going. You know I told you how Captain Woollcott
likes to watch. Yes, distinct advantages, even if it's hell on earth most of
the time—but no use crying over spilled scotch."

Compulsive onchophagia, nail-biting, always the sign of acute anxiety. Spilled milk—no use crying over spilled milk—but he once, during
the war, saw his mother down on her knees crying over a bottle of cream
that had fallen off the kitchen table and broken, spilling the cream all
over the floor with bits of glass scattered in the pools. The Sunday funnies (once read on the radio by His Honor Fiorello La Guardia, Da
Mayor, who never called Kitty Moore a cockeyed Swede—in fact never
got that far uptown to do so. Italians kept themselves to themselves).

. . .

A few doors up the block on their side to Johnny Zillich's stoop, later
remembered by him as the *stop* of the 37 dash whatever 94th Street
block. (Note was taken of the fact that the Zilliches were Lutherans, and
although Martin Luther did write "Away in a Manger" he was also the
one who nailed his protests to the church door starting the Reformation,
which led to Henry the Eighth and his six wives, two of whom he had
decapitated, etc. Protestants were called Protestant because of Luther's
protests. Then once he heard his mother say, "Methinks the lady doth
protest too much," figured that's how women got to be Protestants. Consequently nobody in the parish knew the Zillichs, but Johnny seemed a
nice boy, and although some other parents on the block had tried unsuc-
cessfully to keep their children away from his stoop, Author's parents were
not two of them. Mother said that the business of "outside the Church

there was no salvation" was not *ex cathedra* (whatever that meant) and should be taken with more than just a grain of salt. After the embarrassment of "a salted battery" he forwent asking what that expression meant, but was glad that he had permission to visit Johnny and play cards with him—Crazy 8s, since Johnny said he was too young for poker—which made his grandfather growl that cards were the devil's prayer book, even though he himself played Casino. Johnny taught him the "Look, Ma, no hands!" trick, to which she replied, "Thieves used to have their hands cut off." His brother David said, "It's in Shakespeare too."

. . .

The walk to the wooden church he'd been baptized in. (Wondering what he would nail to the door if he had the nerve. There were plenty of protests in his head and surely not every one of them would make you a Protestant. Apparently ones against indulgences, whatever those were exactly—something to do with sin, which he was too young to commit and remained so until the age of reason, although his grandfather said no boy was ever too young to get the idea, snakes and snails etcetera.)

The trot around the block to 95th Street and Dr. Rooney's office. (Leading to playing doctor and the examination of Tommy Gallagher's smooth, white backside and butt hole on the Gallagher's back yard across the street, and the debacle with Mary Ann Fingerhut in the Fingerhut's garage a few doors up the block. Father Rausch came to the house and after gently chastising him, spoke to his parents quoting St. Augustine on childhood concupiscence, fallen nature and the age of the use of reason, which was the end of the seventh year. (Seven years—plenty of time left to get away with murder—of the kid brother for example.) Engraved forever on his mind, due to the strangeness of it at root and also as his first feeling of camaraderie with big boys besides his brother, is the trip to the Pickle Bridge with David and Tommy Connolly, a smiling, kind of goofy guy—the kind of guy his mother used to call a "gawmey duck"—who was really the nicest guy you could imagine, witness the time Author fell down on the sidewalk and scraped his knee and

Tommy and David washed it and put iodine on it, and Tommy said, "Now, this may smart a little."

It was with Tommy Connolly David always had up to now played convoys on the kitchen table, splashing water all over the floor as the war in the North Atlantic got really rougher and rougher.

Then there was the matter of the Durkee's "pickle bridge" that half-way big kids—the kids around eleven—wouldn't take him to when they went to watch the trains heading for the Elmhurst stations (the trains whose whistles he heard at night along with the foghorns in Long Island Sound), so David and Tommy decided to take him there.

The pickle bridge was a pedestrian bridge built for the employees of Durkee's pickle factory, who had to walk from the residential area in Elmhurst or all the way down from the 90th Street-Elmhurst Avenue El station to get to work. In Elmhurst, once a wealthy village on its own, nearly all the old houses with porches and turrets had by that time been demolished for middle-income apartment houses, which during and after the war the working class was able to afford. Factory workers did not in those days drive to work, although the managers did, and if any among the workers did own a car, he left it at home out of consideration for his coworkers, and so as not to appear to feel superior, using it only on Sundays for rides out to Jones Beach or up to Connecticut where everyone went to look at the leaves turning brilliant colors.

From the top of the bridge he looked and watched the eleven year olds playing chicken on the Long Island Rail Road tracks, while Tommy Connolly and his brother David counseled him never to be so stupid as to play at that game, because sooner or later somebody's number comes up and the cleanup isn't pretty, the railroad workers throw up doing it.

"A hundred years ago," said Tommy Connolly, "the whole country was addicted to pickles. So don't go hiding your light under a bushel and a peck of pickled peppers from Durkee's."

That night in the dark he lay clutching Andy, giggling like an infant and chanting: "*Addicted to pickles, addicted to pickles, addicted to pickles, addicted to . . .*"

8

The first moves out of the house; up off the floor and out the door: a progression. His own Anabasis from the coastline toward the capital of the new country, only not as one of Xenophon's ten thousand but as one of the eight million stories in the Naked City—a thrilling idea and if make-believe, just his ticket. Across the street to sit on the Halloran's stoop with Dolly Halloran (no dolls in it; they talked—or Dolly did).

What doesn't spring to mind is their reason for his grandfather's and his taking the trolley to Maspeth—there were no parts for train sets to be gotten there, and though there must have been a lumber yard, the one in Corona up on Northern Boulevard was where they always went for wood— for instance the plywood used for building the tables on which the new Lionel train set ran, replacing David's cumbersome O set from the '30s.

Perhaps it was simply that he had become excited about riding the trolley, as in the "Trolley Song" from *Meet Me in St. Louis,* to the end of the line (although when he thought about it years later, realizing that the release of the picture postdated the trolley ride by some years, it seemed like another case of "Catherine, you shouldn't have run into the mayor's sled that way"), and Maspeth was the terminus of the journey, the first part of which entailed their boarding at the 37th Avenue stop of the line that had begun at La Guardia airport and ran down Junction Boulevard under the elevated Flushing line and the Long Island Rail Road line, past the great spread of Quonset hut barracks housing military personnel returned from the wars. (His mother's actor friend Eddie Midwinter always said "the wars." Mother said it was because Eddie had played Shakespeare in his early days, and Shakespearean characters always referred to "the wars," but Eddie himself said that, speaking of the theater, it was correct to say "the wars" because in reality there had actually been two of them—only they called them the Atlantic and the other the Pacific, and he had done USO shows in both—one with Marlene Dietrich, for the great blonde star liked to entertain the troops—which confused Author further, since it had been his impression that in plays performed in theaters, what people did was sit around talking.

(Still although since if his mother didn't like a play, she'd call it "a talky thing," there must have been other things they did besides talk. Of course in musicals they talked and sang, and in the opera, they only sang, and always died. But he knew enough to understand that not too many questions could be answered at one time.)

Also "The Trolley Song" invariably led to the song from the same picture, in his version. ("I just adore the boy next door . . . for he lives at 37-15 94th Street and I live at 37-13.") The boy was called Patrick and Patsy, although his real name, in Irish, was Padraig ("Por-ig") Pearse Harrigan, the firstborn of the Harrigan family. ("H-A-Double R-I -G-A-N spells Harrigan.")

Theresa Harrigan across the alley, windows open in spring would sing "It's Magic" (off-key) along with Doris Day on *Make Believe Ballroom*, and his brother David drowning out the sound with the Spike Jones takeoff "It's Tragic," driving Theresa Harrigan into hysterics. "Mommy, he's making *fun* of me—make him *stop!*" (Author's greatest and most shameful cruelty in later years, not to say the stupidest political move in his theretofore successful neighborhood career, was making vicious fun of all the foibles of the Harrigan family, playing smart-ass behind Patrick's back to all and sundry including the dogs in the street and consequently losing irrevocably the good will of "the boy next door" who had always been decent to him.)

· · ·

Catalogue of misheard expressions and ones not understood
    Up and Adam
    A salted battery (why would you sue somebody for one?)

Shot in the dark

Patient n./patient adj.

What the Sam Hill?

Like it or lump it

"Hearts and Flowers"

Tight as a crab's ass. (The horseshoe crab? Where?)

"What is the meaning of this?" (So they don't know all the time either)

A hop, skip and a jump (forbidden games: hopscotch, jump-rope)

Two jumps ahead of a fit

When the shit hits the fan

The dog ate my homework

Absotively, posilutely

Am-scray

Ixnay

Copacetic

Persnickety

Alley-Oop, the caveman in the funnies

The cat's meow

The bee's knees

The cow's udder udder

"The cow's udder what?"

The dog in the manger

Wiseacre

And then there were the uses of "kid" to ponder, considering he was one.

Kid

    stuff

    gloves

    kid(dies)' matinee

The Yellow Kid in the Hearst funnies of his grandfather's day. He finally found the original strips in the New York Public Library.

napped (the kid's nap, thing of the past).

Ory (in David's jazz record collection)

Galahad—Humphrey Bogart as Turkey Morgan, the bellhop turned pugilist in the picture of the same name, directed by Michael Curtiz and also starring Bette Davis and Edward G. Robinson—all of them young: another of his Comeback Tuesday revelations.

His father's name for his mother when they were courting "McCourting?"

(Was the Port Jervis Lothario a married man—and if so did he say, "I love my wife, but oh, you kid?")

-ding around ("Who's kiddin' who? Should be 'whom'—but that's part of the 'expression'— like 'No kiddin'' ")

On the street

   "Jack be nimble, Jack be quick,

   Jack jumped over the candlestick,

   Great balls of fire!"

   "Pile it up in the corner,

   Pile it up in the corner,

   Pile it up in the corner,

   We don't want it here any more."

   (What? Pile what up in the corner?")

   Make him eat crow

Playing dominoes and casino with his grandfather: something important about the ten of diamonds.

At the dinner table

   "Squash tastes like the smell of hay."

Different kinds of squashes: yellow, pumpkin, zucchini, ornamental.

"Italian people call that kind of squash *gagootz*."

With his brother David.

"Where does sugar come from?"

"Sugar comes from sugar cane."

"Like the striped candy canes on the Christmas tree."

"No, that's putting the cart before the horse. The candy canes on the Christmas tree are made of sugar."

"That comes from canes—sounds to me like which came first, the chicken or the egg."

"The egg."

"Who laid the egg?"

"God—a lot of people think when God made the world he laid a big egg."

"Anyway if the Havermeyers went and got all that sugar from candy canes, who went and got saccharin?"

"By nobody and from nowhere—saccharin doesn't grow, it was invented."

"Who by?"

"Louisa May Alcott."

(The sugar question came directly from Havermeyer 0-1234 and the Havermeyers.)

The essay he wrote ten years later in sophomore English about the telephone number at 37-13—actually, he called it "Mrs. Havermeyer's Telephone Number," turned out to be about finding the telephone numbers of famous people and calling them up to shoot the breeze, skipping around from sugar to Degas to Mrs. Havermeyer.

Mrs. Havermeyer's telephone number, Havermeyer 0-1-2-3-4, was known to but the few women she thought of as social peers—to Mrs. Belmont, Mrs. Yakkenfloster, Madame Fullcharge, Mrs. Uptheblock and

Mrs. Hat—and to no men whatsoever: Mrs. Havermeyer was not that sort of woman.

The little band had met to discuss the dreadful scandal of Ljuba Welitsch's performance in the title role of Richard Strauss's *Salome* at the Metropolitan Opera. (She *sat* on the *head* and *sang* those *words!*")

"I remember hearing of the Dowager Queen, when she was still Queen Mary, going to see Marie Tempest in something or other and coming out of the theater in a very querulous mood indeed, shaking her head and declaring, 'Oh, I can't be happy with Mary for that.'"

. . .

On Christmas, the Schmoo, a brilliant creation.

"This Shmoo," David said, "is one of the race called the Shmoon who live on the moon. The man in the moon is a Schmoo. All real live Schmoon have the same face because all Shmoon are identical and completely democratic."

"Like Harry." (President Truman.)

"Like Harry. Also just as there is Andy Panda and Raggedy Andy (who rode on Andy Panda's back until Andy got sick and tired of being treated like a monkey, representing as he does not a monkey but the real live pandas of China), so this inflatable Shmoo represents the real Shmoon, who are themselves in fact inflatable and deflatable, which is how they travel to earth."

(That he gathered was supposed to be subtle, not that the word had ever yet entered his mind.)

Another Christmas a Flexible Flyer sled for bellywopping up on the hill behind the school.

From tricycle with pedal blocks to tricycle without, to bicycle (red Schwinn, *vide supra*); much later, an English racer, three gears.

Ad Deum qui laetificat juventutem meum. I will go to the altar of him who gladdens my youth.

He thinks he remembers somebody actually frying an egg on the pavement on the hottest day of the year. Possible.

The baby lay in his crib, unmolested.

. . .

His mother's ironic bent expressed in Latin tags versus her devout and rather self-righteous side, daily communion, the "Family Rosary" ("The family that prays together stays together." Didn't last very long, what with Big Jim working two shifts and around the clock, pulling down raining cats and dogs bucks), Lenten rituals and the Stations of the Cross, with the sung *Stabat Mater* (later a joke that used to make him scream with *Schadenfreude*:

At the cross her station keeping
Stood the mournful mother weeping—)

And her particular favorite Holy Week devotion, the office of Tenebrae, at which Mercadante's "Seven Last Words" were sung—once by Author in chorus. When he was still in the lower grades at Blessed Sacrament, he was overheard explaining to a Padraig Harrigan that he couldn't come over and help him with his homework because he was serving on the altar at the "Famous Last Words." Put on the carpet at home for saying "famous" instead of "seven" he was adamant, saying, "Is anybody more famous than Our Lord?"

"I'm afraid he's got you there, Catherine," said Father O'Pray.

Even so, when they went out to Northport the following summer people in the village were taken aback, even a little alarmed by the four year old. Beesucker the butcher for one, although the observation that the child's ability to pin down time in relation to events was not all that great seemed a relief to many, even if his sense of denouement was frighteningly impressive—although given the nature of the actual events, perhaps not after all so surprising—but the almost cool and detached way in which the kid late in the summer of 1945 was heard to say that Hitler blew his brains out with a Luger in his bunk bed in Berlin, good riddance, terribly unsettling.

His father grew pensive, as if caught between two opposing questions: *Are* we *responsible for this?* and *What hath God wrought?* Christ in the Temple was at least *twelve.*

. . .

His mother was concerned, his big brother not quite as much.

"Well, I wouldn't worry too much about it," his brother said.

"I wasn't until I heard him telling Andy Panda about the secret weapon. Setting up that school desk and blackboard in the hallway was a mixed blessing, but he was so fidgety and bored and it's too soon for piano lessons. I taught the fourth grade before I married your father, so at least I'm ahead of him."

"Don't be surprised if you're soon not surprised—at the end of the year he'll probably be ready for the Regents Exam."

9

The big day: the trip into the city to buy track for the Lionel trains—
"23-Skidoo," "Chin to the wind," and the original Madison Square
Garden, where Harry K. Thaw shot Stanford White for having "tampered" with his wife Evelyn Nesbit, the Girl in the Red Velvet Swing.

"Is Harry K. Thaw any relation to President Truman? They're both
Harry."

"Don't be silly."

On the train into the city to get some more track for the Lionel
trains—watching the real tracks as the train seems to eat them. Woodside: "If you go into the woods today . . ." and Sunnyside "Grab your
coat and take your hat . . . leave your troubles on the doorstep." Put on
your gaiter galoshes, the streets are slushy.

They took the El train from Flushing from 90th Street station,
where a bunch of old guys clustered around the coal stove, into Manhattan ("The City"). While standing on the platform in the freezing
cold waiting for the train they saw an old duffer pissing off the opposite platform, and the boy got his first good look at a cock—long and
thick as an eel and white as chalk. Wondering was his grandfather's as
big, he heard the old man say, "That bum thinks he's so smart; if he
hits the third rail he'll be electrocuted standing there on the platform.
I hope he doesn't, because if he does there goes our afternoon—we'll
be the only witnesses and we'll have to wait for the police to arrive then
go back with them to the precinct to give testimony for the inquest."
(This was another of the horrible images he remembered his grandfather invoking—others included the time way back in the Yorkville days
when the crazy man who was fixing a girl's skate for her, took it off her

foot and beat her brains out with it, and another the smart drunken socialite during Prohibition who took up the bet of her rich, spoiled, socialite gang and climbed over the fence into the polar bear's den, whereupon the polar bear ambled out of his cave, took one look and went for her, tearing her limb from limb, so all that was left of her was her blood drenched mink coat, for which of course the polar bear had no use.) The old guy hadn't gotten himself electrocuted and the boy had forgotten all about him and the crazy man and the society girl and the polar bear and was standing lost in wonder at the window in the front car, just tall enough to see the approaching diorama of the sublime skyline of Manhattan.

They had crossed over the Long Island Rail Road tracks at Woodside, where in the summer they would get off the El train and descend to the eastbound platform to catch the train to Northport, changing at Jamaica for the great steam-engine, smoke-belching locomotive train. They were now pulling out of Lowery Street past the mysterious Star Hotel, in the factory district, past the Breyer's ice cream sign, the Silvercup Bread sign, the Bulova watch sign, the Chiclets and Spearmint signs, the National Casket Company, the Steinway piano factory, Horowitz and Margareten, kosher matzohs. (Decades later his writing was to find a friend in the *New Yorker* staff writer Naomi Bliven, born Naomi Horowitz, of the matzoh family, and to go to Budapest to stay at the spa hotel on Margareten Island, situated in the Danube between the two cities of Buda and Pest, exactly as Roosevelt Island, Welfare Island that was, lies between the boroughs of Manhattan and Queens, wondering, since there were no coincidences and everything was said to mean something, often enough something esoteric, what vital secret, what sacred message such convergences might contain.)

"Grampa says they're still building New York even without him—he says it'll be a great place if they ever get it built."

At Queensboro Plaza they changed to the BMT coming in from mysterious Astoria, where they never went (but which his mother joked about a lot, about her almost being in motion pictures, silents, but he knew all motion pictures came from Hollywood, some in Technicolor, and all of them talking), where the Hellgate Bridge carried freight trains and the New York, New Haven and Hartford passenger line from Penn Station up into Connecticut and on to New Haven, Hartford, Springfield and Boston. Another time than this they would be taking the IRT all the way to Grand Central for the Jerome Avenue IRT to go up to the Bronx to fix Grandma McCourt's chairs—1912 Loring Place. Imagining Catherine and Elizabeth Goodbody as girls like his cousins Miriam and Marcella, in long Holy Communion dresses. Aunt Lizzie says, "Papa was thrown out of the Goodbody family for marrying a Catholic, can you imagine? The Goodbodys were Quakers—People said Quakers came to America to do good, and stayed to do well. They certainly didn't do well by papa, not even decently, but he made his own way very nicely, thank you very much."

(He had no idea at all why she was thanking him; most of the time she was barely civil—a word he'd heard to apply in such situations, but which confused him further by making him wonder what connection it had to the Civil War in which his own great-grandfather had fought in the Wilderness.)

The Woodlawn line—he would watch for one red and one green lamp on the head car as it pulled into the station. The last stop, Woodlawn cemetery. (Granma said he was going into Calvary back in Queens, which they had passed on the IRT, between Rawson Street and Queensboro Plaza.)

If one went up the elegant way, which he did upon occasion with his father, taking the New York Central from Grand Central Station, one detrained at High Bridge, walked through Highbridge Park and up Burnside Avenue to Loring Place, turning left up to 1912 on the right side. (High Bridge, the former aqueduct, still spans the Harlem River, but the station and the park were demolished ages ago to make way for the Major Deegan Expressway. Author has always despised the Major Deegan Expressway; his visits to the park with his great Aunt Lizzie were essential to his coming to understand the world.)

—

Ruminations. By then they had passed through Sunnyside, Woodside and Long Island City at Queensboro Plaza. From there the IRT went to Court House Square, then into the tunnel to arrive at Times Square via Grand Central, whereas the BMT crossed over the bridge to connect at 59th Street with the Third Avenue El, which they take to 23rd Street where the hardware store was, the one with the Lionel trains and all the track and the stations and the level crossings with blinking lights—and sometimes all the way down to Chinatown to walk over to City Hall and the statue of Patrick Henry—"Give me liberty or give me death!"—and look at the Woolworth Building and the Singer Building, then amble down to Battery Park to watch the ferry boats going to and from the Statue of Liberty and Staten Island, the *City of Keansburg* going to New Jersey, the excursion boats going up the Hudson to Poughkeepsie, Nyack and Bear Mountain and the boat to Rye Beach, which went around the Battery, past Governor's Island, up the East River, through the waters of Hellgate, past City Island, River's Island and Towe Island, New York's potter's field. (Why "potter's field" for paupers' graves? His grandfather said it didn't much matter how or where you're buried if you were going to rise up again on the Day of Judgment. All graves are damp . . . and out into Long Island Sound over to the south shore of Westchester County to its destination.) You could, by staying to the south shore of Long Island Sound, sail all the way to Northport by way of Little Neck, Great Neck, Oyster Bay, Cold Spring Harbor, etc., all the way to Charlie and Flossie Moore's dock, but it would have to be in a private yacht such as the Vanderbilts had just opposite Moore's Hotel, directly across Northport Harbor in Counterpart. Starting nearly two decades later, trips in from Idlewild airport along the Long Island Expressway, reaching the overpass leading to the Queens Midtown Tunnel, passing virtually over the graves of David Matthew, his wife Mary Ann and Author's father and mother: Next of vision, either brightly in the day or dimly in the night: the beginning of

"The dream-crossed twilight between birth and dying." Then shapes, outlines, silhouettes. Sightlessness however is not a privation; the only privation is hunger. The devil and all his works and pomps may have been renounced by Aunt Elizabeth, godmother, promissory by proxy, but the dark shadows were not inhabited by angels and the sounds on the radio were not the starters orders of the heralds of gladness. Laughing friends moreover seemed ready to deride, but nothing of any kind, seemly, unseemly, seeming, unseeming, could be taken into account until the days of reconstructed memory, in which no second personality would be revealed—what else after all was the point of being clever if under the hypnosis even of high art some uncontrollable alter ego should emerge over which one was utterly powerless, to make one's life unmanageable to say the very least of it?

. . .

He loved the game of falling between his father's legs while his father recited,

> *One-two-three O'Grady*
> *I spy Mrs. Sadie*
> *Sitting on her bumba-layly*
> *All fall down!*

. . .

He was ill equipped. Catherine had drunk very little in the pregnancy, or smoked, but as she told him decades later, she'd developed a compulsive attraction to the smell of nail polish remover—the smell of course a question not of "scent" but of the inhalation of noxious chemicals.

A few years later at Doctor Rooney's office, Catherine said, "He's become lackadaisical."

"Melancholia, Catherine?"

"I'm not laca-whatever. I'm thinking."

"Don't contradict your mother, James, or you'll get coal in your stocking on Christmas morning."

"Melan-coal-whatever?"

If he did get coal he'd know where it came from—across the alley at the Harrigans' and the Smiths', who had the only coal-burning furnace on the block, or probably in the whole neighborhood. And he'd know who put the coal in his stocking, too–Mr. Lavan dressed up in his Santa Claus suit—so maybe he'd better not contradict Mr. Lavan either.

David: Author asked if it was true as Fr. Daly, the Jesuit, said that the Jews murdered Christ.

"That is another fallacy."

"What about Jewish people? In the Mass it says pray that the Jews may—"

"See the light? That's got to go. The Jews invented the light—or they were the first to write down that God did. 'Let there be light, and there was light.'"

"I know they're God's chosen people. 'How odd of God to choose the Jews.'"

"Noel Coward said that, I think."

Rome wasn't built in a day around and atop its seven hills: God took six days to make the world; on the seventh day he rested. They say it was on a Sunday, but his grandfather told him the Jewish people say it was on a Saturday.

Mrs. Goldberg: If it got to be noon without David going down the hall to the Goldbergs' apartment on Weeks Avenue, the phone would ring, "Hello, Mr. Moore, this is Mrs. Goldberg. I'm missing my little Davey, when is he coming down to see me?"

"Was Mrs. Goldberg related to Molly?"

"A relation almost—the two Mr. Goldbergs are cousins."

—

Jewish shopkeepers in the neighborhood: Milton and Leon's soda parlor on the corner of 94th Street and Polk Avenue. ("Mother and Father go out at night to Leon and Eddie's nightclub in Manhattan—we go up the block in the daytime to Leon and Milton's.") The Silvermans' bakery next to the Polk movie theater. Fay and Hymie's soda parlor and candy store and newspaper shop with bottled sodas on Polk Avenue between 94th and 95th Streets. (My mother's favorite Jewish joke: "Hymie, I heard you had a fire!" "*Sssh*—next week.") Al Tiffany's, the dry cleaner, two doors down from Fay and Hymie's toward 94th Street. Papisch's drugstore on the corner directly across from Milton and Leon's. (They filled prescriptions for Doctor Rooney and his daughter, Virginia, the pediatrician, and her husband Vito Pagano, the neurosurgeon, who also acted the role of family doctor and prescribed all the new miracle drugs that came in after the war, which Author loved to take because they zonked him only enough to stay home in bed, where he could still read and play at the Land of Counterpane. When he prescribed those drugs to Author's mother, along with really revivifying vitamin B-12 shots—their mystery only revealed a decade later—he'd always say, "Now down these, Catherine, with a couple of belts of good scotch.")

There was also a third Doctor Rooney, Virginia's father, so the Rooneys had the business tied up. The first wake Author ever went to was old Doctor Rooney's and he was waked in the front room of the house on 92nd Street. (There had been a spy picture called *The House on 92nd Street*, but of course that was East 92nd Street, upper Manhattan, a stone's throw from the Yorkville his parents grew up in, where the Irish kids used to stand along the curb sucking lemons on 86th Street when the old German marching bands of the *Musikvereins* marched along, yelling out "sucking lemons!" in an effort to get the horn players to pucker up their lips and make pitch mistakes. (They called the Germans *Heiniekablotzes* and made fun of their accents the same as George Hermann did in his *Krazy Kat* comic strip and as Rudolph Dirks did for *The Katzenjammer Kids*.)

. . .

Little Christmas: The Feast of St. Nicholas, December 6—his grandfather's birthday to kick off the season of advent wreaths and Macy's windows (which had in fact been in place since Thanksgiving Day Parade: there were only two windows he ever cared to look at, Macy's and Tiffany's), and the big Santa Claus charade on Christmas morning (the stockings were hung by the chimney with care—although there was no chimney, no hearth: they'd turned the piano around and covered it with brick paper, pasting the picture of a hearth fire cut from *Better Homes and Gardens* at the center). Then Midnight Mass, the twelve days of Christmas, the Feast of the Holy Innocents, December 28 (what did Herod *do*, eat them?), everybody pixilated on New Year's Eve, the Feast of the Circumcision (whatever that was, nobody ever said, except to remark that the Italians didn't do it), and finally Epiphany and the Three Kings (which for Puerto Ricans up in East Harlem and Washington Heights—where his mother taught often tutoring Spanish-speaking children after hours—was the most important day, called *Reyes*, the Kings). And that was it. Down came the tree, which was then taken up the block to a vacant lot and added to the pile for the big bonfire. Then back to school and January and David's birthday on the 19th. Next stop, Groundhog Day, Lincoln's Birthday, Valentine's Day and Washington's Birthday and February, and usually Ash Wednesday. In March St. Patrick's Day and the March winds.

He lived as if he were the sole event of the day until, as the motion picture put it, there were eight million stories in the Naked City. Whereupon the idea of being naked with 7,999,999 others was both frightening and exciting—there would be both men and women. Would they be kept separate the way they were in public toilets and Catholic elementary and high schools and colleges?

It was said that in Japan men and women bathed together and that in Poland during the war men and women were burned together in ovens (the horrors of what had happened to the Jews, never discussed in his home, but shown he knew at the Guild Newspaper theater opposite Radio City Music Hall and told in detail by Johnny Zilch, whose Lutheran family called down the wrath of God on Nazi Germany).

Also in a house up on the corner of 94th Street and Elmhurst Avenue, there lived a family of escaped German Jews called Mittel, who had moved in at the end of the war and kept very much to themselves. In front of their house was a great Dutch elm, which perished along with all the other elm trees of Elmhurst in the Dutch elm blight of the 1950s. The two Mittel boys were pale, wore thick glasses, yarmulkes on their heads and curious curls on each side of their heads (when every other boy in the neighborhood wore his hair crew-cut), and were not permitted by their parents to associate with what Author at last learned were the *goyim*—Christians. The family did not even give their custom to Mr. and Mrs. Silverman.

. . .

On June 16 (as it turned out), 1958, he went down to Wilentz's Eighth Street Bookstore and bought James Joyce's *Ulysses*, to be surprised to find in it a newspaper item telling of a very real New York disaster, the famous *General Slocum* fire on June 15, 1904, a thing his grandfather used to talk about: people cramming down at the shore to watch passengers burning to death and the pleasure boat finally sinking into the East River. The sight of *Ulysses* sitting on the desk in the bedroom he shared with his younger brother brought on such a ruckus that he'd had to call his brother David in Seattle to get the bitch off his back yet again and to wonder again what kind of shit he could get on her around questions of sexual hypocrisy: "Methinks the lady doth protest too much." He swears to this day that at that point in his life he knew somewhere deep in his cold heart there was something. He wanted more than anything to destroy her hold on him, but his father wasn't available as an ally (perhaps having started his affair with "the other woman").

He'd had his first sip of beer on his first birthday and thereafter was allowed to sip from his father's and his brother's glasses. His grandfather, a nondrinker, is furious, but they say if Jimmy learns to drink—it was in those days considered a skill—as he grows up he'll never be an alcoholic.

When his father said they ought to pour Schaefer beer back into the horse, he asked if they should do the same with Budweiser, since they already have the Clydesdales. His brother then says Budweiser is a good beer and Schaefer gets theirs out of the horses in Central Park. Remembering this in later years always somewhat tilted the experience of the "romance" of nocturnal hansom carriage rides around the park.

"Poor Jimmy, for him the world is booby-trapped."

The noise of the B-29 bombers coming into Floyd Bennett Field to be recalled and refueled.

English war song "The White Cliffs of Dover" sung by Vera Lynn on the radio about Jimmy back in his own bed again.

"Where had Jimmy been?"

"They had to take him; they had to take all the children out of London because the Germans had started bombing it. The Germans call it 'blitzkrieg.' It means 'lightning war.' The Londoners call it 'the blitz.' They send their kids to places in the country—evacuate them in case London is destroyed."

"Are they going to evacuate New York—"

"No—New York is never going to be destroyed. We're going out to Northport again for the summer—but we're not being evacuated. We're fighting this war along with the British so people will never have to be evacuated again. You know, pal, out in California they evacuated the Japanese-Americans called Nisei—many of whom have been U.S. citizens for generations—and put them in detention camps."

"They evacuated people in the hurricane on 1938—it blew down the St. Philip Neri's steeple in Northport."

"On a wooden church, yes—it didn't do a thing to St. Patrick's."

"New York will last forever."

—

Bliss Street: A stop on the El train to Grand Central and Times Square.

Associations over the years from the misunderstanding of "bliss" for blitz and blitzed, heaven, beatific vision, sight of God, nonstop orgasm, sex in the factory district, the enigmatic Star Hotel (transients). So many ideas, so many transformations as the life progressed—from the magic closet elevator to the "middle floor"—later echoes in "coming out of the closet" becoming for him coming out into a magical world where things look the same but were in another dimension. Also the deep attachment to the stage, deeper even than to motion pictures. The latter were dream states with variously dissected people: floating head, close-ups on hands, backsides—as with Marilyn Monroe's walk in *Niagara*—but the legitimate stage was actual worlds somewhere between real life and the whole landscape of the Land of Counterpane: full bodies talking or singing or dancing—and as to the supposed ridiculousness of opera plots, he thought detractors were just being stupid.

The City on the Hill: New York is its own hill and its own city, too.

. . .

"I'm under ownership here, Andy, but one day I won't be anymore, I'll be a grownup. . . . I'll be free like Quiet Love."

There was nothing really wrong with the streets of Jackson Heights—they were perfectly long, straight runways for takeoff into the wild blue yonder of the imagination. The streets of Greenwich Village were known to curve and crisscross in labyrinthine fashion. When really shaking with nervous terror over these images and sayings which kept coming to him in the night, he asked his grandfather had he not played with Jews as a child down on Grand and Delancey Streets, and his grandfather said yes, but they were not Jews Christians had herded into gas chambers and then burned in *ovens* (he had heard that if you killed somebody and got caught it was either the electric chair, hanging or the gas chamber).

Apart from anything else, that was for him the end of *Hansel and Gretel* at the Metropolitan. And what about Mrs. Goldberg up in the Bronx? Well, we haven't seen the Goldbergs now in many years, but it's pretty likely that some of their relatives back in Germany perished.

It was a horror whose magnitude in numbers he could not grasp— the newsreels had disappeared into the more or less secret army files and the vaults of television stations in that period of deliberate amnesia that lasted until the middle 1950s in which the Jews themselves, the survivors, wanted no more rocking of the boat, because there were Catholics all around the place saying the Jews had got what they deserved for murdering Christ.

"They wanna make a lampshade out of my grandmother." (Movie line quoted by his brother David, making his mother shudder.)

Everybody thought the kid brother was such a brave kid because he wasn't afraid of the dark—but he always fell asleep the minute his head hit the pillow—obviously he had nothing to think over—*and then* they'd turn out the light.

(Big deal, he has nothing to think over, he's pretty as a picture and dumb as a rock, but I do and I lie awake. If there were shadows on the ceiling I wouldn't care—they'd remind me of things—but the dark is terrifying, so sue me. And Eddie Midwinter agrees with me, and he's old. "As Herbert Hoover once said, a good many things go around in the dark besides Santa Claus.") Whoever Herbert Hoover was—the FBI guy on the radio's brother?

Hands down there can never have been a more rotten brother than he. And it was all so stupid because deep down, as he had to admit to himself early on, he loved the little guy—he was so funny and you could sit and look at him for hours he was such a beautiful-looking kid. But he'd always fit in anywhere without making the slightest effort, and that . . . anyway for being such a rotten brother, Author would probably get his comeuppance, starting from the time the little monster got big enough to kick the shit out of him, but not on that account alone, but apparently from what he understood about America (but not New

York, so he might never leave it), for being a smarty-pants and growing up to be a wise-ass. You were just plain asking for it once you pulled that caper. (But yes, maybe if he never left New York. . . . There were smart-asses everywhere who never seemed to get their comeuppance, although his mother used to say of some that they were "educated beyond their own intelligence." That would take some doing in his case, he decided, or else why were they making such a fuss about whether or not to skip him a grade, maybe two. When they decided not to, he was relieved. The way things were left, he could do the work in ten minutes, then dawdle.)

Mother's perfect boiled egg: put egg into boiling water, lower heat, say three Hail Marys at reverent speed. Remove from water.

"I'm not running a Bickford's!" (Meals at odd times: later recalled at the hustler's Bickford's on "the Deuce," 42nd Street.)

Another name, his favorite, his father called him by—always while vigorously drying his hair after a bath, and his favorite—was Ichabod. So after reading and then seeing *The Legend of Sleepy Hollow* at the Polk, he made a little valley in the Land of Counterpane and put in the center of it a decapitated equestrian guard in a British uniform he got in a trade from a boy serious about his collection but willing to trade one of his prized Home Guards for a session playing doctor with Author—whose fame after the Mary Ann Fingerhut incident had spread and would in fact last for years, ironically enough insulating him from the earliest "faga-toon" charges. He seemed to be the only boy on 94th Street who had ever stuck his finger into a girl's pussy—and by that time he was already lying, saying that they'd gone on meeting in secret down in his cellar and he'd stuck his dick up her slit, which sounded so much more rugged than the action involving a finger. He was coming to prefer hard, honed lan-guage to soft, tentative expression. When he persuaded Tommy Quilli-gan to pretend he was joining the army, the "doctor's exam" consisted entirely of Author's holding the studious boy's balls and telling him to cough three times, but even at that, so much clear goo drooled out of the boy's cock, Author started masturbating the boy until he broke out into the shivering convulsion of a dry orgasm and passed out—only to awaken seconds later, too young as yet to be terrified of the priest in confession telling him he was going to hell, but terrified nonetheless—of Author's power to make him feel like he'd just gone to heaven and then died, which was getting the whole thing backwards.

Finally the Raggedy Andy doll, which he'd always disdained, what with all the well-dressed men seen everywhere in New York, met its end. One day his brother David found it torn to shreds. Author offered the excuse that Andy Panda had attacked it out of jealousy, but David said that no panda would ever do that, that they were peaceable animals who sat around all day eating bamboo shoots. He told the boy to get rid of the evidence or the shit would hit the fan, which delighted him. "And *don't* try that alone in the house, all right?"

On a windy day, walking to the 23rd Street BMT subway, his grandfather explained "23 Skidoo." The wind off the North River blowing toward the East River skidding pedestrians along, their hats blowing off and women's Gay Nineties hairdos unrolling and flying all over the place. My clavicle.

A dypsomatic search.

Sticktoitiveness.

There wasn't much of a mystery about "Mairsy Doats," except that some women called his little brother Brendan a "dote" which meant a sweet, good-natured kid who right off the bat started talking in the "deez, doze, and dems" way and could not be corrected, but his looks redeemed him, in fact it was thought the bad pronunciation and grammar actually enhanced his appeal and that "he oughta be in pictures." But what was the meaning of "Hudsa broad on the rillarod hudsa brawla, brawla, brawla?"

. . .

"Season of mists and mellow fruitfulness." In the autumn mist arising, he sees from the top of the only hill in Jackson Heights the smoky gray outline of the phantom city veiled in mist.

Burning autumn leaves and Joan of Arc (the next parish over, closer to the city, a wealthier parish than Blessed Sacrament).

They all talked about Catherine "thinking out loud" and joked about Creedmoor and *The Snake Pit* (the movie), but he actually began at an early age—in the schoolroom in the hallway—to listen to her. While "doing his lessons" he could hear her at the kitchen table, when the radio wasn't on, reviewing situations and planning things. Because of the war, he thought right away of "logistics," "strategies," and "campaigns" and even more so when he became aware of Cold War matters and club politics and his father and older brother on opposite sides. Then she went on the radio, at which point he could tell she was thinking up things to say, but more and more he began to construe the whispering as having to do with secrets—old ones he thought, because she raised her voice a little when "thinking" of contemporary things. And finally he began to associate all of it with rehearsing lines for plays.

There was the statue of the BVM in her altar, crushing the head of the serpent beneath her feet, the inscription AVE-EVA etched in gold underneath on the marble facade. Obviously there had been no call for BVM to visit Ireland, but Mae O'Flaherty said she finally went anyway to a place called Knock, where then they put up a shrine to her, now the holiest place in Ireland, replacing the Hill of Tara.

"What's a Marian appa—"

"Apparition," his brother said. "It means to appear, so it's whenever the BVM appears to children. Also when Marian McSherry comes to dinner."

Years later when he went on a Comeback Tuesday at the Polk to see the movie *Cobra Woman* he was knocked sideways by the experience of Maria Montez's wild dance and roundup of the islanders to be thrown into the volcano as human sacrifice to propitiate the gods, the terror of the Last Judgment and of the possibility of damnation for all eternity was trumped absolutely by the erotic thrill of the performance. Mass, Benediction, everything in church took place in a lighted church and the priests were in charge, where in the movie the priests were fools and the priestess all-powerful, taking place as it did on a 40-foot screen in incredible Technicolor in a darkened theater—like something the cat-

echumens in the catacombs in Rome might have gone through. Later
he understood perfectly why Maria Montez as Cobra Woman became
such a majestic and powerful icon for a whole generation of homosexuals. Next to her Bette Davis as Margo Channing in *All About Eve* was
merely an amusing pal, which of course was wonderful, but could not in
the end compete on the mythic level with the fairly annihilating force of
Maria Montez's dark pagan religion (also, he longed to embrace Sab) and
he knew that homosexuality would always be that for him, a dark, pagan
religion, for which in his daytime one he would be sent straight to hell.
The seeds of a nervous breakdown were sown.

He was developing an interest after hearing Grace Moore on the
radio singing "What'll I Do?" and learning she was a big star, not snooty
like European divas, but a "rip" who had very sophisticated weekend
parties at her place in Connecticut, where guests were all asked to sign
the guest book in the hall, and when Garbo refused, saying she never
gave autographs, a taxi was ordered to drive her right back to the station
after lunch. *Garbo!*

"Grace is a Southern woman, from Tennessee; Tennessee women put
up with no guff from anybody."

So he started to love the Met broadcasts, especially *Madama Butterfly*
with Licia Albanese and *Tristan und Isolde* with Helen Traubel and Lauritz Melchior, and *Aida* with Rose Bampton and *Carmen* with Risë Stevens, *and* then was taken to hear Jarmilia Novotná in *La Traviata* and
welcomed backstage afterward where his mother and the beautiful diva
had a warm and lively conversation. Jarmila Novotná was Czech: the
Czechs had been betrayed by some English fool called Neville Chamber-
lain, who ran England before Churchill took over to win the war, and
now it was run by Clement Attlee and the Labour Party everybody said
were communists who would do away with the monarchy—the poor
stuttering King and the feisty Queen who had been so brave during the
war, and the princesses Elizabeth and Margaret Rose.

. . .

If anything they were eating dropped on the sidewalk, they picked it up and kissed it up to God before finishing it.

"It is just as well not to provoke altercations with Neanderthals," David said.

"What's a Neanderthal?"

"A race of marginal human beings who once lived in a valley in Switzerland."

(People made of margarine? He supposed they hadn't melted because it was always cold in Switzerland.)

"Were they making cuckoo clocks—making Swiss cheese? What makes a Mexican jumping bean jump, its nature?"

"The worm inside. They put the Mexican jumping bean in a bottle of tequila—the fire water they drink down there—and the tequila gets into where the worm lies, and it's worse than fire water to the Navaho. The worm goes berserk and the bean starts jumping around.

"And speaking of worms, when you die and the worms crawl in and the worms crawl out, in your stomach and out your mouth, sometimes some worms susceptible to embalming fluid act the same way as the Mexican jumping bean and that's why you hear about people rolling in their graves."

"What's sep-acle?"

"Part of receptacle. Susceptible means prone."

"What's prone?"

"The opposite of supine."

"What's that?"

"I'm trying to teach you things."

"I think they're the same."

"You're not alone—Einstein hated school."

"They call me Einstein and I don't go yet, except in the hall."

"You have to stop going in the hall, that's what the bathroom is for."

"You're tormenting me."

. . .

Hubba, hubba, zing, zing,
Baby you've got everything,
What a face, what a figure
Like a cow, only bigger.

Serious illnesses and miracle drugs, and days in the Land of Counterpane.
He fell in love with the Land of Counterpane and unlike his obsession with
Oz, never got over it, becoming in adult life one of *les grands horizontales,*
working in bed all day like Marcel Proust, connoisseur in degenerates. He
dreams of fires, floods and hurricanes, imbibing when on his sickbed his
drugs of choice: Brown's Mixture and Stoke's Expectorant. Years later Ter-
penhydrate and codeine cough medicine and prescriptions for Darvon for
sinus headaches. Later paregoric and Hennessy cognac. Later still Dexamyl
and Seconal. Finally tequila and Percodan, then maybe after all sudden
death and resurrection—something like it anyway.

The mystery of the "leakage" of liquids out of glasses put on the
mahogany tables and causing white rings and of pitchers of iced tea,
lemonade or Kool Aid on the kitchen table or on the card table out in
front of the house where he sold the stuff for two cents a glass (and the
further mystery of how, no matter if the liquid was milk, orange juice,
Coca-Cola, beer, a highball or anything else, it was always water that
seeped through), whereas none of the milk bottles, beer bottles, bottles
of juice or soda, pitchers of lemonade, iced tea or Kool Aid there in the
refrigerator ever leaked.

Pause now for station identification (since forgotten) on journey out
to Los Angeles on the Super Chief. It happened on one of his many train
trips to Los Angeles. They had gone beyond the waving wheat and the
elephant-eye-high corn down into the drier land—perhaps in western
Nebraska, and whistled at a town with one long street visible out the
window. Somebody said out loud to nobody in particular, "The guy who
invented Kool Aid was born here—he *made* this town."

"Really? God bless America."

10

The two kinds of rugs, summer and winter—the latter wool of rich oriental design, meant, he was told, to picture a Persian garden, and once a
year during Spring cleaning beater with a wire beater while hung on the
fence in the back yard, and the former of straw in bright colors, which
unhappily the dog Tiny when he was nervous in a thunderstorm tended
to piss on, leaving bleached-out spots—but straw rugs were cheap, and
the members of the household understood even less the direction that
Tiny's neurosis was taking than the labyrinthine paths down which their
own had led them into places their guardian angels would have wished
them never to visit, much less frequent. Therefore until the fatal day
when poor Tiny's schizophrenic brain entered the arena of raging psychosis, primed for instinctual, primordial attack, and struck out at the
world in haste post haste in the form of biting Author's mother on the
cheek, sending her to Doctor Pagano to have the wound cauterized and
Tiny was put down that same afternoon, his periodic and unfortunate
debility was tolerated, as might be a child's who wet the bed by any
decent, loving parent. (Children of course were also known to bite their
parents, but were generally not "put to sleep" for doing so.)

He himself was said to be defiant. (Children must not be defiant to
their parents; parents on the other hand could be defiant to their children whenever they felt like it; there was no such thing as kids being
defiant to other kids; and if he tried being defiant with his older brother
all he got was laughed at; such were the rules.)

Both willful *and* defiant, so they said—especially when cornered,
having been discovered *in flagrante delicto* or in open licentious-
ness. When you got mad you were supposed to see red; he'd see white

flashes, split-seconds long, which seemed to command him to stand his ground—stand his ground or be crushed, yet nobody had ever lifted a finger against him since the day his mother threw a whole bucket of cold water over him as he was having a tantrum standing on the turned-down toilet seat. Strange the defiance; worrying, and he'd been told so *ad nauseam.* (These Latin expressions they used all the time were something—something he knew you didn't hear in other households in the neighborhood.)

11

Mary Ann Fingerhut was having a great time, giggling and giggling when he put his finger in and was stiff as a pencil down there and remembered what the older boys said that you stick *that* in, so he pushed his finger in, all the way—up to the first knuckle—and still she was giggling and giggling and he was feeling dizzy and like he was going to piss when Mrs. Fingerhut came into the garage, saying, "Mary Ann, what are you giggling about?" And then there was a banshee shriek and poor Mary Ann was being dragged away by her long hair, screaming and later saying that he made her do it and it hurt, but he swore to God that she'd been giggling the whole time—even turned to her mother and said, "You *know* she was, Mrs. Fingerhut, because you heard her through the kitchen window and came into the garage asking Mary Ann why she was giggling—and when your eyes adjusted to the dark you started screaming so loud *she* started screaming and now she says I hurt her, but she was giggling, you know she was." And Mrs. Fingerhut said later he frightened her not only for what he had done but for the tone of voice as he tried to get out of it, as cool as you please, with no feeling in it at all, so cool that he must be possessed by the devil.

Father Rausch was called in (absent the candles and holy water) for an exorcism. Things were explained on both sides. Would he save it up for his first confession? Best to forget it and remember not to do anything like it again, whether Mary Ann Fingerhut was giggling her head off or not.

Next day he took the dishtowel down from the dish rack, which he used to try to hang himself (found on the floor by his grandfather, having kicked out the kitchen chair, snapped the wooden towel rack).

He was hastily shooed away to the back bedroom and nothing was ever said about it, not to him, anyway, although the close cold eye was on him from then out for a long time. (He himself had forgotten the next day what his reason or thinking was, and he could never bring them up out of the deep dream state.)

Although his grandfather had apparently kept silent about the suicide attempt, he had quite a temper, and it would indeed flare up, but when it did aimed always at one of two targets, the Republican Party or his daughter (voting Republican, along with her husband, in reaction to Franklin Delano Roosevelt's defiance of precedent in winning a fourth term in office and to rumors of his foreknowledge of the attack on Pearl Harbor) who would give back as good as she got, which was interesting to watch: she had real histrionic flair and was not to be deterred by any sense of filial piety, as much as she loved the operas of Giuseppe Verdi. In fact it seemed to Author that she and her father flat out despised one another. He'd go into his room at the back of the house to, as she always put it, "cool his heels."

The boy had no idea what that could mean.

. . .

More language.

"hang fire"—hanging on the towel rack while the house burns down.

"the hang of it" "hang out" in the interim during the war the wash on the clothesline, shirts and sheets froze.

"Handsome as all get out."

"Gosh all get out."

"Let's see you get out of this one."

"And now get out!"

Spic and span. The spics (for the "Porta-Rickans," not nice).

Also the human life span: they say it's getting longer every year. ("That makes sense," Big Jim says. "They keep inventing more work to be done.")

The passions that concern self-preservation turn mostly on pain and danger.

. . .

One night he decided to give a party on the middle floor—his fiefdom. He had crept out of bed, taking Andy with him, while the grownups' party beyond the kitchen was going strong—his mother at the piano, everybody singing—pushed the button on the wall, gone into the closet elevator and ridden downstairs to welcome his own guests on the floor between the floors. The Shmoo and all the Schmoon. Soon he was at the piano banging out show tunes too, while everybody was drinking cocktails and dancing up a storm. Next thing he knew he was waking up in his own bed, with Andy next to him (hung over?).

What had happened was the baby brother had jolted awake, crying, and David had gone in to check on him, found Author missing—as the Irishman said, there he was, gone—then found him in the closet and put him back to bed. Had the proprietor of the middle floor accidentally revealed his secret?

Analogues to his experience: Not yet to *L'enfant et les sortiléges* ("*Il est doux, il est bon.*" He is sweet, he is good) but definitely to "The Teddy Bear's Picnic." ("If you go down in the woods today, you're sure of a big surprise . . .") He wasn't going into any woods that day or any other; his great-grandfather had gone completely off his rocker in the woods in The Wilderness. They whose vocation it is to go into the woods do so, chop down trees and bring in the firewood for those snowy nights when he'd hear all about looking into the heart of an artichoke. They could get him on the annual school picnics which were to come to trek with them through the Nature Trail at Alley Pond Park, along which at a certain bend one could look through the wire fence across the Grand Central Parkway at Creedmoor.

Years later, at his official coming out at Cherry Grove on fabled Fire Island, "If you go into the woods today, down to the sunken forest— sunken that is beneath sea level and common decency both—the *people*! The *manners!*"

("There are undoubtedly rough edges, but I find the Hairy Bears Picnic far more congenial than the Old Trolls Turkey Trot at the Belvedere.")

. . .

Sputnik was a new object in the sky. Strangely, he had been sitting in the dark smoking Luckies right next to the extremely extravagant and beautiful sand castle their gang had been working on at low tide in the afternoon, watching the dark, rising tide, directed by the moon, drawing nigh, intent on the destruction of their Xanadu, when an old voice behind him declared, "Forget about the London blitz, dear, or Dresden or Hiroshima and Nagasaki for that matter. Courtesy of Alger Hiss and the Rosenbergs, those devils could pack enough shit into the next one of those they send up to wipe out New York, Chicago, Los Angeles and the District of Columbia—such a darling little town where the black folks know their place, and *soooo queer*—in one gay night."

Take two (Revision): He should feel sorry? He should get involved? With a fifth of gin and a bottle full of Darvon? He had better things to do, the apprentice, unseen, unacknowledged legislator, deeply immersed in his first attempts at serious writing in diary and commonplace book form (as if he had all the time in the world, which from the present viewpoint . . . although Cherry Grove with all the mouthy affluent amazing queers and their attendant funked-up boy losers, and an army of lesbians, butch and femme more formidable than anything dreamed up by Kleist in his masterpiece *Penthesilea*, augmented with a platoon of hapless but kicky fag hags, turned vicious when drunk, plus W. H. Auden, all swarming around Duffy's and the Sea Shack, was no common place, but one always full of rude with and shapely eloquence: ephemeral cartoon dialogue in hot air balloons, slipping from their grasp and floating out to sea ("because nobody remembers anything at the Grove").

("Duffy's Tavern. Duffy ain't here.")

Free association, use of by historian-memoirists with uncertain but compelling goals: The Age of Chaos (which has thoughtfully provided at the start its own theory).

FOUR

1

*P*ortal to the Sublime.

Four freedoms, four spacious skies, four years of age in Paradise, four clusters of days at the end of a dreadful four-year war that changed the world forever. In the early fall of 1945, right after the end of the war, his mother gave him the assignment of telling the story of what he had done that summer to Marian McSherry when she came to dinner. She would be bringing the stenography pad from her days as a secretary and write it down in Pitman shorthand. (Marian was no longer a secretary; she now worked for Schenley Industries in an office in the Empire State Building, the last building his grandfather had worked on. His grandfather had fallen off the scaffolding while building the Empire State Building and his leg was crushed, and the surgeon in the hospital replaced the crushed leg bone (connected to the O.K. thigh bone), with the bone of a sheep's leg. That was a miracle.)

Unlike people who could only afford to go to Rockaway and maybe rented a shanty there for a week or two and had to settle for Tillyou's *Playland*, fake, grotesque, suggestive, or several rungs above them, the owners of the gated community of Breezy Point, "the Irish Riviera," the McCourts and Mr. Moore in those years went out to Northport, beautiful former fishing village on Long Island's North Shore, for the entire summer. Author and his grandfather, his mother and the baby went out on the train; his father and brother David in the green Plymouth carrying the luggage.

His brother David showed him a map of the route from the City.

"You could do it on your tricycle if you wanted to. Here, I'll draw you a map from the house all the way there.

"Go straight up 94th Street on the sidewalks over Bellywop Hill to Northern Boulevard. Turn right, with the Manhattan Skyline at your back, and start peddling through Corona, Flushing, Bayside, Little Neck, across the city line into Great Neck, then through Manhasset and the Miracle Mile, then to Syosset, Oyster Bay, Cold Spring Harbor, Huntington, Greenlawn and finally at the old trolley crossing on 25A, Northport. Some stretches between towns don't have sidewalks, so the safe thing to do where the sidewalk stops, is to cross over to the northern side and keep going facing oncoming traffic, and watch out for the big trucks—one of those houses on wheels could squash you like a bug."

"Snug as a bug in a rug."

"Maybe later in bug heaven, but not right away—only after your bones and blood and guts, and your head squashed like a watermelon had been scooped up and put in a garbage pail and the emergency street cleaners made the road look presentable again and the traffic west was resumed.

"Sidewalks will turn up from time to time. At the old trolley crossing on 25A take a left and continue all the way down the hill—it's much steeper than Bellywop Hill—hold tight onto the handlebars, until you reach the harbor. Turn right down Woodbine Avenue all the way to Charlie and Flossie's.

"Pack a knapsack, so you can eat snacks on the way. Sleep well in from the road so the headlights don't wake you. It should take about two weeks. You'll make the front page of the *Northport Wipe* and maybe even the *Daily News*. Flo Mulligan's brother Arthur is a reporter on it and he may get a Sunday feature out of you. You'll find that you're in the rotogravure—how does that sound?"

"Like too much work."

"Something you were not cut out for."

"Mother says I do everything the hard way."

"So you'll take the train with the others, and stick your head out the window when the train goes round the bends so you can see the locomotive and get a cinder in your eye.

"Of course there are other ways to get on the front page of the *News* and the *Mirror*, and you don't have to work for it at all—just go murder somebody."

FOUR YEAR OLD GUNS DOWN ENTIRE FAMILY
AT DINNER TABLE

"They told me it was a cap pistol."

"Neighbors declare 'we've always thought of him as a polite little boy—funny eyes though—shifty, and an odd cast to them sometimes. At times he'd look at you in the oddest way, or look through you is maybe a better way to put it, as if you weren't there—or, it sounds funny, but as if *he* wasn't there. I don't mean *not all there*, not at all, but like he was somewhere far away—never mind over the rainbow or with the fairies, but like on Mars or someplace. They're saying it's a clear-cut case of insanity often found in geniuses. I feel so sorry for the parents or I would anyway, if he hadn't wiped them all out—all except for the older boy who they say has gone into seclusion with the father's people in the Bronx but visits the child every day over in Bellevue where he's under observation and kept in isolation, bringing a stuffed panda called Andy along with him for company.'"

"And I knew you'd be home late from school; I heard you telling mother."

("She was active in the parish, as you know.")

. . .

All the way on the train trip Author sat musing on trolleys—the journey to Maspeth, the trolley in the middle of the road, and all the cars had to stop while you stepped up and found a seat and then the driver would ring the bell and they were on their way again to Maspeth with a change at Woodhaven Boulevard, and the sight of Newtown High School towering over Elmhurst.

(He had come to understand there was some kind of stigma attached to going to Newtown High—to do with rough kids and as with all the public schools in the area—P.S. 149, P.S. 148 where they held the outdoor dances in summer—a last resort if you got expelled from Catholic school, and so an automatic ostracism of a sort. Idiotic, paranoiac Catholic propaganda—for most of the teachers were Jews.)

. . .

On the train on the way out, with the windows open because of the heat and cinders occasionally flying in so they had to be careful of their eyes, a big black woman a few seats up had apparently gone stark, raving mad and was being taken in a straitjacket by two attendants to the insane asylum in King's Park, the next stop after Northport ("King's Park, St. James, Stony Brook, Port Jefferson").

"Maybe she killed her whole family at dinner," Author said, "and got off on an insanity plea, committed for life in the insane asylum—better than getting the chair."

"Jimmy, please, as the Jewish people say, 'Relax yourself.'"

In later years he would come across hundreds of drunks and drug addicts mumbling incoherently, manic depressives sitting staring at the wall one time and another going great guns, but always connecting words and phrases in some coherent or semi-coherent pattern. It was not until the AIDS epidemic struck that he again heard people, many people, in the final stages of cytomegalovirus, stark, raving—what the Irish called "barking"—mad: disconnected phrases, fragments of memories, fantasies, visions of heaven, visions of hell.

. . .

Northport was made possible entirely by David's willingness to turn over the greater part of first his soda jerk and then his longshoreman's salary—considerable in itself—to finance the vacation home for his brothers and his grandfather. The parents went along with the deal, but he didn't do it for them, but to buy his own freedom from the whole set-up. To have for the first time in his life, for the two weeks in August in which his father went out to Northport to suffer the family himself, the run of 37-13 and the run of himself, of Jackson Heights and beyond—all of Broadway or Yankee Stadium for sixteen blissful days and nights. His brother missed him, but those were the breaks—sometimes the breaks broke your heart. The Northport train station was actually in East Northport, not a village so much as a small throw-together of shops and a couple of sneaky road houses with the distinctive look of small-scale Long Island honky-tonk. City people didn't spend their vacations in East Northport.

The taxi driver, driving from the train station in East Northport to Northport village, was expounding on local Northport history.

"The idea back then was to connect the station to Northport Village by trolley, but then 25A cut right across, and the hill down into the Village was so steep they'd have needed to put in a San Francisco cable car, so the line started at the top of Main Street and went straight down to the town dock. Then they had the bright idea of extending the line down Bayview Avenue past the bandstand to St. James Landing, but Charlie and Flossie Moore and the other residents wouldn't hear of it, and anyway the automobile took over, same as it did out in Los Angeles when they ripped up all the trolley tracks out there.

"So as not to leave their guests stranded at the station the dock, Charlie would send the two trucks down to pick them up with the kit and caboodle they brought down for the whole summer—in those days most folks stayed same as you do over the garage, but the war put a big dent into even modest lives of leisure. Before the war came, things hadn't changed much in Northport, not like what happened when the automobile came in and brought out all the city people, and the taxi business came to exist. In those days there was no call to drive over to Centerport—the Vanderbilts kept liveried chauffeurs waiting at the station, and you should've seen the looks we got from them when the first taxi fleets got organized. Of course in those days to turn a steering wheel without wearing soft leather gloves and a cap, but with your bare hands and bareheaded was considered—well, a city woman still won't get behind the wheel of an automobile without putting her gloves on. Of course the minute the war ends, the first thing Rosie the Riveter is going to do when she gets laid off is throw away her old work gloves and put on her new satin ones and paint the town red with some . . . returning service man, no introduction necessary. Well, it's a funny old world we saved for democracy—twice. Interesting to see what it's going to look like when they put it back together."

"My grandfather says New York will be a great city if they ever get it built."

"No doubt—I haven't been there since the World's Fair."

"I wasn't born then—Mother says I was in God's pocket and Dorothy O'Sullivan says I was but a gleam in my father's eye—which is why, since I got into the picture, there's no more gleam. He watches me all the time, but there's no gleam. Maybe he thinks I really would wipe out the whole family."

The boats at the town dock ranged from small motor craft to modest sailing vessels, but across the bay was anchored the Vanderbilt yacht. Dave Moore used to look across at it and say, "The Moores fitted out many a craft of that type, all sail, down in Philadelphia, oh, and it must be a century ago now."

By this time the cab had crossed 25A—which was the direct extension of Northern Boulevard, so Northport was really in a long bee-line from Jackson Heights and ran along the top ridge of the moraine to the four important roads, pathways to origination in the Northport experience: Scudder Avenue, Main Street, Bayview and Woodbine Avenues down to the apartment over the hotel carriage house, or rather the garage that used to be the carriage house.

"A baby carriage house?"

"No," said his grandfather, "a horse carriage house—before there were cars there used to be horse carriages and horses in the stable, don't-cha-know."

"Like in those pictures on the wall in your bedroom back in Jackson Heights?"

"That's right. Back in ought-seven when your mother was born, there were still horse carriages all over New York—just like the ones we saw there in Central Park."

Northport was a village right off a cover of the *Saturday Evening Post* as pictured by Norman Rockwell that in and of itself, to look at and walk around, could never lead to a sense of dismay—for him. Or maybe it was Mars, where they often said he'd come from, and maybe he'd come home.

His brother David for example pretty much hated it, too much bosom of too much family and dead as a doornail so far as things to do. He probably would have been relieved to have been later home from school the day of the big gun-down—and if there was a way to bust out of jail they could hop a freight together to California and now that the war would soon be over, lead an adventurous American life. David could work as a road-house bartender and he could put on shows.

Marcus O'Sullivan said that when Charlie and Flossie were younger Moore's Hotel had a certain North Shore glamour mixed with the aura of a waterfront saloon in a Eugene O'Neill play, right out of *Anna Christie*.

"It was before your time."

"Same as most things—not the war, though."

Main Street, Bayview Avenue, Woodbine Avenue, Scudder Avenue, St. James Landing. The broad oaks and chestnuts and the big sycamores, the beeches, the giant elms vs. the skyscrapers: two types of the sublime, greatly influenced by the difference between summer—his time—versus the three seasons, all school time, their time.

.   .   .

Summers and the ludic sublime. Playtime. Blissfully happy all day long, day in, day out, yet what is wonderful leads always to a sense of dismay— he was caught by surprise time and again—by fireflies in the dark, by low and intermittent sounds and shadows, or as in the moment sitting in the old Ford, right front door hanging open off the hinge, in Jo Normoyle's victory garden in Greenlawn—ducking in out of the sun so as not to burn to a crisp, his hands on the wheel, turning this way and that, ecstatic in the blazing light of July.

Then came the cloud and the rain and a terrifying story. Father Frank O'Pray had been an army chaplain recently relieved of duty on compassionate leave and sent back stateside for a rest. It seemed he had upon returning stood in the pulpit of St. Ignatius Loyola up on Park Avenue and preached a sermon in which he gave an eyewitness account of the liberation of the Nazi death camp Bergen-Belsen. Then after the dead silence that held for several minutes, his voice changed, his eyes filled with tears and he informed the congregation in no uncertain terms that the horrors of the camps just then coming to light constituted the ultimate manifestation of evil in our century and that however many Jews perished in the gas chambers, and whose bodies were burned in the giant ovens constructed by the Nazis (Author shuddered thinking of the Silvermans and their oven and the hot-cross buns they made for the parishioners of Blessed Sacrament parish at the beginning of Lent) they were the people who had suffered persecution for justice's sake, so that, according to the eighth beatitude of the Sermon on the Mount, theirs was the Kingdom of Heaven.

People were beginning to speak in terms of millions, that however many there had been, so many Jews, on that bright Sunday morning he was speaking to them, all arrayed in robes of glory, all gathered around the throne of God.

And the cardinal couldn't do a thing about it except recommend a summer's rest in the country.

. . .

Author's fourth birthday on the Fourth of July was fast approaching, the president had died and been replaced by a funny little guy called Harry. People started going around singing

Harry, Harry, this is my answer true
I'd be crazy to marry the likes of you.

There won't be any marriage
If you can't afford a carriage,
For I'll be damned if I'll be crammed
On a bicycle built for two.

He liked President Harry because they said he played the piano—
said he'd played piano in a St. Louis cat-house when he was starting out
but not what kind of a house that was—maybe a road house like the one
up on 25A where they teased his mother she could pull down a good
buck playing cocktail hour on weekends. There must have been lots of
cats there running up and down the piano keys.

On the radio H. V. Kaltenborn said the end of the war was in sight
and that it would be remembered as the most terrible war in the history
of mankind.

Gabriel Heater said, "There's good news tonight."

For Mark O'Sullivan there was a glamour to the moraine, glamour
being a word he'd never have used except when saying from time to time
that he married Dorothy because she was all woman, not some empty-
headed glamour puss out of a fashion magazine, or perhaps when speaking of a spell cast over the earth, it lay in the mystery of the moraine
why the ice Age had as they used to say ended in Mineola, ended exactly
when it had, and why had the ice begun to recede exactly from the ridge
of the moraine, exactly from 25A, millions of years ago? Obviously to
pave the way with sand and gravel for Charlie and Flossie's famous hotel.

The last Ice Age, and the next, as the glacier creeps back down, beginning a long period of winter carnival ending with everybody who hasn't
headed south—like the Jews in Miami in winter—frozen to death and a
new cycle beginning—that is unless the next meteorite strikes, in which
case to make a long story short . . .

"Tell the long story, we're here on vacation."

"You're a card Jimmy—the Jim of Diamonds."

Somebody was a card if they said funny things a lot. Marcus
O'Sullivan said he was a wild card. He wouldn't be called the Joker—the

Joker was Batman's mortal enemy, so Marcus started calling him the Jim of Diamonds.

"Marcus O'Sullivan is truly smart, but I don't think he's as smart as my father even if my father doesn't tell you much."

"That's quite a wise observation on your part."

"I'm pre . . . something."

"Precocious."

If the street leading down to Charlie and Flossie Moore's hotel has been called anything else but Woodbine Avenue, the connection between the word and the smell of honeysuckle would not have been made—also Woodbine was close enough to Woodside, the neighborhood adjacent to Jackson Heights, but also the same as the common name of the sweet flower, honeysuckle and therefore to the song "Honeysuckle Rose." As a result Author set about to learn as many names of flowers as he could—not necessarily matching them to the plants—many of the names were names of exotic orchids for instance which women wore as corsages, also camellias and gardenias—all heavy scents.

Whereas if a man put a carnation in his buttonhole, it looked stupid and smelled of nothing, and if he put a rose in, there was something very much the matter with him—although the paper rosette of the American Legion was admirable.

His favorite elm tree, the last one on the southwest corner of Elmhurst Avenue and 94th Street, had followed him to the Moore's Hotel in Northport because he will be getting just old enough to climb to the bottom branches, given a boost up by Keevey the gardener/handyman. But in time he preferred to sit under the sycamore and look over at the elm, thinking how lucky he was to be where he was and not on the streets of Jackson Heights.

. . .

"Why is it called a blue moon? It's white like it always is."

"It's an expression."

(Everything they couldn't explain was an expression—like the catbird seat. Every time Red Barber said it on the radio, he would ask what it meant and they'd tell him it was an expression. Despairing of a true answer, he never ventured to ask what a catbird was.)

"Eddie Midwinter knows what a blue moon means"—his friend Maggie Lewis told him; they had been on Broadway together in *Dark of the Moon.*

"Another expression."

"Not entirely—you've seen a night when there is no moon."

"I just thought the man in the moon was busy or something."

"Gone up to visit his grandmother and Aunt Lizzie in the Bronx."

Eddie Midwinter visits because Kitty Moore used to play for him on the Strand Roof along with Marie Kelly, Ruby Stevens and Hope Miner and because he was a friend of her beloved Uncle Jimmy O'Keefe who had first taken her to the Metropolitan Opera to hear Enrico Caruso and Rosa Ponselle in *La Forza del Destino.*

(*The circus*: make-believe—the tightrope walkers? If a tightrope walker missed the trapeze and fell and was killed, would that be make-believe? The clowns, yes, with the car, they were make-believe, but the menagerie and the freaks? Another world, a scary world, but make-believe?)

He told Andy in halting words that he knew they didn't believe in him—that they all said they did but they didn't—except for David; David did, and explained things to him in simple words (a little too simple sometimes if he was not to hide his word progress under a bushel).

"Whatever Andy says it's true"

"Well, I certainly wouldn't contradict Andy on any salient point— pandas are very wise creatures—and God has a special regard for their ancient Chinese patience."

"My brother David says Andy is a screwball—more of a screwball than Charlie Chan—but Andy's not Chinese, he comes from Rumplemeyer's."

. . .

Sunburn. The first time it had happened, his Aunt Betty had fallen asleep in the sun holding him and they both woke up with blisters, and he wound up at Doctor Jacobi's covered in plaster and bandages, being given strong pain killers and then kept indoors for two weeks, but it happened almost every summer and every time it did they would wrap his arms and legs in gauze soaked in witch hazel and make him sit under the sycamore tree for three days until first the pain and then the itch went away. He would read an Oz book and watch for the brief afternoon storms to come across the bay, fascinated by the fast approaching sheets of rain, and safe under the sycamore unless there was lightning, in which case sitting under a tree was the worst thing you could possibly do so you ran indoors. The Oz books were good, you could get the whole story with a little help and by looking at the pictures, but he hated being sedentary because it prevented him from moving around and hearing what they were saying about him, so he'd get up and go into the hotel kitchen.

"Hi Flossie."

"Hello, Jimmy, you coming to help peel some potatoes?"

"I'm too young to use a knife. My grandfather cuts my meat for me, except on weekends when my father does after he carves the roast. He always recites the same poem, 'Jack Sprat' something."

Jack Sprat could eat no fat
His wife could eat no lean,
And so it was between them both
They licked the platter clean.

"That's it."

"You could probably use the potato peeler—it works much better—but we'll leave that for another time."

"My brother David says I'm the only kid he knows could cut himself holding a pencil. Anyway I just wanted to ask you what's the latest—what are people saying about me? "

"I don't have time to listen, but I'm sure you could read it in Walter Winchell's column—he sends stringers out to the country in the summer."

"What's a stringer, is it like a string bean, like the strings on a fiddle? You say 'fiddlesticks' a lot, what are they?"

"You are the most inquisitive little boy I have ever known."

"Pain in the ass, you mean."

"Now you know when you talk like that, when you use bad words, they—"

"Beat me black and blue—you want to see the marks?"

"No I do not, and you know why; because there are no such things on you."

"Things that aren't so attract attention. So what's it like running a hotel—fun?"

"I don't know as I'd call it fun, but sure beats working in a factory making airplane parts. You get the same characters coming back year after year, only instead of coming here to the kitchen door, they waltz up the front steps proud as you please and half in the bag, asking for the bell hop and room service from the bar. I tell them they want to make the acquaintance of bell hops and room service boys they should paddle right over to the Vanderbilts'—only maybe they should try the servant's entrance to get the lay of the land first."

"Charlie says where you find all the stray cats is a mystery—he says you never leave Northport and people hardly ever hear you on the telephone. My mother says they must be like swallows, or homing pigeons."

"More like queer ducks—they're all my old suitors, didn't you know?"

"But they don't wear suits."

"Old beaux then—old boyfriends I once walked out with—and walked out on."

"You would never walk out on Charlie, would you?"

"Not likely—my you are full of beans today."

"Queer ducks can turn out to be swans. That's what Russell Crowley said in the rowboat—he rowed us across the harbor to the Vanderbilts'. He says they're friends of his, he plays polo with them and they have a better beach and so there was this old guy sitting in his bathrobe in a beach chair on the lawn, and the old guy talked to us for a long time. He was like Eddie Midwinter, in fact he said he knew who Eddie was—or had been. He said 'Eddie was great once upon a time but he's an old has-been now. Same as me,' and he laughed, like that was really funny."

Russell Crowley was a rough-edged boy who the older boys said referred to his teen boy penis as his "swizzle stick" and to his hanging testicles as "the boys downstairs," but never in the hearing of the younger kids, to whom he never made the slightest sexual reference (in spite of teasing them about their pissing contests, which at the time was not viewed as the harbinger of corruption, even by the Methodists and the Presbyterians, and you certainly never told it in confession) much less an inappropriate move, and in fact acted as their lifeguard when they went skinny-dipping in the "secret" cove up at Eaton's Neck. To his coevals, he solemnly declared that Jesus was right to say what he did about bringing scandal to his little ones, but that millstones were in short supply in those days and since they were up on the North Shore, miles and miles from the ocean, that men who "tampered" with kids should be shot and put in cement shoes (there was a plenty of cement around the building sites), and their bodies thrown into the Sound just like the big-city goombahs did with those who betrayed them in the East River.

"After the hike, you can skinny-dip all afternoon if you feel like it, and run around bare-ass naked—it's summer and it's healthy. You can air out your privates but they're still your privates. Anybody gets weird around you or tries any funny business—and some of those rich sons of bitches off the boats down at the dock have the best candy—you come to me."

"Jesus, Mary and Joseph, Jimmy," Flossie said later, "don't tell your mother you let that Russell Crowley row you all the way over there and back, or she'll have a fit. Didn't anybody tell you never to talk to strangers?"

(Even strangers who are friends of the Vanderbilts—*especially* strangers who say they are friends of the Vanderbilts and the Rockefellers and the Whitneys and their entire ilk?)

"In his bathrobe in the middle of the day—I suppose he calls it a *dressing gown* or a *lounging robe*, but I call it a bathrobe."

"Mother says when you wear it on the beach it's called a beach robe."

"Too hoity-toity for me."

"Jewish people say that—Molly Goldberg says it on the radio."

"And I'll tell you something else free of charge you won't get out of a box of Cracker Jacks. The bathrobe is the official uniform of the confirmed alcoholic."

"Russell Crowley isn't a stranger—he's not a child molester, either, I don't think."

"I don't know where you hear the things you say—except I do; the old queer ducks saying things that aren't so. Russell Crowley isn't a bad boy, but he's reckless—*never* get into that old jalopy of his, rumble seat or no rumble seat. Stick to your big brother, even if you have to wait for the weekend. Sit under the sycamore and read your books, or go with Butch and Marsha O'Sullivan to Crab Meadow. Dorothy will always pick you up in the four-door wreck she drives—no rumble seat though. And don't go getting any more poison ivy."

"My brother got confirmed when he was only a kid not much older than me, up in the Bronx. They all used to live up there. We go up to visit my grandmother. I hate my grandmother. The bishop slapped my brother's face—I think my grandmother would slap my face if she thought she could get away with it, but Aunt Lizzie wouldn't let her. I had colic when I was a baby—I kept them up all night. My mother says, 'I like your grandmother very much, she's feisty, but there's no question she can sometimes be a witch with a B.'"

"So what's an alcoholic? My father gives me rubbing alcohol back-rubs after my bath on Saturday night."

"An alcoholic is somebody who drinks too much—and not water or soda pop—in fact in some desperate cases, rubbing alcohol and mouth-wash and even after-shave lotion."

"Like the guy who was getting a back-rub and broke his neck trying to lick the rubbing alcohol off his back?"

"You should definitely sit under the sycamore and read your books, and keep away from those first floor hall windows right over that porch roof."

"Am I an al'cholic?"

"Well, you sure do like your beer, the little of it you're allowed to drink, but I don't see you on Skid Row just yet."

"They say but for you and Charlie, Eddie could have ended up on Skid Row."

"Never you mind about that. Do you wear your bathrobe all day long out on the lawn sitting under that tree?"

"No."

"Well, then you're not an alcoholic. But you shouldn't be going around all the time saying things that aren't so."

"Eddie's a good egg—a little scrambled though."

"I'll bet you a cookie I know where that snappy remark came from. You're a good comedian, you choose good material—some day you're going to be stiff competition for Jack Benny on the radio."

"A stiff is a dead guy, right?"

"Stiff is lots of different things. The Vanderbilts and the Whitneys and the Rockefellers and all their ilk are stiffs. The backbone of America, they call themselves. Well, it's a miracle we ever won the war if that's the backbone of America. Murderers, that's what they are, or at least their grandfathers were, plain murderers—not the Astors though, they made their fortune in furs and were originally good Jewish people."

"The murderers—did they get the chair, Flossie?"

"In a pig's eye. The rich never get what's coming to them, except for their inheritance."

"What's inherance?"

"Inheritance is what you get when your parents—Oh, never mind: scat now and let me peel these potatoes."

"Grampa says Rockefeller used to throw loads of dimes at people."

"Trying to buy his way into heaven on the cheap, like a typical Protestant."

"I know what Protestants are—they go to the white church across from St. Phillip Neri. Some people say they'll never get into heaven, but Father Frank says that's nonsense, although Martin Luther may still be in Purgatory along with Henry the Eighth whoever that is. Mr. Beesucker is a Protestant."

"Mr. Beesucker is a Christian gentleman, a good thrifty man of the Lutheran persuasion—now don't go around discussing it with that pal of yours, that Andy. Wait till your brother comes back on Friday night and talk to him about it. People overhear you talking to that panda."

"Fuck 'em."

"Jesus. Mary and Joseph, Jimmy—do you *want* to get your mouth washed out with Lifebuoy soap?"

"My father says Mr. Beesucker puts his thumb on the scale in the butcher shop—says you'd think by now he'd know what his thumb weighed."

"Your father is a fine, educated gentleman with a dry wit. Anyway it was only one of those Vanderbilts over there sunning himself, no doubt with a royal hangover. Those Vanderbilts all drink like fish, same as three quarters of the rich—"

"Sons of bitches?"

"All right, you got me—all the rich sons of bitches on the North Shore."

"Charlie calls the Astors the assholes, you know."

"Little pitchers have big ears, that's what I know. And the Astors go to Newport, in Rhode Island, across the Sound.

"Anyway, I like a good couple of drinks myself. I like my Singapore Slings and a few laughs and some songs with the happy crowd, especially with your mother at the piano, but I wouldn't give that hoity-toity crowd house room—they're all Masons."

"Masons like James Mason? My brother David likes James Mason."

"No, not like James Mason. The Masons are a secret society; they hate Catholics and desecrate the host during their mumbo-jumbo shenanigans—and they have nothing to do with the movies; Jews make all the movies, and Jews can't be Masons, they're barred along with Catholics. There are some good ones though—Masons. Mr. Truman is a good Mason."

"Then we should get Mr. Truman to put the bad ones in prison—or burn them at the stake—except they made a mistake burning St. Joan of Arc."

"The English burned Joan of Arc—they're always making mistakes, although you've got to hand it to them, they were very brave throughout the war.

"Anyway, no can do, the Masons are protected by society—they even have their own state, the State of Utah."

"I'm learning the states and making a map of them. The first thing you do is draw a wiggly line right down the middle for the Mississ–uh–"

"The Mississippi River—it runs smack dab down the middle of the country."

"My brother David showed me on the map—he says, 'Notice how it looks exactly like the part in your hair.'"

"I agree—now go sit someplace quiet—it must be time for your nap—or go and read your book. I've got to get dinner started. What book are you reading now?"

"*Lucky Bucky in Oz*. David's helping me with the dif'cult words; it's got a big whale. He's reading a book about a giant whale too—he's been at it forever—an enormous white whale."

"*Moby-Dick*, I suppose."

"Yes, that's the one. I asked him was it anything like *Pinocchio*, and he said no, it's a lot more thrilling. It sure is longer. He said he'd read some of it to me pretty soon, after I finish with *Lucky Bucky*."

"You've got a very good big brother—as they say in the army, he's got your back."

"Whatever that means, he's my hero. He's my hero and Andy is my confidence."

(In August would they be able to find Moby Dick on a whale watch out of Orient Point?)

"You know my baby brother was probably dropped in Mis'ra-cordia by the fairies pulling a switcheroo and the real kid, the one who looks like the rest of us, they took away."

"That's balderdash."

"Another expression—anyway last weekend we finished *The Tin Woodman of Oz*. He's my favorite character of all."

"Jack Haley."

"Who?"

"Jack Haley in the movie. Ray Bolger was the Scarecrow and Bert Lahr was the Cowardly Lion. And of course Judy Garland was Dorothy, and Margaret Hamilton was the wickedest wicked witch you ever saw, and dear Frank Morgan the most loveable Wizard. If they ever bring the picture back, make sure you catch it."

(That would be some kind of catching anyway: he couldn't catch a rubber ball to save his life.)

. . .

"What's up with that kid—somebody tell him he's the goddam Second Coming?"

"He's made quite a reputation for himself since the family started coming out here. "

"Half the time you can't figure out what he's up to, but whatever it is, he's got some crazy *plan* going and the brains to work it."

"Since he's always up to what he's up to by himself, that seems to make sense."

"But that's just it—is he? It looks like he is, but I have my doubts."

"Kids like that are good at leading invisible platoons."

"Charlie, you'll be givin' the kid ideas."

"That kid's not going to need my help getting ideas—would you say, Dave?"

"He just gets bored waiting for his big brother to come out on Friday."

"Right now he says he's sick of painting clamshells with water colors, and he's stomped on all of them—first I thought he was having one of his tantrums, but he put the pieces in a box and says he wants to make a color clamshell jigsaw puzzle. That's on rainy days. Today he wants to go and sit on the porch and look at the Florilegium from the Bronx Botanical Gardens and smell the honeysuckle on the honeysuckle bush. Or go down to the end of the jetty with his binoculars and look across at the old guy sitting on a lawn chair in his bathrobe."

"He spends the whole day yakking at that panda."

"All little boys talk to their teddy bears and their pandas—I've seen Andy, he has intelligent eyes; I'd talk to him—and don't ever call him Andy Pandy, 'Andy is not a *pansy!*' Eddie Midwinter's not a pansy either—my mother says so—that it's just mean gossipy. She calls him a 'soft man,' which means kind and gentle—and he used to be an important actor on Broadway and friends with the Lunts, whoever they were."

"The Lunts *are* still—probably the biggest stars on Broadway—it's Eddie who isn't any more. Eddie is a has-been."

"He told me—but he said, 'Better a has-been than a never-was.'"

"Can't argue with that. Anyway he's a funny kind of a kid. Kids like that, you expect to find them moping around, but not him. When he hasn't got his nose stuck in a book he's got his ears glued to the radio. 'I like the real world,' he said—which would be news to a lot of people around here."

"I asked him what his favorite show was—you know, expecting he'd say, *Uncle Don* or maybe *The Shadow*. You know what he said? *The Bickersons*. The Bickersons! And next after them, *Fibber McGee and Molly*. But he will admit that on the night *Batman's* on, *Batman* is his private favorite. Andy, he says, likes Jack Benny and Baby Snooks and the *Green Hornet*."

"*The Bickersons*. It's not so surprising when you think of it—he likes smart, sarcastic women."

"I gather you mean like Kitty."

. . .

He was sitting on the hotel's front porch in the company of Eddie Midwinter, retired Broadway actor.

"You seem like a happy young fellow—a regular Sunny Jim. I think when you wake up every morning and go into the bathroom to brush your teeth—"

"After I pee—I pee first."

"Yes of course—but when you do brush your teeth—"

"We only use Colgate—Ipana is disgusting, it tastes like soap."

"And comb your hair—once in a while."

"My mother says it looks like I comb it with an egg beater, but it's O.K."

"Well, then, let's you and I drive into the village for a hot fudge sundae. In for a penny, in for a pound, as our cousins across the waters will say, so let tongues wag themselves ragged. And the truth is a hot fudge sundae does ever more than Milton can to justify God's ways to man—and boy."

"Milton makes a great hot fudge sundae back home in Jackson Heights."

"Wouldn't he."

"Sometimes Milton makes them and sometimes Leon does."

"It is the way of the world—put your shoes on."

"Okay."

"That was a lovely show, *Oh, Kay!* Starred Gertie Lawrence.

"In any case when you look in the mirror there he is grinning back at you—Sunny Jim—ready to get up to some new mischief. You really like it here I think—but all the same I think you like the honky-tonk of Rockaway Beach."

"My mother says it's so peaceful here it would be a great place to spend the last three days of your life."

"There's that."

"Sometimes in my dreams I float up to the ceiling and look down at me sleeping."

"That's you keeping your guardian angel company; it's a lonely job looking after a sleeping boy."

"My brother David says I talk in my sleep."

"Well, that would make their job less difficult—it's very considerate of you."

"My mother walks around talking to herself—she always says she's thinking out loud. My brother David says next stop Creedmoor—but there's no station there, I asked my grandfather."

"I didn't know David was a head shrinker."

"Cannibals have shrunken heads—plus they eat one another. Anyway, Eddie, what's a mart'net?"

"A martinet is a gentleman—or nowadays a lady—who likes to drink martinis."

"Really?"

"It'll do."

"They said martinets have bloomers."

"I think that was probably 'plumage.'"

"What's that?"

"Plumage? Plumage is feathers—from the French *la plume*—which also means a pen."

"Feather pens—I've seen them in kid's books. And what's *callamy*—is it like calamity—sounds like."

"*Calammy?*"

"Somebody said don't go spreading calammies."

"I think you mean calumny—I think that's what you heard—they were talking about me, weren't they?"

"Um . . ."

"Oh, it doesn't matter really: people who are the least bit different are subject to it—scurrilous obloquies, flouts and calumnies of the stripe broadcast by Winchell and Cholly Knickerbocker to name but two—sniffing the ground beneath great oaks like truffle pigs, in search of peccadillos. People who never got around much, not back when or ever after, will go on sitting in rocking chairs on boarding house porches summer after summer until the end of time, looking out at well-mown lawns as if they were Homer's gods perched on mountain crags surveying the wine-dark sea. One gets used to it in a way, although equanimity can hardly be said to arrive. Some though are more wounded by calumny than by death. Whoever said that sticks and stones may break his bones, but names can never harm him, simply had no knowledge of the world. Nevertheless, what can't be cured must be endured—and contrary to popular fancy, age adds little wisdom to its creaking, overburdened hoard of knowledge."

"Is callamy a mortal sin?"

"St. Jerome thought so, if it is the cause of somebody's death, such as committing perjury as a witness in a murder trial. In general though it's more like what St. Thomas Aquinas says about getting drunk: it lessens the fervor of charity."

"If I murdered my little brother, they wouldn't put me on trial because I'm only a kid—but it would be a mortal sin against charity."

"Your brother is a lovely child, a quiet child for now."

"I still don't get what calumny is."

"Calumny is usually the result of false pride, thinking one is so much better than other people, and pride goeth before the fall."

"And summer too."

"You're a clever fellow, they are alike, pride and summer."

"But summer isn't a sin."

"Only in a certain sense—of betrayal. Come now, put a shape on you. And we're off."

(Eddie said the funniest things; did Author have a shape already—wasn't he in good shape for a kid, even one with strange fears that often crept up on him on sunny summer days? Summer wasn't a sin, even with the heat that everybody calls hot as hell, and the sunburns if you don't have the sense to keep out of the sun, which he didn't, but since he started using Coppertone his brother said he turned brown as a nut, which made sense because he was a nut case. David could kid him like that and he wouldn't feel afraid.) As they were eating their hot fudge sundaes, Eddie Midwinter told Author about Puck, a boy about his size and age who serves Oberon, the King of the Fairies—already Author was suspicious: on the one hand "fairy" is a term of insult, but on the other hand, although he has been supposedly visited by the tooth fairy and has heard Irish people talk about the fairies, the Little People, the Good People, The Other Crowd, and their mischievous ways, stealing babies and leaving a fairy child as a "changeling" (this particularly fascinated him), all these things happen, if they happen at all, in Ireland, and not anywhere in America. In America children are kidnapped and held for ransom and often found murdered like the Lindbergh baby back in the '30s. Then there is the threat "I'll give you back to the Indians."

Flypaper and the omnipresence of death ("Little fly upon the wall . . ."). Eddie Midwinter went on to tell Author the fantastical story of *A Midsummer Night's Dream*, the Shakespeare play that Puck appears in, while his image is of the cartoon of Puck on the front page of the Sunday *Journal-American* looking down at the comics page and saying, "What fools these mortals be." Author has also seen this Puck character on a building in Manhattan his grandfather has shown him, the Puck Building—so this Puck whoever he is, and he's not real, must be somehow some kind of big shot to have a building named after him when every other tall building in Manhattan that has a name has the name of a real person or a company, like Woolworth or Singer or Chrysler or the *New York Times* on Times Square, or of something bigger even, like Carnegie Hall, the Chrysler Building and the Empire State Building. And Eddie Midwinter said Author is like Puck—he's "puckish," then told him about Puck Fair in a town in County Kerry, Ireland, where once a year in summer they crown a goat.

. . .

When he'd stay in the water too long and come out with a sunburn, never as serious a one as that first time with his godmother, Aunt Betty, he was always made to put on Coppertone or (more interesting to him) Dorothy O'Sullivan's mixture of iodine and baby oil that really did turn his pale skin almost chestnut brown over his body except on the underside of his arms and when he took his red, white and blue trunks off, his "privates" and his backside, as white as Tommy Gallagher's on that afternoon in the Gallaghers' back yard, leaning against the cellar door. He really was a Yankee Doodle Dandy, especially after they all went into the village to the school supplies department of the five and dime, bought a box of silver stars of the kind the teachers used when they turned in more than satisfactory (red star), but not yet excellent (gold star) work at school and stuck them all over his trunks. He was happy to show Butch and Marsha O'Sullivan the dramatic contrast between his nut brown parts and his white ones, and for some reason Russell Crowley also when they all piled into Russell's jalopy (in the rumble seat) and drove up to the "secret cove" at Eaton's Neck to go skinny-dipping (Russell's sixteen-year-old athletic boy privates another story—happily not one of "tampering," and not really a "story" in the sense of telling one, but the expression meaning thing, or instance, or example or fact-of-life).

But not his brother David, because in front of him when it came to taking his clothes off, now that he was allowed to take his baths alone, he was profoundly shy, and the last thing he would ever have shared with him was funny business that made his little boy dick stand up and practically sing "The Boogie-Woogie Bugle Boy of Company B."

"I don't want females looking at my privates," he told the O'Sullivan kids, although as a tomboy Marsha didn't count, which made her proud—"and that means my mother and Doctor Virginia or anybody else. I'm housebroken. And I don't take baths with anybody, except once in a while with the tadpole: he gets a kick out of the Alka-Seltzer speedboat." (And the Lifebuoy soap "lighthouse game," but that was instinctively unspoken.)

Catching fireflies ("lightning bugs") in glass jars—always perforate the tops to give the fireflies air. Was a glowworm the same as a firefly? No. Fireflies did not hatch out of glowworms the way butterflies hatched out of caterpillars.

"The caterpillars of the Church?"

"*What?*"

"The Caterpillars of the church." (He giggled.)

"So saying, he plunged to his death," his brother David would say whenever he'd come out with one of those quips, turned on his heel and sauntered away or as they were to say many years later on the opera line, "*E se n'andava.*"

2

"Pistol Packin' Momma," sung by the chorus in the bar while Author dances around in his cowboy outfit, bought for him at the rodeo in Madison Square Garden. "Handles his weapon with an easy competence, implying a long familiarity with cap pistols."

Jackie Carmody, Mary's son (his father Ted played trumpet at the Roxy), about the same age as David, lived up on Prospect Place at the top of the hill that ran down to 25A. (There was a bellywop hill if he could only get out to Northport in winter, to a house his mother sometimes visited with which Author fell in love.) Johnny Zilch palled around mostly with Russell Crowley, who drove his old jalopy up and down Main Street with no muffler on the exhaust pipe so it sounded like a B-29.

A few years later in Jackson Heights he got Johnny Zilch to sneak him into a Mae West picture, *She Done Him Wrong*, in which Mae West, all dressed up in her Gay Nineties finery, sang "Frankie and Johnny were lovers . . ."

Although Frankie Galliani and Johnny Zilch lived directly opposite one another on 94th Street, they were never seen together (maybe because Johnny was a Protestant). Anyway Frankie was into sports and Johnny was into the Egyptians and the Greeks and the Romans and astronomy and the Facts of Life which he knew cold, and was not only a Protestant but a Lutheran: Martin Luther was the most prominent villain in the Protestant lineup, worse by far than Henry VIII, because he had been an Augustinian monk and therefore a major "prostate."

"That's apostate."

"Father Leonard had a major apostate operation, I heard you telling Mrs. Uptheblock on the phone."

"That was a prostate operation—and stop listening to me on the phone."

"Okay, promise, cross my heart, but you say the same things on the phone that you say when you're thinking out loud."

The nuns said that when Martin Luther nailed his famous theses to the door of the church it was as if Jesus Christ was being nailed to the door as well, crucified a second time. Hence no Bach in church, except for the Bach/Gounod "Ave Maria," which somehow got snuck in, but only Palestrina (which in strictly musical terms was not really a comedown, in spite of Bach's being a universal musical genius and Palestrina being essentially an opera composer for Catholic ritual).

Johnny Zilch also had a circle of admirers, Author included, and for a time, kept a praying mantis in a little cage made out of matchsticks—he said the Japanese did the same with crickets which they considered lucky, not that any crickets like Jiminy Cricket in *Pinnochio* had been much use to them in the war.

There were certainly enough of them on our side, you could hear them making a racket all summer long at night—according to Johnny by rubbing their legs together and fucking.

Anyway Frankie Galliani palled around with a guy called Tommy Carbone—Tommy, not Johnny. Frankie and Tommy were boyfriends. In fact there were very few Johnnies in the neighborhood—all the Johnnies were obviously driving cabs in the City.

. . .

His mother said about something, "I wouldn't . . . in a fit."

Memory of the girl having a fit (a grand mal seizure at Mass in Blessed Sacrament).

There were other fits—rage, pique, of dresses, of suits, of shoes, of the kid brother into Author's hand-me-downs; "fit company" (Eddie Midwinter for him)?

On his fourth birthday—Jimmy's fourth Fourth—he is given his grandfather's diamond stickpin to wear on his polo shirt for the day.

"Diamond Jim" (the ironworker with the diamond stickpin and the pearl formal shirt studs who sent his daughter to convent school on the danger money he made high in the sky over the streets of Manhattan). Thus all the chatter on such a festive occasion—fireworks that night over the town dock and a big clambake on the beach about Diamond Jim Brady and all the flashy Jimmys in the public eye—Jimmy Walker, Jimmy Cagney, James Thurber (little garden slug at the Algonquin Round Table), Big Jim McCourt, the gent on the waterfront, Jimmy Dorsey. There were more U.S. presidents called James than any other name: Madison, Monroe, Polk, Buchanan and Garfield.

"Wouldn't you like to be president one fine day, Jimmy?"

"No thanks."

"Why not?"

"You have to go and live in Washington—no skyscrapers."

"Jimmy is a New Yorker, dyed in the wool."

"Wool is in the winter, it's cotton in summer."

"Sunny Jim doesn't complain about conditions."

"Not even the rain."

"I like the rain—my mother says I was born in the rain."

So instead of complaining he set about setting things to rights, he lets them be; he knows the score. He knows that if he kills his little brother to set things to rights, he'll get the chair, the hot seat.

He quoted the score from the Yankee two-night doubleheader of the day before. Then at noon, when the whistle in the firehouse went off, he checked the watch for accuracy. They were by then up at the top of Main Street for the start of the big parade down to the dock, turning right down Bayview Avenue and then let into the town park and the bandstand, the older kids chanting "Oh the monkey wrapped his tail around the flagpole, so he could see his little asshole," and getting away with it under the patriotic blare of the Northport High School marching band playing John Philip Sousa's "Stars and Stripes Forever."

Father Frank O'Pray, a former army chaplain just back from Germany and in somewhat rocky shape, was visiting in Northport, staying at the rectory of St. Phillip Neri and saying daily Mass, which Author and his mother attended. Father Frank was of course a great hero to the boy just turned four (and liberated from naptime as France had been from the Nazis the year before). When he hears Father Frank was at the liberation of Buchenwald, he almost mentions that he's there now at his own liberation, but knows enough not to, that it would be a stupid goof, because Buchenwald was a Nazi death camp, his grandfather having already told him what they were, and that the Nazis would have put Molly Goldberg and Fanny Brice and Jack Benny in one of them if they could have captured them, so just says he's four that day and won't be going in for a nap. Father Frank says these days he's more than glad of a nap: "*Somne quietis rerum, placidissime somne deorum pax animi,*" O sleep, repose of all things, sleep, gentlest of the gods, peace of mind, then waking with terrible dreams rectified.

"I don't have those."

"I'll bet not—you live in a happy family; all happy families are alike."

"The O'Flahertys downstairs are like us, so they must be happy— they own the house. Not the Harrigans next store though: you should hear that fishwife whine."

"*Legis plenitudo caritas*, Jimmy. Justice lies in wealth of charity."

"I'll be learning Latin when I become an altar boy and get the use of reason."

"How do we know Christ spoke Latin? Picked it up in his travels? It's possible. After that 'Render unto Caesar' quip, the Romans started keeping an eye on him. Pontius Pilate thought he was a real wiseacre like all the Jews, but he liked a good laugh, and the palace guards' humor bored him, and the wife wouldn't tolerate it at all."

"He probably learned it from the Jesuits, same as my father."

"Jimmy is a happy boy, but he worries," said his grandfather.

"'*Nada te tube, nada te espante. Quien a Dios tiene, nada le falta,*' nothing disturbs you, nothing frightens you, if you have God, you'll want for nothing." Father O'Pray said. "That's Saint Teresa of Ávila."

"That's Spanish, isn't it? It sounds like that Mexican guy on Jack Benny, you know, who has a sister Sue and she sews and then Jack Benny says, 'she sews?' and the Mexican guy says, '*Sí.*'"

"Father works with Spanish speaking people up in Spanish Harlem."

"Harlem is jigaboo country."

"Not on the East Side," his grandfather corrected. "On the East Side it's all Puerto Rican—and what have you been told about words like 'jigaboo?'"

"Sorry. Charlie says 'Porta-Rickan.' My brother's going to take Spanish Spanish at Manhattan Prep."

"Someday in New York Spanish will be spoken as much as English—it'll be like it is in Montreal."

"But why do they speak Spanish in Montreal? Isn't Montreal French Canada?"

"They don't—I was giving an example by allusion."

"Illusions aren't real, right?"

"I wouldn't take him on if I were you Father, he can go on like this until you need another nap—a long one."

"My mother calls Saint Teresa of Ávila Big Teresa, because she's a big shot, not like the Little Flower."

"Strictly speaking, all saints are alike in importance."

"Anyway, they're both Caramelites—Caramelites are more important than Domicans, the Amityville crowd, my mother calls them. The Spark Hill Domicans are better though. The Caramel come from Our Lady of Mount Caramel. They have a novena every year in the Caramelite Church in the City. My parents made a mistake leaving the City—but we get by with lots of excursions in to see important things like Bear Mountain and Ashokan Reservoir.

"Anyway I'm not a Caramelite, I'm a Franciscan. My middle name is Francis after St. Francis of Assisi and St. Francis was *not* a sissy! He was mild mannered like Clark Kent, who is really Superman."

Changing the subject, somebody suggests they plan on going on the August Whale Watch sailing from Orient Point to Nantucket. Author is excited and wants them to promise he can go.

"So you can get swallowed up by Mostro the whale like Pinocchio and light a fire in his belly to make him sneeze you out? You're a little too fond of fire as it is."

"Because of the firemen—they're all brave volunteers."

"And speaking of Pinocchio, that nose of yours has been growing at an alarming rate this summer."

Anyway Father "O'Pray" was a funny name for a priest, but real neat.

. . .

The clambake at sundown, the singing of patriotic songs and show tunes (the new "clambake" song from the musical *Carousel*). Finally, the red, white and blue, stars-and-striped birthday cake Flossie had baked was brought out: the celebrant easily blew out all four candles.

The big kids, his brother and Russell Crowley's gang, sang the song about Casey and the band playing on, but some drunks sang the dirty version—"Got hit with a bucket of shit," "Married the runt with the strawberry cunt"—and were thrown out—eighty-sixed Flossie said, like the Street in Yorkville with the stop on the Third Avenue El.

"Don't you see there's a four-year-old kid here, trying to enjoy his birthday party?"

"You're makin' a mistake, Flossie. He could've learned the lyrics in fifteen minutes and gotten enough attention to last him the summer—maybe."

Then later inside, with his mother at the piano, they sang "Danny Boy," "Galway Bay," "I'll Take You Home Again, Kathleen," "The Rose of Tralee," Tom Moore ballads and Victor Herbert operetta songs (Kitty insisting on some quality material), Balfe's "I Dreamt I Dwelt in Marble Halls" (from *The Bohemian Girl*), "The Wild Colonial Boy," "The Fields of Athenry." Then in honor of Dublin, where the Moores had originated, "Molly Malone."

She wheeled her wheel barrow through streets broad and narrow
Crying "cockles and mussels, alive, alive-oh."

"Cockles and mussels—ah now that'd warm the cockles of your heart."

Listening to his mother sing "I Dreamt I Dwelt in Marble Halls," which he'd never heard before and which enchanted him, he was stricken by something like his visions at the title of *The Bohemian Girl*. So Eddie Midwinter, a guest, told him the opera's plot. Also explained the phrase, "the cockles of my heart."

The boy was interested in the latter, but harped on the former, until Eddie Midwinter explained Bohemia and the derivation of the idea of artistic bohemians both from the fact that when Rudolph was the Holy Roman Emperor, Prague had been a center of alchemy and magic and that many gypsies had once come from that country until they were driven out of Hungary—to Transylvania and Dracula's realm, with the Infant of Prague—they had a statue of him at home in Jackson Heights, which they dressed in many different colors—bright red, bright green, shining white and bright purple, according to the liturgical seasons.

. . .

"Charlie, what does 'iota' mean?"

"Like 'I owed her a dime?'"

"No—io-*ta*."

"Iota? Iota is a state out west with nothing in it but farms—no cities at all. The corn is as high as an elephant's eye and the waving wheat can sure smell sweet when the wind comes right behind the rain—except for the tornadoes, the twisters. They have twisters there, just like in Kansas, like in *The Wizard of Oz*."

He walked away looking suspicious, wary; he'd been made fun of.

"You shouldn't be doing that to the kid, he asked an honest, straightforward question."

"Should I fear reprisals?"

"Not right away, not just now, not this summer, but as he gets older better watch your back—he'll be out to get his own back one fine day."

"By which time I'll be good and dead."

"That won't stop him."

What did that mean? One man said David has his back, but *he* has his back, his own back—and shoulders too, and the sunburns to prove it. And how could anybody watch his own back? Then he remembered the fitting room at Weber and Heilbroner's down on Wall Street where his father had taken him to look at the grownup men's clothes he so much wanted to wear—long pants and suit jackets and ties and fedora hats. He stood watching his father being measured by the guy with the tape measure (and asked a question that made no sense, but his father answered it, which made no sense either).

"What side do you wear yourself on, sir, right or left?"

"The left."

Nearly forty years later at their father's funeral when he told his brother David the story, David said, "That's got to have been the only thing that was left about him."

But what with the slanting mirrors he could indeed watch his back—however you couldn't carry a bunch of mirrors around with you all the time, now could you.

To run free
to gulp the breeze,
to bite the grass,
to fall from trees,
to be impressed
with little money,
to laugh because
there's nothing funny,
to spend hours
throwing stones,
to know nothing
about bones,
to work magic

with knives and strings,
to eat strange
sickening things
to be proud
of mere strength,
to keep elders
at arms' length,
to disobey
from sheer joy—
such are the duties
of a boy.
         —John Rand Weaver

"Sweet—I'll buy it all except being impressed with little money."

. . .

That night before bed: watching Donald Duck's hands go around the dial—like all children with a new watch he couldn't stop looking at it, when his brother David came in.

"People who can't stop looking at their watches end up in Creedmoor."

"Or King's Park—like people who can't stop being afraid of the dark."

"We've already agreed on that issue, agreed that there's nothing to be afraid of.

"'There is nothing to fear but fear itself.' FDR."

"I'm watching Donald's hands move."

"That's not why it's called a watch."

"He's giving important sema . . . something."

"Semaphore signals?"

"Yes—to the imaginary boats on the cardboard sea—"

"Ships, not boats—you know how Pop feels about people who should know better calling a ship a boat."

"Yes—those aren't boats down on the waterfront that people take over to Europe and have big champagne parties on before sailing with the tugboats blowing their whistles like crazy tugging them all the way down to the Narrows—"

"That's *towing*, not tugging."

"Then what I say is they should be called 'tow boats'—and the Norman-d-da that . . ."

"The *Normandie*."

"Yes—that the sabotages burned at the pier—"

"That's *saboteurs*—and what they do is *sabotage* and that comes from the days of the French Revolution where saboteurs wore wooden shoes called *sabots*."

"Like the Dutch do?"

"Same idea—only they were called *sabots* in French and because the saboteurs used to go around kicking and smashing things—"

"You told me Scarlet Pimple guy was an English spy in the French Revolution, but he never wore wooden shoes—he dressed up in fancy clothes."

"The Scarlet Pim-per-nell—I pronounced it for you the last time, remember?"

"'Don't eat meat on Fridays.' He's Catholic, and the French relutions are trying to destroy the Church and send all the priests and nuns and nuns to the Gilly–um–"

"*Guillotine.* G as in God, Y as in only, O as in oh boy, teen as in Ovaltine."

"Or like Russell Crowley. I asked him about the pimples on his face and he said all teenagers get them. You don't have any pimples like Russell or the other guys in the village."

"Knock on wood—*kinna hurra*."

"What's *kinna hurra*?"

"Same thing—but stronger; Mrs. Goldberg up on Weeks Avenue way before you were born used to say it."

"Anyway ships drop anchor and dock at piers, boats dock at docks—sailboats especially. A hundred years ago ships used to have enormous sails but then they changed to steam engines and men had to go down and keep the furnace burning coal all the time and hardly ever saw the light of day on the long voyage home, and Grampa says the family business which was ships' chan–something—"

"Chandlers."

"Chandlers, because chandel was an old word for candle you said and that's why they're called chandeliers because there used to be hundreds of candles stuck on them. There were no electric lights anywhere, they hadn't been invented yet by Thomas Edison, only whale oil lamps and the sailors used candles to write home by and read books by and The Bible and everything. And the business was in Philadelphia which also had a thry–thry–"

"Thriving."

"Yes, big shot waterfront. But nobody uses candles these days—Pop says there's not the call for them that there was—except in church on the altar and in front of statues of the Blessed Mother and the Sacred Heart and the Infant of Prague and St. Jude, the patron saint of impossible causes, to pray for the boys overseas, like the O'Flaherty boys downstairs. Ships don't use candles these days except in fancy dining rooms and that's not enough to keep a ship's chandler in business, so the Moores went belly-up, *kaput.*"

Also to put into pumpkins—candles—to make jack-o'-lanterns once all the pumpkin stuff had been dug out to make pumpkin pies and faces carved in the empty pumpkins so to look like Jack Pumpkinhead in the Oz books. And Flossie Moore said people like the Vanderbilts across the harbor, when they sat down to dinner with God only knew how many hundred people sitting at a table a city block long were always going in and out of rooms to turn out the lights, because they were so cheap and hated to burn electricity from the new LILCO installation in Northport, and couldn't wait for big storms to knock out the power lines so they could use their hurricane lamps—a more flattering light for old bags to be seen in, she said.

"Grampa says two things about dinner. 'If you can't eat it, don't put it on the table and 'I like to see what I'm eating.' And the Irish."

"The Irish—what about them?"

"They go chasing after moonbeams and light their penny candles from the stars—Orion and the Big Dipper stars and the morning star and the evening star which Grampa says are both the same star but isn't a star, but the planet Venus, our nearest neighbor in the solar system. But Eddie Midwinter says that's all crap about the Irish, seminal crap—"

"Sentimental—and you've got that song all twisted around, but that's all right."

"Grampa says I twist things around to suit myself. Yes, and that the fighting Irish are not the football team out at Notre Dame, but the Irish Publican Army, who are like the rebels who burned down the Wilderness."

"Burned out—you burn down a building, you burn out a forest— and it's Republican, not publican. A publican is a barkeep in Ireland."

"What's a barkeep?"

"A fellow who runs a bar—and a bartender is called a curate."

"So anyway they went out of business down in Philadelphia and Grampa's father Matthew—but this is where you came in, right?"

And his brother David said, "Watching Donald's hands is not why watches are called watches—but there is a definite connection with ships—the watch of the night—and stars, because ships used to navigate by the stars. The Northern Star in particular until they went below the Equator and then the Southern Cross took over. Remember I told you that's where they found Moby Dick the great white whale, in the South Pacific, below the Equator."

"Where the war is. And Ignatz escaped alone to tell us."

"Ishmael—but also on land, the Watchman of the Night and today in office buildings and offices where the night watchman makes his rounds."

"Tomorrow I get to play with my other birthday present, the yellow tractor Grampa gave me. I'm going to dig a ditch."

"That's excavate."

"To put in a foundation. How do you make concrete, anyway?"

"With sand and gravel and water."

"If I can get a concrete mixer—maybe the electric mixing bowl—and I'm going to get started early, and it's probably going to be pretty noisy, so I hope nobody has a Bromo-Seltzer hangover. The lightning bugs are just getting started out there."

"I'll bring you one in a jar."

"O.K.—only don't forget to poke a hole in the top."

"I wasn't born yesterday."

"Me too—I'm four; that's a big deal."

"One for the books—and I'm fourteen. Next month Pop's going to be forty, and in December Grampa's going to be seventy."

"Then dead. You know they'll be keeping me awake anyway singing songs in the hotel bar. You know what I heard today at the parade? Some guy dressed up like George Washington singing the one about the beautiful four spacious skies. What four? I only see one."

"That's because you haven't been anywhere yet."

"Northport's somewhere, isn't it?"

"A matter of opinion. Two schools of thought. Anyway, you're looking up at the Eastern sky. There is a Southern sky, a northern sky and a Western sky; that's four."

"Grampa says you never know what people will do. Remember his story of the crazy man who bashed the little girl's brains out on the sidewalk with her own skate?"

"Which is exactly why you need your rest to keep on your toes. Now blow taps, bugle boy, and lights out."

"I'm with my own?"

"You're with your own."

He lay there in the darkened room talking to the panda, the smell of the citronella candles to ward off mosquitos rising up from the holiday celebrants below. With the singing in the background over at the hotel,

he could hear them talking about him right underneath the window—
the things he could overhear people saying about him, and the vastly
greater number of things either he couldn't hear or they weren't saying
were all occurring to him.

"He pestered everybody on blue moon and nobody knew, until he
asked Eddie Midwinter who told him and everybody else sitting at the
table."

"It was fascinating—I never heard the explanation and it had never
in my life occurred to me to ask. Trust an actor to know the elaborate
answer and quote chapter and verse in Anglo-Saxon yet and summing
up by saying blue moon stood for rare instance and that was that. Perfect timing."

"He's apt to get pretty confused, the poor kid, and scared by the
strangest thing. For instance, you know how a lot of kids go through that
phase of not stepping on the cracks in the sidewalk—Well, if you tell
this kid there are places, whole towns, where the sidewalks are red brick,
he'll look at you as if you're crazy, but also with a really frightened look
in his eyes. 'Houses are made of brick,' he'll say—'some houses, not ours.
Apartment houses—but sidewalks are made of concrete.' Then if you say
the Big Bad Wolf can huff and puff and blow a brick house down, but
he can huff and puff until Doomsday and not disturb a brick sidewalk,
he'll ask you 'What's Doomsday?' The fact that he doesn't know what
Doomsday is obviously in his mind makes everything you tell him about
brick sidewalks a lie."

"Ever think of the fact that there are too many cracks in a brick
sidewalk not to step over? Could be that. Anyway, you know how he
is with his words and printing them in those big letters. The kid can
really read—phonics, Kitty says, she teaches him by phonics. So first
his grandfather tells him bust is the opposite of boom—the '20s were
boom, the '30s were bust, and after the war's over it'll be boom again—
a big one like after the last war. Then he hears somebody say, 'Somethin'
I trusted done rusted and busted,' and 'Don't bust a gut over it for God's

sake,' and then everybody is going around singing 'June is bustin' out all over' in the bar, but since it's now July he doesn't see how that's worth singing about. Then there's the boomerang which his brother says if he throws it out across the water, it'll come back and hit him in the head with maybe a Vanderbilt head stuck on it."

"Ginger Crowley said Kathryn Grayson has the biggest bust in Hollywood. . . . Well, he would've forgotten all about it if Ginger hadn't thrown in the D cup. That got him going again, but his brother said D stood for Dixie cup, so it turns out Kathryn Grayson is walking around Hollywood wearing big Dixie cups. Big Jim says he doesn't know how phonics can clarify that one."

"And remember, this is a kid who *likes Spam.*"

3

$2003.$ *Moriarty here.* It was just last night in Dreamland that he was riding with his brother on the carousel, but they were rising and dropping on their horses in syncopated seesaw fashion so that each missed snatches of the other's voice, a difficulty made worse by the steam calliope playing "Stars and Stripes Forever."

"So where were we?"

"The building blocks incident—you've forgotten."

"Tell me again then; I've got to remember these things to write this book."

"Psychoanalysis . . . the past beyond the limit of the previous . . . living in the strictly non-existent now . . . as such things always have."

"*Credo quia absurdum est,* I believe because it is impossible."

"Absotively posilutely."

"Accent on the wrong sy-*lla*-ble."

"It's not possible I could have understood what I was saying—"

"Much of the time, but just as often you did—in outline, in concept."

"The ships' chandlers discussion."

"Practically word for word."

The horses were suddenly going up and down in perfect unison.

"And two years later, in that last summer in Northport you were completely fluent."

"Fluent and very sad—they go together."

"Summertime, when the livin' is easy—I never saw a fish jumping— but there are flying fish."

"On the road to Mandalay. They can't play in the road for too long, though, and the road must be the kind of one that runs right alongside the water, the kind that floods at high tide, unless that is the fish are fish that can breathe out of water. Flossie would say, 'Why are you moping around like a fish out of water?'"

"The whales on the whale watch jumped up in the air, though they didn't fly—but a whale isn't a fish, it's a seagoing mammal. But we're mammals right?"

"That's right."

"So then if we go to sea on one of the big ships docked on the North River on the West Side, are we like whales?"

"Exactly."

"I think you're pulling my leg."

"Does it hurt?"

"No."

. . .

Their summer clothes are made of cotton, and their winter clothes were made of wool and rich people's clothes were made of silk that came from silk worms.

"On the Silk Road."

"Our shirts and our pyjamas—they're made of cotton all year long, because we have steam heat, of seersucker in summer and flannel in winter, unless we get rich, if Pop hits the jackpot on the ponies, and then everything we wear will be made of silk."

"Why some people are called flannel mouths nobody I ever ask knows.

"And rich women and Jewish men wear furs in the winter. Raccoon coats don't count. Mother sold furs to rich women during the Depression to keep their morale up, she says. She was a traveling salesman—like the Fuller Brush Man, only with fur coats. She used to wear foxes over the shoulders with their tails hanging down, and their faces sn–sn—"

"Snarling with bared teeth."

"In the fall she wears a black velvet coat and in winter a black cloth coat with a Persian lamb collar to go to the theater and the opera. When we get rich she'll wear ranch mink."

"Or sable."

. . .

Ships dropped anchor and docked at piers on the North River, while boats docked at the town dock in Northport or at the marina in Bayside.

"Docking. Who was it first showed you how at the Everard?" Moriarty asked.

"I shall call him Matthew Swan, a gentleman to his fingertips."

"In three syllables—what was he at the time, about eighty?"

"One didn't think it polite to ask. He died there one cold December night, Christmas Eve in fact, in 1957."

"Whereupon you—he—one—started having the docking nightmare—a pip."

"Not exactly a nightmare, more a transformative dream experience, or so the Jungian called it."

"That German ventriloquist taught you a lot, didn't she. What was her name?"

"Doctor Pontius—Anneliese Pontius. I imagine it still is."

Whereupon the dream within the dream, like a window without frame, sill, sash or edge opening before him in the thin air into which things disappear.

He was standing in his father's empty office on Pier 88, North River, the French Line, with *Normandie* tied up at dockside, when one of the dockers came in—a rugged man with a kindly face—walked over to him and pulled down first his pants and then his own, revealing an uncircumcised cock. He pushed the cocks together, covering Author's circumcised corona with his own long foreskin, masturbating them both, and pulling so hard he pulled Author's cock right out of its socket. Author screamed for help and into the room strode Father Rausch, Father Tausig, the Emperor Rudolph and the court alchemist.

"You told me in confession," said Father Rausch, "that you'd taken off the robes of the Infant of Prague to examine him and found he had no—you had trouble saying penis."

"So now without at penis—a cock—" said Father Tausig, "it would be no sacrilege for you to start dressing up as the Infant, changing your silken robes with the seasons of the Church year and putting on his crown to hold back the Turks. Thus, as St. Paul says, we make ourselves eunuchs for God. And think of what a singing career . . ."

Distraught, Author turns to the emperor and the court magician.

"Can you help me?"

"I think we'd better," said the Emperor Rudolph, "they won't allow you onboard in your present condition (put a shape on you), and we have no time to wait. The saboteurs are on their way in from the safe house in Maspeth to blow this fucking ship to smithereens. Theophrastus Bombastus, do your stuff! It's cold as a witch's tit out here and the imperial cabin awaits me."

Author feels tingles of excitement over the idea of sailing with the Emperor Rudolph to Europe and overland to Prague. He awakens into the carousel horses dream with a stiff erection, the kind they said men got when riding real horses through the sagebrush out on the range.

"A hundred years ago ships used to have 'normous—"

"*E*-normous."

"Huge big sails but then they changed to steam engines, and the sailors had to go down and keep the furnace burning coal all the time on the long voyage home, and Grampa says the family business, ship chanlers—"

"Chandlers."

"You're reading a book by a guy called Chandler—Raymond Chandler —*Farewell, My Lovely*; can I read it next?"

"Next year maybe—you're pretty sure to be able to handle it by then. Could you read the title?"

" 'Chandler' and 'farewell,' and Russell told me the rest. It doesn't make a sentence. Farewell my lovely *what?*"

"Geraniums."

"You mean like Grampa's in the flower pots on his windowsill—did you remember to water them this week?"

"I did."

"You lie."

"No I don't lie, I did."

"You lied about the fucking title. I can read the word 'geraniums.'"

"Don't say 'fucking' or 'fuck' around here—the walls have ears—and they don't use Lifebuoy they use lye soap and you wouldn't like the taste."

"I have a deal with the walls."

"I'm not going near that one."

. . .

In the morning of the day after, July 5, 1945, he was up at the gravel pit behind the hotel, playing with the yellow tractor when a visitor approached.

"What are you up to out here, Jimmy, you watching the big guys?"

"They're men."

"No kidding. You learn something new every day—and what are they up to, the men?"

"Building houses."

"Right—They're building houses for the G.I.'s home from the war—going on all over the country. That sand pit looks like the Grand Canyon."

"Ferde Grofé wrote the *Grand Canyon Suite.*"

"Good for Ferde Grofé—friend of yours maybe?"

"I think my mother knows him, through Flo Carmody over on Prospect Place. They went to high school together—my mother and Mary, not Mary and Ferde Grofé—like my grandfather went to high school with Al Smith, the Happy Warrior. But he never comes to dinner—not Al Smith but Ferde Grofé. Flo Carmody's a talent scout; she discovered the Silver Masked Tenor, only Mark O'Sullivan said 'If that's a tenor, I'm Helen Traubel in drag.' Helen Traubel sings at the Metropolitan Opera. What's drag? Nobody will tell me, not even David."

"You drag your yellow tractor through the sand, no?"

"That's a verb—an action word; it's not the name of anything at all."

"Drag's just an expression—what are you building?"

"I'm not truly building anything—I'm pretend building. I would like truly to build something some day. My grandfather built half of New York an' he took me to see it."

"Like it?"

"It's a wonderful place. My mother says if it ain't New York it ain't. Ain't. She doesn't usually say 'ain't,' but my brother David says she's making a strong point. My grandfather says the whole thing could be blown to kingdom come same we did to Dres–"

"Dresden, yes, in Germany. Don't go having nightmares. Harry Truman will never let that happen. You talk like a big boy—are you a big boy?"

"I'm a genius. I'm only supposed to know words with two . . ."

"Syllables?"

"Yes—and that's three—so's 'grandfather.' My father used to work for McCormack Sand and Gravel in Roslyn, now he works on the docks on the North River; he's a timekeeper, he keeps track of the time."

"Makes sense."

"I guess so—anyway despite rigid work skedaddles he's very popular with the long—"

"Longshoremen."

"Yes."

"Your father's a gentleman."

"He's got a sardine wit—I don't know what that means."

He had already concluded that underneath what they called his reserve his father was a funny man—although so far as the word 'reserve' went he'd only ever seen it on a Schenley's whisky bottle label.

So the family made a novena, and that got Aunt Katy out of Purgatory.

. . .

A passage in time might be represented in many ways. The Bakelite disc on the coffee table back in Jackson Heights might start spinning out of control, but it showed nothing but the date of the month, so one would have to watch carefully to count the months, an impossibility at that speed of rotation. Better the old motion picture standby of the pages falling from the wall calendar or the wind blowing the pages of the desk calendar forward. The child's favorite however, the one he used to imagine, spinning the lit-up globe of the world carried back and forth from Jackson Heights to Northport so as never to lose sight of the idea that there were innumerable places to go, innumerable trips to make. Spinning the globe however wouldn't necessarily take you into the future unless you could get Superman to piggyback you as he flew faster than the speed of light—Mark O'Sullivan said there was no such thing, so you had to make believe—around the globe, from east to west to go back in time and from west to east to go forward. So might they take off from the top of one of his grandfather's tall buildings—the kind Superman could leap over in a single bound—and head off into the time when the war would be over and land back at the exact same spot years later—you always landed back in the exact same spot.

Otherwise the days just passed one after another in the normal way and one day he just happened to be back in the same spot as he was that August afternoon in 1947, having become a different boy, or so they said—

("What happened to the little whippersnapper who made everybody laugh so?"

"Someone told him the story of Pagliaccio."

"From a Caruso record?"

"You're nearly right—from a Saturday afternoon Met Broadcast—Jan Peerce, I think.")

—when the same man came to welcome him back.

"Do you remember the first afternoon you brought your yellow tractor up here to help the men build all the houses? Well, now they're built and the grounds all landscaped and people have moved in, and we've got a little village within the village."

"Charlie says it's an invasion—says we got through the whole war—German submarines right out in the Sound and all—and were never invaded. It took peacetime for the invasion to happen, the water in the harbor to get polluted with the oil from all those guys in the houses and boats, so no more clams and no more clambakes. And soon there'll be a golf course and a country club and lots of money so new the green will come off in your hand, God bless America—but I don't think he's being sincere in that last part."

"You're a different boy from the one with the yellow tractor."

"My father says I'm a gentleman and a scholar, but I don't know. I know I'm smart, I can read books—and not kid books—but I don't think I'm a gentleman. Maybe when I get to wear knickers and then long pants. My father wore knickers when he played baseball, and I think he was a gentleman then."

"Now why do you say that? You already act the part, you're a veritable Jimmy Valentine. When they sprung Jimmy from the joint—he had been framed—they decked him out in a suit of villainously ill-fitting ready-made clothes and a pair of the stiff squeaky shoes that the state issues to its departing guests."

"My brother says I can't wait to go to school so I can be kept in. Those clothes don't sound so bad—better than these short pants and stupid sandals. My grandfather says the Irish built our jails and the Irish filled our jails and Gentleman Jim Brady was no gentleman, despite his proper grammar and painting the town with the beautiful Lillian Russell, a loose woman, whatever that is. Maybe a woman who doesn't wear a girdle. My mother wears a girdle. Proper grammar doth not a gentleman make, she says."

"You'll be a gentleman, all right, and do something big and brilliant one fine day—you have your whole life ahead of you."

"I just wish it would start."

On the basis of previous summers, his reputation had preceded him. The sympathetic reader may imagine the village's reaction on one of two levels—or on both. On the model of the German submarine

landing at Amagansett and the subsequent capture of the three spies
in the safe house in Ridgewood—not difficult to conjure up since submarine periscopes had been detected off Block Island in Long Island
Sound, that a landing could be made at Eaton's Neck—and more than
possible the Vanderbilts would be in on it and that they would bug the
area—but as somebody remarks of that if they managed to get somebody to bug the porch and the bar and the trees around this place, all
they'd hear would be a lot of Irish songs and American show tunes
and a lot of talk on one main topic, the kid from Mars—a pun on the
fact that he devours the candy bar "Forever Yours" made by the Mars
Candy Company. (He was not so interested in somebody telling him
they were forever his as in being able to tell someone he was forever
theirs: gender specifically forever his own gender—"You're with your
own," as his Aunt May always said.)

"I say there are too many bugs on the porch already."

"More or less, yes."

And on the model of the party line, this. Most times nobody heard the
click and if you didn't say anything or sneeze you could listen all day long
to run-on sentences, duets, trios and even choral effects like the birds in
the trees . . . *Bee's knees, cat's pajamas—I know it's terrible, but my Fred says
he's a little horse's ass, says he could do with a good shellacking.* The meaning
was unclear: he called it stupid—but then he told himself he had to stop
calling things he didn't "get" stupid. To be ignorant of something wasn't
such a terrible thing unless you stayed that way, although Eddie Midwinter had said ignorance was a delicate and exotic fruit—touch it and the
bloom is gone—a jumble of words that had made no sense to him and
he hadn't even bothered to ask his brother David. Anyway "stupid" and
"ignorant" were always being used to mean the same thing—which was
a stupid thing that ignorant people who were going to stay that way did.

Shellac was that gooey stuff you bought in a can at the hardware store
that smelled so weird you could get dizzy and pass out sniffing it that
you put on the floor and on chairs to make them shiny, only you have to

let it dry all day and if you light a match anywhere near it while you're pouring it out of the can it will ignite and burn your face off for life, so Grampa always put his pipe away while he was working with the stuff. So do you pour this stuff all over some horse's ass or some kid—him for instance: he wasn't slow in figuring that out—and let it dry? Or take a match to it and burn his face off for life. Nice guy, whoever the son of a bitch was. You never could tell who was out to get you—snakes in the grass: they were everywhere except in Ireland; St. Patrick had driven them all out. Where was St. Patrick when you needed him? Back in the city of course—and his great-great grandfather McCourt had carved the stone work over the big front doors.

That's a terrible thing to say, Myrt, we had entirely too much of that in the Depression when kids got farmed out to families not their own and that sort of thing happened all the time for no good reason. Of course you do get provoked—city people. City indeed. What I think is he should be sent off to Bible camp, but those Catholics don't go in for the Bible do they—say it needs to be interpreted, *when there it is on the table and all you have to do is go and open it to any page and it's as plain as the nose on your face—and no face powder either out of those compact mirror things you always see them pulling out of their purses and looking at themselves in. City people.*

I myself heard Flossie Moore say he does spend a lot of time standing in front of that hall mirror in the hotel. Maybe so, but Flossie told me he's far and away the most unusual child she's ever come across. "So you're going to be six," she said to him. "My, you're getting on in years." "I wish I was seven or eight." "Don't be wishing your life away." "What life?" Now that's frighten-ing, that's what that is.

She thinks he's almost certainly a genius and that the parents are doing a very good job, not pampering him—except in that "Forever Yours" business, and the older brother too. "A penny for your thoughts," she said. "Make it a dime and I'll do my new routine." Imagine—bold as brass. You do have to admit though he comes out with the darndest things.

"At least if I had the use of reason I might know what I was talking about—but my brother David said why did I want to be different from

*everybody else?" Wiseacres, the whole family, if you ask me—city slickers—
although Big Jim as they call him is very well spoken and Catherine plays the
piano very well.*

*Flossie said she watched him one morning last week looking at that cat
that Charlie calls a regular tramp and sets a bad example. Flossie was thinking they should get her fixed so she'd stop dropping litters—the child had
already seen her drop one—we never let the children near any cat when she
was delivering a litter, only later when she's got them all cleaned up and we
could say the cat stork brought them.*

*Anyway he sees the tom mount the cat and goes and asks Flossie about it.
"You are the most inquisitive boy I have ever come across." "Well, the farmer's wife cut the tails off the three blind mice, are you going to cut off the cat's
tail so the tom cat won't be trying to play with it all the time?" "I don't think
so—anyway I'm not a farmer's wife; I run a harbor hotel." "We pick pussy
willows at Crab Meadow and my mother puts them in vases—my father says
vah-ses, that* vay-ses *is Upper Yorkville."*

*"You know," says he, "I was looking at my Long Island beach towel, at
the picture of the girl sitting under the big beach umbrella, but Dorothy
O'Sullivan says you can't go near Jones Beach until you've worked up a good
tan—she puts iodine in baby oil and smears it all over herself and Marsha
and Butch, and what's the point of sitting under a beach umbrella all day
long—if you can't go in the water, but she says the undertow is far too tretch-
something for a four year old, even if he can swim. That Rockaway is a
warm bath by comparison and in the water you burn worse than you do on
the beach, and that defeats the purpose of going over to the ocean in the first
place." He wanted to know if when people burn in hell it's worse than sunburn? I said what is he a Presbyterian or something?*

Then Marcus O'Sullivan said he agreed with Dorothy, that the ocean
was way too dangerous for a four year old, even closely watched, that
there are sea pussies that would drag you under and maybe some mines
the Germans left behind. He wonders what a sea pussy can be, concluding it must be a big catfish, a kind of fish with whiskers, concluding for
the moment to table the motion on Jones Beach. (Table the motion

is something he's heard and sees the kitchen table in Jackson Heights, a bunch of papers called motions stacked on the linoleum tablecloth.) All that kind of scared him; you could tell he couldn't figure out the sea pussy part even after Mark said it was a monster catfish more prevalent in the waters off the South Shore than sharks off the Jersey coast or whales up New England way, and Flossie said he went away then across to sit in the grass under the sycamore tree and think it over. *Well, I better get off this line and think over what to give those ravenous wolves for dinner—besides somebody might be trying to call in a kitchen fire—I'll name no names.*

Suddenly the boy started screaming into the phone; while Russell Crowley stood by with his father's shotgun cocked. Russell fired. The women on the line all started screaming at once. Russell laughed so hard he wet his pants.

Decades later in analysis he realized the truth: that before Northport nothing had ever really *occurred* to him. For instance that the things he could overhear people saying about him, and the vastly greater number of things either he couldn't hear or they weren't saying were all occurring to him.

. . .

By that time, instead of asking Flossie Moore what they were saying about him, he would climb up the vine to the roof of the porch and sit and listen for hours on end. It seemed to him he was still the most talked-about boy in the village, in the summer anyway.

"Surely by now he must be interested in his kid brother."

"Except to say, 'Can't you shut him up? I'm trying to read,' he might as well be looking at a horseshoe crab. He's jealous of course, the little kid's about the best-looking little kid you'd see anywhere."

"'You could give him a tranquilizer,' he said, 'they gave one to the lady who went hysterical when she got herself locked in the upstairs bathroom at the hotel.' He's just not interested in you unless you want to talk to him, which is why he idolizes his brother David, and during the week he's now got this imaginary Moriarty in addition to the panda. David got Moriarty from Sherlock Holmes. Jimmy had said he had to have an enemy, that you're nobody unless you have an enemy, and the panda of course is his next best friend after his big brother. All kids talk to their stuffed animals, but they don't usually put in Europe. He already knows the Americans, the Russians, the French and the British partitioned Vienna and Berlin into sectors after the war, that they had war crimes trials in Nuremberg and hanged the biggest Nazis, also that we hanged Tojo and now he wants them to prosecute Moriarty and some kid back in Jackson Heights he calls Johnny Zilch—claims to have the inside dope on their fifth column activities during the war, with the German submarines, in New York Harbor, no less."

"That Sunday morning, time they told him he'd been a bad boy and couldn't go to Mass with them—and when they came out of the church there he was standing waiting for them at the top of the steps, no explanation forthcoming—he started getting very strange after that."

(Often in later years, indeed nearly four decades later, on the night preceding the early hours of the morning in which he died, at dinner in the restaurant just cross 59th Street from the New York Coliseum, his father still wondered about it, for it had never been explained. For some reason, he said, although there was no logic in it, he wondered what Author had done, what the nature of the infraction was that had incurred the punishment. The rest might reveal itself—likely as something like being cruel to his little brother—but none of the three at the table could remember anything but the aftermath. His mother said the nature of the translocation was the result of a too severe and inappropriate punishment and who could tell but that something beyond what anyone understands had intervened to let him or her know so.

Whatever of that, it had been the beginning of his legend, the one in his own mind as much as the one so often spoken of at parties, and even again at Big Jim's wake. ("Kitty says they were having dinner together that night and Jim brought the story up again. You'd think it was the *Transfiguration*.")

. . .

"He didn't know what a bust was until Flossie asked Kitty should she show him on her dress dummy upstairs in the sewing room, and Kitty said fine, but if he asks you what they are *for* better fudge the answer, because he was bottle fed. Tell him they're for show, he'll like that."

His brother David said no picture was ever as good as the book, not even *Gone with the Wind*—that the best pictures were the ones where they thought up the story from scratch—like in *Casablanca*, or used real-life stories like in *Citizen Kane* and *Back to Bataan* and *The Best Years of Our Lives*.

And he was finished with Oz now. His brother David had just finished a great book for English class—called the *Odyssey*. Sounded like Oz, but it was all about the ancient Greeks and sailing all over and getting shipwrecked and gods and goddesses and beautiful sorceresses casting weird spells such as turning his crew into a herd of pigs.

David said it was better than *Treasure Island*, that he'd help with the ten-dollar words, but he told him he thought that's what dictionaries were for, and by the way, his pocket *Webster's* was no good, he needed the *Webster's Collegiate* and he'd just as soon not wait till Christmas.

The remark is made that in actual fact the boy doesn't talk snappy all the time—not even most of the time—only when he does, it's memorable.

"For example, Captain Marvel in the comics; he'll say, '*Shazam!*'— only he won't know what he's saying—and he starts talking half the time like something out of Damon Runyon and the other half like something out of Kaufmann and Hart."

"Is Eddie Midwinter like that old wizard in the *Captain Marvel* comic books, I wonder?"

"Wizened, yes, wizard, no."

"Eddie's played with Barrymore."

"Did you ever see Barrymore's Hamlet? Greatest thing I ever hope to see on a stage. What a sad end, an old washed-up rummy throwing his talent away on cheap Hollywood trash."

"I wouldn't call *Dinner at Eight* trash—and he was very good in it—almost as good as Jean Harlow and Marie Dressler who was the best."

"Type casting—a washed out old rummy who turns on the gas. 'So long, suckers—see ya in the funny papers.' And once the Great Dane—"

"The Danes were great during the war, gutsy people, everybody said so, had been brave as hell and helped the Jews, who had trusted them, escape to Sweden across the frozen strait between Helsinfgors and Helsingborg and taking over their property, their homes, their shops, so the Germans couldn't tell them apart from the real Danish ones, running their businesses, keeping them all shipshape until the war was over and they returned every penny of the profits, and no charge for caretaking or upkeep."

"I say trust nobody."

"People can't live that way—better say trust only the man whose outlay matches yours."

"*Legis plenitudo caritas.* Justice lies in wealth of charity. Father O'Pray told me."

. . .

"Some people call my mother Katy, after her Aunt Katy, and they sing that crazy song.

> *K-K-K-Katy, K-K-K-Kay-ty*
> *You're the only g-g-g-girl that I adore*
> *And when the moon shines over the outhouse*
> *I'll be waiting at the k-k-k-kitchen door.*

"Over the *outhouse*—are you sure about that?"

"My grandfather says they used to carve a hole in the shape of a crescent moon in the door of every outhouse—but they don't have them any more, except in the Sunday comics—*Barney Google* and *Snuffy Smith* and *L'il Abner.* My father says there's not the call for them that there was. I guess that's the truth."

"You know what Oscar Wilde said about the truth? That the Irish had too much respect for it to drag it willy-nilly into every conversation. A word to the wise."

He had been listening to Charlie Moore on the Russian threat if they ever got the bomb.

"Well, for now anyway," Marcus O'Sullivan said, "but there's a worse threat and no atom bomb in it."

"What do you mean, Mark?"

"I mean the Chinese, the Yellow Peril. They don't all run laundries, and restaurants you know—they're not going to tell you their plans in fortune cookies either. They're not all clever houseboys or clever private eyes and they don't all lie around in opium dens playing Chinese checkers. China is being run by a puppet supported by the Americans and his maniac of a wife, but the Red Chinese have a leader called Mao Tse Tung who's got big plans to do what the Japs failed to do and take over Asia—and this time we aren't going to fight them off—they've got a standing army of ten million men—and women. Within five years they'll take over and then mayhem. Payback for the opium wars; look for the bullet ridden bodies of Christian missionaries hanging off the Great Wall."

"So we drop a few more A-bombs over there."

"No can so easily do, although General MacArthur would dearly love to. There's such a thing as the United Nations now—with *our* China a member—but within five years our China will be exactly the size of the island of Formosa—largely because it will *be* the island of Formosa, which is approximately the same as if the United States shrunk to the size if the District of Columbia and all the forty-eight states formed another union with the capital in New York, say, where it was when Washington was inaugurated—in order to do direct business with the United Nations. How long do you think the four divisions of the District of Columbia would last as one of the five permanent members of the United Nations Security Council?"

"And just where in Manhattan would this new Confederacy put up shop—where the executive mansion and the congressional buildings and the House of Representatives and the Senate, Congress, the agencies and—well, I don't suppose they'd let us have the Library of Congress."

"Staten Island, of course—Todt Hill would make a much more impressive site than the so-called Capitol Hill, which really ought to be called Capitol Knoll—except for the executive mansion and the Supreme Court which would fit very nicely right in the middle of the East River on Welfare Island—the old lunatic asylum could easily be converted into an executive mansion—or torn down altogether and one of those Frank Lloyd modern things thrown up to attract the high hats of the world. China will be our deadliest potential enemy."

"Not Russia?"

"Russia is currently too busy annexing Eastern Europe. Harry can handle the Russians, he's a tough little bastard. Anyway Russia doesn't want us for an enemy—we've got the bomb."

"And I still say we should use it on the Chinese. '*Fiat Justitia Ruat Caelum.*' Let justice be done although the sky fall down."

"Chicken Little."

"That's correct, Jimmy, Chicken Little—or little chickens."

. . .

Pregnancy and the hotel cat—whether to get her fixed so she'll stop dropping litters of kittens. Charlie Moore calls her a regular tramp. He sees the Tom lurking around one day and watches as he mounts her, then goes and asks Flossie Moore about it.

"The cat stork brings them of course—he's a smaller bird than the baby stork, but he works harder carrying all those litters of five, six, seven and eight kittens per consignment. By the way, how are you measuring up on the marks on the wall? You seem to be shooting up real fast this summer."

"I don't know; I am what I am; I don't need to know what I was when."

While the adults played cards—bridge, pinochle, poker, hearts, the children played over and over their favorite, Monopoly. Monopoly was great, especially the railroads. Flo Mulligan said they all ought to go down and look at Atlantic City. She hadn't been there since before the Depression, when they'd stayed at the Chalfonte-Haddon Hall opposite the Marlborough Blenheim.

"Compost *mentis*?"

"Compost from the victory garden. I'm sure he had no idea at what he was saying—he seemed to be taking a comedian's chance in it getting a laugh, and when it did, a big one, you could see the brain filing it away for some future date when he would understand what *compost mentis* means."

"It doesn't mean anything."

"Stay tuned."

. . .

He was getting good at climbing trees by then. They asked him to come down from the sycamore's lower branches then watched him descend.

"Easy is the climb to heaven—Ziegfeld had all those girls doing it every night for years—but it's the descent that's tricky (for men grow cold when girls grow old) like Jacob's angel on his ladder."

"'Jacob' in the Old Testament translates as James—let's hope James has a good guardian angel."

"Eddie says my guardian angel watches over me when I sleep—sometimes I float up to the ceiling to keep him company."

"You've got the wings—or the beginnings of them" (the delicate blades jutting out from beneath his small shoulders) "and when you're ready you'll fly not just up to the ceiling but then out and all over the village and then one day all over the city, over the tops of buildings up there with the airplanes looking in at the passengers."

"Eddie taught me a prayer to my guardian angel:

Be near me when my light is low,
When the blood creeps, and the nerves prick

And tingle; and the heart is sick,
And all the wheels of Being slow.
                    —Tennyson

I don't understand some of it—the part about the wheels being slow, but I say it anyway, because Eddie says guardian angels know everything and we must never do the things that make them weep."

"Low and intermittent sounds and shadows bring about feelings of the sublime. . . . The passions which concern self-preservation turn mostly on pain and danger."

Eddie said about the church melodrama, "But the fairies would never have taken him to the church—they have a scunner against the Church."

Dorothy O'Sullivan said Marsha and Butch learned all about babies watching the cats—the whole show from the female in heat to the tomcat mounting her to the pregnancy when they could feel the little lumps squirming in the cat's belly, to the cat giving birth and cleaning the kittens and nursing them. Later on in Jackson Heights, he never saw Calypso with the tomcat who came around to the alley at night, but she was allowed to have one litter because he insisted he wanted to observe the process, and they kept one kitten and the two kittens used to torment Tiny, the Spitz Pomeranian who was the one big mistake of those years—a schizophrenic animal, said somebody nobody knew who came to an open house with somebody else everybody did and made all kinds of predictions, about the dog, about Author, about his grandfather, who would die in a very few years, and about the dark cloud that would not descend on the house but ascend—creep *up* through the floorboards and eventually drive the family out. Somebody said that sounded like a fire that would start in the cellar or on the O'Flaherty's floor, but the visitor said that although the O'Flahertys would be responsible, it was not a fire—that the family would be driven out by the dark cloud but the dark cloud was not smoke but spite and more mental illness.

"The kid from Mars" and "Forever Yours" had stuck with him. Mars, the red planet. Blood. Mars, the Roman god of war. The canals (like the Gowanus, the only canal he ever heard talked about—because of its foul odor) except the ones in Amsterdam and Venice. When New York was New Amsterdam the canal that now was Canal Street.

The people like it or not had no say in the matter: the British had just marched in and took over and named it New York. They were like that, which is why we threw them out in the Revolutionary War. Swell, they got theirs, as Eddie Midwinter said—although they were terribly brave and stiff upper lip, whatever that meant and inspired the world with their courage—but boy, did they make boring pictures, always the second feature and impossible to make sense of, until a few years later when they came out with *The Red Shoes* with that gorgeous Moira Shearer. Not *Norma* Shearer, Moira Shearer—Norma Shearer was cock-eyed, worse than his mother (it was not polite to say cockeyed—especially when you were cockeyed yourself—you should say, 'a cast in the eye'), and couldn't act her way out of the john.

At the moment they were out on the porch listening to *Fibber McGee and Molly*. (His father often called the boy McGee—was this because he was a known fibber? They never confronted him on the issue; were they keeping book on him?) (Another of his father's expressions, to do with horses, the racetrack, the bookie, which was illegal, and something called the numbers racket. A racket was a lot of noise.)

"The old man is uncanny with the ponies," his older brother said. "Big biscuits upon occasion." His grandfather said the horses could bring you to wrack and ruin. What was *rack* besides the towel rack? (In due time he found out—the meat rack.)

"How much wood would a woodchuck chuck if a woodchuck could chuck wood?" Was a woodchuck the same as a gopher? Or a groundhog like at Groundhog Day in the winter? (Were winter questions all right for summer?) They couldn't be all the same. Somebody called the question metaphysical—it had to have been Eddie Midwinter "and therefore can have no relation to the facts of life as we know them." (The facts of life—Johnny Zilch said he'd tell him when he was older; he decided he'd rather ask David, who was fourteen and must know.) "I played it once—*The Importance of Being Earnest*, by Oscar Wilde—in school. And as a matter of fact that very part, Gwendolyn. No girls to play girls' parts in an all-boys prep school. Rather like Shakespeare in his own day." (Strange.)

The fast approaching official age of the use of reason came about, out of the realms of the sublime to the first of the long, never to be porous, and never curvilinear, halls of learning, the first grade of Blessed Sacrament parochial primary school.

He could commit neither a mortal nor even a venial sin until his first communion; but he could, and did, practice, delighting in the last months, then weeks, then finally days of his last freedom. Unwanted intelligence, surplus to requirements.

. . .

The calendars blew pages back instead of forth in the wind until it was late July, 1945, and Author was in Jo Normoyle's victory garden, with the florilegium from the Botanical Gardens open on his lap, pretending the garden was full of flowers and no vegetables—and thinking of The Land of Counterpane again from Robert Louis Stevenson's *A Child's Garden of Verses*, in which there were no vegetables or any fruit either. No flowers, no weeds, but only words.

And Flossie was saying "Eddie Midwinter's got the boy all het up with that Shakespeare stuff so he's chasing all around the kitchen garden looking for magic herbs and being disappointed because he wanted to turn Charlie into a donkey and have Kitty, if you don't mind, fall in love with him. Well, Kitty's welcome to him any time she likes."

"You know, Flossie, there are already rumors of loose talk on many fronts in this venerable establishment."

"To hell with them—did we sink any ships? No."

Jo Normoyle said there were lots of flowers you could eat: roses, violets, nasturtiums, and the best of all those yellow Italian zucchini flowers—which she shows him. He thinks the zucchini are cucumber—there's a lot of cucumber and tomato salad round in the summer and he has never eaten zucchini, much less zucchini flowers which anyway are weird and don't look a thing like flowers. There is also a watermelon patch.

"But I have to be careful of earwigs. If an earwig crawls into your ear when you're asleep at night, it wiggles all the way into your brains and eats them."

"That is an old wives' tale. "

"Charlie Moore told me."

"Same difference."

Funny expression, made no sense, none at all.

"Anyway, no orchids for Miss Bandage, isn't that the truth, Dave?" David said to his grandfather.

"Who's Miss Bandage?"

"It's Blandish—as in bland Miss Blandish? Ask your grandfather—he knows, don't you, Dave."

"Grampa, who's Miss Bandwhosie?"

"Miss Blandish is that socialite I told you about—in the polar bear den, don't-cha-know, and the polar bear ripped her arm off. She had on a white orchid corsage. Almost bled to death, but the doctors at Wickersham Hospital—stopped the blood flow with boiling hot tar—lucky there were workmen on the street right outside the hospital putting in new tarmacadam road."

"Boiling hot *tar*?"

"Sure thing—an old remedy, don't-cha-know: they used to use it at sea in the days of the big sailing ships when a sailor's arm or leg had to be amputated—saved the girl's life."

"They were going to amputate your leg, but they put a sheep's bone in instead."

"That's a fact—I'm one for the books, don't-cha-know."

(Did the doctors feather her too and run her out of town on a rail? A tall story—it had to be.)

David said, "So can it with catching earwigs and dropping them in the baby's crib."

"I never did that—I was only asking."

. . .

What is immense leads always to a sharp sense of dismay. August 6, 1945, Hiroshima, August 9, Nagasaki. The bomber *Enola Gay*, the bombs Little Boy and Fat Man.

Sunday, August 6, 1945, his father's fortieth birthday, had begun as usual with Mass at St. Philip Neri. Then straight out to the O'Sullivans (who were not practicing Catholics) so Author had baptized both Butch and Marsha right there at the holy water fountain in the baptistry in the back of the church because he heard you could in wartime. He baptized Butch Brendan. Butch was not a Catholic name; there was no St. Butch, so he baptized him after St. Brendan the Navigator, who had discovered America a thousand years before Columbus.

. . .

At Crab Meadow they went collecting pussy willows to put in vases—or *vahses*—back at the apartment over the garage that used to be a carriage house while they talked about the promised excursion to Fort Salonga. The British attack on Long Island was kiboshed by the North Shore Volunteers. They listened to Author remark that had the Germans had submarines in Long Island Sound in those days, they could have destroyed the whole fleet sailing over from Connecticut, because the Germans were on our side in the Resolutionary War. Then, arriving at the beach umbrella, the blanket and the long beach chairs, the boy announced that he and Marsha had been playing Duel in the Sun with Pistol Packin' Momma's pistols—he has enough of a tan due to Dorothy O'Sullivan's iodine and baby oil mixture to go out bareheaded, but wearing sunglasses so as to be able to focus to shoot. Butch was Marsha's second and Andy was his. It was a draw.

Father O'Pray, sipping a Singapore Sling, remarked, "Jennifer Jones does not make a convincing Mexican. I liked her much better as Saint Bernadette."

"Father, you've seen *Duel in the Sun*?"

"Twice—in the line of duty, you understand, I understand in Hollywood they're calling it *Lust in the Dust*."

Everybody but everybody had started calling it that, including Father O'Pray, just returned stateside, and those who had rejoiced on VE day with songs and prayers of thanksgiving, had that day, Big Jim's fortieth, put behind them in a tightly locked box the key to the cataclysmic event that turned out to be the turning point in world civilization, the absolute annihilation of humanism which would be nothing more from that day on than an object of wistful nostalgic referral, the day when Homer, Virgil, Dante, Shakespeare, Cervantes, Goethe, Tolstoy, Melville, Dickens and the Victorians were hung out to dry, forever stripped of any relevance in the mirroring of world affairs. The day of the invention of the post-human. And the band did play on—they'd been paid after all.

Mark O'Sullivan had said there were seven hills in ancient Rome that were still there and that was the meaning of "old as the hills." Then it was that the older boys came running down the beach yelling "*Banzai!!! Banzai!!! Banzai!!!*"

He had nearly completed the Flatiron Building at the water's edge when the boys jumped on top of it, savagely kicking it, reducing it to sand rubble in seconds. And just that morning he'd been thinking of the word "stampede." The few cows he'd come across so far seemed far too lazy.

"Obliterated in a flash of white light!" He remembered the instantaneous flash of white light he'd once seen as he stood at the window in the front car of the IRT train, watching the Manhattan skyline grow closer and closer . . . and now there were voices close by: his mother's and Dorothy O'Sullivan's.

"It had to be done, Catherine—they just would not admit defeat, and the kamikazes were dropping onto our carriers all over the place."

"Yes, I know—but Dorothy, a whole city, gone like that."

His terror was such as to be neither assuaged nor forgotten all his life.

"The Germans would have done it to New York—consider that."

(Age that he was, he had not yet imagined death could undo so many.)

Hiroshima and later Nagasaki were two examples; after them the Japanese must surrender.

Then back at the hotel listening to President Harry on the radio, and to Father O'Pray speaking at the same time saying, "If we can do that to Hiroshima, what's to prevent somebody else doing it to New York, Chicago, Los Angeles, San Francisco . . . nobody was ever invincible. The cities on the plain, Nineveh, Babylon, the original Jerusalem with Solomon's temple housing the Ark of the Covenant—all disappeared. The Bible says it plain: 'we have here no lasting city.'"

. . .

As he lay in bed wanting another brandy in milk, a four-door sedan came down the driveway, and as he looked out the window he heard his brother's voice. "Enter the celebrated Shermans, stars of opera, radio and Wilshire Boulevard." He looked down and thought he saw characters from the old circus wagon.

Marie Kelly had been a friend of his grandmother's, later of his mother's, who'd played rehearsal piano for her, too. His grandfather said he'd rather listen to Marie and Lee Sherman (a former Italian tenor, Luigi, Marie's second husband, who now owned a plumbing parts company in Los Angeles) sing than to Jeanette MacDonald and Nelson Eddy every time. Marie Kelly and Grace Moore were his two favorite singers. And Lee was as good a singer as Jan Peerce, if not as good as the greatest tenors, Caruso or John McCormack.

"Marie's being a divorced woman and being married out of the church—"

"Now, now, Catherine let him who is without sin—"

"Gene McCann was a bum who used to beat Marie senseless."

"I love Marie, but she asked for it—all that temperament."

"Ask and ye shall receive—knock and the door shall be opened to you—you'll be pulled right in and beaten senseless."

"On that account, Catherine, you'd be in trouble if Jim were a Gene McCann. Marie didn't ask for it, or anyway she didn't know what was in store for her in that period when she took up torch songs and ended up living them. So it was chuck the bum and back to singing in *The Student Prince.*"

They were talking about music when he put a shape on himself and went down to join them.

"Catherine, just look at him he's shooting up, growing like a weed."

"As far as that, all the Strausses and Franz Lehárs, who's better than any of them, everybody shares them or there would be rioting in the streets."

The Second Viennese School? (Schoenberg, Berg, Webern.)

"Horrible, awful, ghastly—noise, noise, noise, noise."

"Strictly insane asylum music—all written by Jews."

Lee flinched. "Hitler said the same thing—must be some truth in it." Dead silence.

("God almighty, talk about the perfect squelch.")

"*Ach, Wien—die bestes Zeit meines Lebens,* the best time of my life. I'm strictly a Lehár girl—Lehár, Rudolf Friml, Victor Herbert, Sigmund Romberg—Ricky Korngold said, 'You should have seen Novotná in *Giuditta.*' Lehár sure knew what he was doing when he wrote it for her. We were talking with him one night at the Liederkranz Society—"

"Liederkranz is stinky cheese. When we go to Al Mueller's after the Circus, Pop eats it with raw onion on some kind of black nickel bread."

"Pumpernickel."

"Yes."

Unfazed, Marie went on, "*Liederkranz* means crown of song—and Ricky said it was ridiculous how people keep going on about Paula Wessely and Helly Möslein and Miliza Korjus—remember rhymes with *gorgeous*? She lives in Los Angeles now, up on Mount Olympus, teaches, and sings now and then at the Society and the Hollywood Bowl, still getting out those high A's. Ricky's taken quite a shine to her. We see her for bridge now and again—gorgeous, not Novotná—still going strong. The Viennese slighted her because she's Czech of course, which in those days was the same for them as being a Jewess. *Unserer Wien*, our Vienna. We were a merry crowd back then."

"More than half of them were merry Nazis," Lee Sherman said.

"But Weegie, you sang for Mussolini and made him cry—you told me so."

"At his funeral, dear—and his mother cried; it was the highlight of my career."

"Nobody knew Weegie was a Jew boy. He even ate shrimp and clams and lobster—the same as we did. Did you know that whenever Nellie Melba ordered lobster and they brought it she'd ask, 'Is it a *cock*?'"

(Who killed cock lobster?)

The cock crowed three times ("Cock-a doodle doo!") and Peter denied knowing Him.

"Does the boy cock his head like that all the time?"

"Pretty much—the same as Catherine."

"Are you the Weegie that takes dead people's pictures in the street?"

(Temperament—*temperamental*; subjects for further research.)

His mother had also dated Jack Naish, the brother of J. Carrol Naish who played Luigi on *Life with Luigi* on the radio even though he was Irish. There was Show Business and coincidence (the two Luigis in the one night when he hardly ever heard the name in real life, or many other Italian names for that matter except for his mother's best friend Alma Monaco, the names of characters and singers on the opera broadcasts— such singers as Ezio Pinza, Licia Albanese, Eugene Conley, Jan Peerce, Jarmila Novotná, Helen Traubel, Lauritz Melchior, Richard Tucker, Risë Stevens, Zinka Milanov and the purest and most beautiful tenor voice in the world, Jussi Björling. Arturo Toscanini conducting on the New York Philharmonic radio broadcasts).

"Anyway," Marie said, "we could all use a couple of stiff snorts and some happy songs to blot out the noise of this terrible day. I never understood politics and war myself."

Lee said, "Marie thinks everybody ought to just make the best of it and get along—like in opera companies."

"Of course we did our part: we sang for the boys at the Stage Door Canteen."

"Well, let's have a song or two now," his father said. Lee sang first "*O sole mio*" and then Governor Jimmy Davis's "You Are My Sunshine."

(Sunny Jim.)

(In 1955, visiting the Shermans in Beverly Hills, Author is looking at the map and asks Lee why they don't live in Sherman Oaks. Marie is quite ruffled. "*Sherman Oaks*? Why not *Encino*? Why not *Tarzana*? Now let's talk about the good old days—everybody in Los Angeles talks about the good old days.")

(The conversations are ones he seems to remember, and he asks his mother weren't the same things being said out in Northport on Pop's fortieth birthday, Hiroshima Day?

"Practically word for word."

How the mystery of "recall" elucidates itself.

"I thought from the beginning backward—they don't know anybody in Malibu. I know Novotná is still alive—is Miliza Korjus?"

"I believe she is."

"On the Late Late Show anyway.")

That evening in the bar/lounge with Kitty Moore at the piano, they sang selections from *The Merry Widow*, his grandfather and deceased grandmother's song when they were "walking out together," which Marie had sung many times in her career on cross-country tours. "Vilja" and the songs about Maxim. Also from *Show Boat* Marie's haunting renditions of "Can't Help Lovin' Dat Man" and "Bill" "as good as Helen Morgan ever was, with the 'catch' in the throat," "People Will Say We're in Love" from the smash hit *Oklahoma!* he was too young (goddamit) to be taken to, and finally each a solo, she "Musetta's Waltz" from *La*

Bohéme and he *"Vesti la giubba"* from *I Pagliacci*. ("Canio was a clown, and his wife Nedda was having an affair with a local yokel, so he stabbed her to death.")

Then after the "recital" Marie Sherman tied one on and sang "Zip" from *Pal Joey*. Author wants to know who "Soap-and-Water" is and is told by Lee he was a famous German egghead, great pal of Nutsy, who was the creator of Superman.

"Nutsy Fagin?"

"That's the guy."

Marie said Jimmy ought to run away with Novotná and the opera. There are opera parts galore for him—"Trouble" in *Madama Butterfly*, the child who introduces Parpignol in the second act of *La Bohéme*, the Tzarevitch in *Boris Gudonov*, Yniold in *Pelléas et Mélisande*.

. . .

The day before the family's departure for Jackson Heights and the city that was still there and that his grandfather said was sure to last as soon as they got it built found Author behind the wheel of Charlie Moore's pickup truck, a map of Japan unfolded on the seat beside him, examining the dashboard, deciding the way to drop a bomb was to pull out the choke with the determination of General Douglas MacArthur, and about to take off and fly across the four spaces skies of America, and across the Pacific over Pearl Harbor, all the way to the Land of the Rising Sun on a mission to flatten all their cities with atomic bombs, even though they'd surrendered unconditionally, so they'll never be able to destroy Los Angeles or Chicago or New York or Washington in two minutes flat.

. . .

Two years later, when he was in the first grade and just after their fourth and last summer at the apartment above the carriage house, with the yellow oilcloth table cloth, back in New York, after another day out in Central Park and another ride on the carousel, he came home with a temperature of 101 and was put to bed. Doctor Rooney came over, gave him a shot in the backside, and gave his mother a prescription which this time the kid brother was sent up to Papisch's to get filled—but there was to be no shot of scotch for him, but anyway he'd tasted it and hated it, it tasted worse than Listerine. He was delighted at the prospect of a few more days in the Land of Counterpane, fell asleep and dreamed a dream of the carousel in which his mother sat playing the waltz from the musical *Carousel* on the steam calliope, the horses ran on an outside track while his father and a couple of bookies in flashy gabardine suits and Hawaiian ties and fedoras tilted up on the backs of their heads watched them race. He was dressed not in his western costume, but in his jockey costume all silk in many colors and riding an Arabian stallion, not a palomino, passing all the couches on the carousel—David had said that people get on the carousel to carouse—where he could see and hear everybody from Moore's hotel talking about him. You'd think they'd have something better to do, he said to himself, now that the family is gone for good—next year they've decided they're going up to Windham in the Catskills where his father used to go before he and Kitty Moore were married—but he guessed they didn't. Although he didn't know how, why, or even the word, the McCourts and old Dave Moore had become the stuff of legendary nostalgia at Moore's Hotel.

. . .

They'd cleared the shipping lanes in the North Atlantic; he knew when the *Mary* was in and that the *Île de France* had been restored from a troopship to its former glory. Resuming lessons in the hallway schoolroom, he descended time and again to the "middle" floor to discover the Bakelite calendar, the exact replica of the one on the top floor, instead of showing the date in the windows, on one side showing newsreels of the aftermath of the war in a devastated Europe and a running travelogue of America the Beautiful on the other. Father O'Pray was no Barry Fitzgerald or Spencer Tracy, or Bing Crosby, either, in the pulpit at St. Ignatius Loyola on Park Avenue—risking censure by the Archdiocese for omitting in the Mass the prayer for the conversion of the Jews and equating their murder with the crucifixion of Christ, who need he remind the congregation was a Jew, and who if the congregation remembered was nailed to the cross under the mock banner INRI, for Jesus of Nazareth, King of the Jews (in Latin), but finding the Jesuits as usual impregnable—they're with their own—the Archdiocese demurred.

. . .

Back on August 6, 1945, the moon had set, the hour was late, and they'd run the gamut a fair way and the longing for sleep had overtaken them.

Things sure got different, and quickly—nothing was ever going to stay the same. He was being put to bed by his big brother David.

"Are you going to wear your clown face to bed?"

"I think my guardian angel will get a kick out of it, don't you?"

"Definitely."

"Could you leave the globe on—and could you show me where Hiroshima is?"

"Tomorrow, O.K.?"

"O.K."

"You want to know something important? Terror can become a kind of beauty too when two fellows stand up to it together. I'll leave the little night light you like on instead—but just remember, there's nothing in the dark that wasn't there before."

"There *is*—the *dark*."

As he drifted off to untroubled sleep, the voices over at the hotel seemed to have died down, but for a lone singer, his mother at the old upright.

Now, laughing friends deride,
Tears I cannot hide.
So I smile and say
"When a lovely flame dies,
Smoke gets in your eyes."

ACKNOWLEDGMENTS

The author wishes to express his heartfelt thanks to Robert Weil, an exigent master and the best editor I have worked with in over thirty years, for his heroically grueling and exhaustive editing of *Lasting City*; to Will Menaker, the best editorial assistant a writer could wish for; to Don Rifkin, who as before made dozens and dozens of corrections on a manuscript rife with errors, pleonasms and other grammatical infelicities; to Nancy Palmquist, for her patience and generosity in matters of a budgetary nature; to Darren Haggar, with his brilliant realization of the city as a plenitude of fragments as tall buildings, he has contradicted an old maxim: in this rare instance you *can* tell a book by its cover; and to Vincent Virga, guardian and life companion for 49rrrr years!

ABOUT THE AUTHOR

JAMES McCOURT was born in New York City and was educated at Manhattan College, New York University and the Yale School of Drama. His novels are *Mawrdew Czgowchwz*, *Time Remaining*, and *Delancey's Way*. He has published two short-story collections, *Kaye Wayfaring in "Avenged,"* and *Wayfaring at Waverly in Silver Lake*. His nonfiction epic is *Queer Street: The Rise and Fall of an American Culture, 1947–1985*. His stories, articles and film and book reviews have appeared in *The New Yorker*, the *Paris Review*, *Grand Street*, the *Yale Review*, *Vogue*, *Film Comment* (contributing editor in the seventies and eighties), *SoHo Weekly News* and the *New York Times* and *Los Angeles Times* book sections, and he commented on the 1995 Oscar presentations for *Buzz*.

James McCourt has taught creative writing at Princeton and Yale Universities. He lives in New York City and Washington, D.C.